Worlds of Print

WORLDS
of PRINT

The Moral Imagination of an Informed Citizenry
1734 to 1839

JOHN SLIFKO

Westphalia Press
An Imprint of the Policy Studies Organization
Washington, DC
2020

WORLDS OF PRINT: THE MORAL IMAGINATION OF AN
INFORMED CITIZENRY, 1734 TO 1839

Westphalia Press
An imprint of Policy Studies Organization
1527 New Hampshire Ave., NW
Washington, D.C. 20036
info@ipsonet.org

ISBN: 978-1-941472-24-8

Cover and interior design by Jeffrey Barnes
jbarnesbook.design

Daniel Gutierrez-Sandoval, Executive Director
PSO and Westphalia Press

Updated material and comments on this edition
can be found at the Westphalia Press website:
www.westphaliapress.org

ABSTRACT

Plato, Aristotle, Baron Montesquieu, and Jean Jacques Rousseau argued that you could never have a democracy bigger than the geographic size, intimate oral habits, and embodied rituals of face-to-face communication, and walking distance of a Greek city-state, French town, or small Swiss city. However, in the years surrounding the 1776 American War of Independence and accelerating into the 1800s in the American northeast and mid-Atlantic, there was a significant cultural transformation in the transition from oral/aural cultures to an increasingly literate citizenry. A consequence of this transition was an expanded geographical range of democratic engagement. I argue that freemasonry was representative and played an important role in this transformation and helped articulate the moral imagination of an informed democratic citizenry via fast emerging worlds of print. A metamorphosis occurred through worlds of print anchored at home in the routine lives of local community and transmission in space across networks of place. Communication and political participation were enhanced in early America through a growing range of print vehicles such as pamphlets, newspapers, declarations and books of all types concerned with ancient and modern learning. The formation of local civic associations and reading libraries further contributed to this growth of available print documents. In this work I examine the vital roles that freemasons played in this print transformation.

TABLE OF CONTENTS

LIST OF FIGURES

VITA

John Slifko

Founding Member and Board of Directors Hannah Mather Crocker Society, Notre Dame University

http://hmcsociety.wix.com/hmcs

Education

M.A. 1989 University of California, Los Angeles, Los Angeles, California

B. A. 1987 San Francisco State University, San Francisco, California

Articles

Paper presented at *2015 International Conference American Political Science Association*, San Francisco, California, "The Moral Imagination of an Informed Citizenry, Crocker, Hall and Freemasonry."

"An Historical Geography of Louis Goaziou and the Early Years of L' Ordre Masconnique Mixte et International 'Le Droit Humain', American Federation of Human Rights: the Significance of the Industrial Monongahela Valley of Western Pennsylvania." *Journal of Research into Freemasonry and Fraternalism.* Latest issue Vol. 4. No 1-2 (2013), *Woman and Freemasonry.*

"Hannah Mather Crocker." *Le monde maçonnique des Lumières: l'Europe, l'Amérique et de ses colonies, prosopographique Dictionnaire.* Cécile Révauger and Charles Porset, eds. 3 Vols. Paris: Champion, 2013, Vol. I, 908-917.

"John Dunlap." *Le monde maçonnique des Lumières: l'Europe, l'Amérique et de ses colonies, prosopographique Dictionnaire.* Cécile Révauger and Charles Porset, eds. 3 Vols. Paris: Champion, 2013, Vol. II, 1058-1062.

"Philipp Morin Freneau." *Le monde maçonnique des Lumières: l'Europe, l'Amérique et de ses colonies, prosopographique Dictionnaire.* Cécile Révauger and Charles Porset, eds. 3 Vols. Paris: Champion, 2013, Vol.II, 1228-1229.

"Hezekiah Niles." *Le monde maçonnique des Lumières: l'Europe, l'Amérique et de ses colonies, prosopographique Dictionnaire.* Cécile Révauger and Charles Porset, eds. 3 Vols. Paris: Champion, 2013, Vol. III, 2100-2103.

"Benjamin Russell." *Le monde maçonnique des Lumières: l'Europe, l'Amérique et de ses colonies, prosopographique Dictionnaire.* Cécile Révauger and Charles Porset, eds. 3 Vols. Paris: Champion, 2013, Vol. III, 2424-2426.

"Isaiah Thomas." *Le monde maçonnique des Lumières: l'Europe, l'Amérique et de ses colonies, prosopographique Dictionnaire.* Cécile Révauger and Charles Porset, eds. 3 Vols. Paris: Champion, 2013, Vol. III, 2635-2638.

Paper presented at Liberal Arts Masonic Center, Grand Lodge of California, in collaboration with the Roosevelt Center for the Study of Civil Society and Freemasonry. "Freemasonry in Early American Worlds of Print: Building the First Internet," 2011.

International Conference

2014 Conceived and Organized an *International Academic Conference* in collaboration with the Roosevelt Center for the Study of Civil Society and Freemasonry and Liberal Arts Masonic Center. "At a Perpetual Distance: Universal Freemasonry and Its Historical Divisions", Los Angeles California.

Research Assistant

2012 Research Assistant to Professor Margaret C. Jacob, Distinguished Professor of History, University of California, Los Angeles, Department of History

Fellowship

1988-89 Cotton-Beland Fellowship, M. A. UCLA School of Architecture and Urban Planning

Memberships

The Founder and Co-Director of the Roosevelt Center for the Study of Civil Society and Freemasonry.

Founding Member and Director at Project A.W.E.

American Political Science Association

American Historical Association

Historical Society of Massachusetts

Historical Society of Pennsylvania

Library Company of Philadelphia

CHAPTER 1

INTRODUCTION

A. ORGANIZATION OF THE THESIS

In this work I argue that freemasonry as one civic association in early America was representative and partially constitutive of the early development of American deliberative democracy and civil society.[1] I claim specifically that freemasons supported and contributed to the moral imagination of an informed citizenry via worlds of print as central in furthering the multifaceted deliberated ideals and experimental acts of maturing democracy.[2] The geography of print culture began with a core network of places of deliberation, face-to-face communication (the spoken word and embodied performance), and networked printing capacity running from Washington D.C. and Baltimore to Boston with outliers, such as Charleston.

Everyday life in the early American Atlantic coast was transformed in new ways because of the rapid growth of literacy and use of print technology. Growth included the promise of economic gain by job-printers, newspapermen, publishers, merchants involved in advertising, work for the government, no less the public printing of arrival and departure dates for maritime commerce. Legal codes, regulations, and governance of the states and their ports, counties and cities were also facilitated via the printed text.

---

1 The idea of deliberative democracy is grounded on the principle that legitimate democracy is the result of the public deliberation of citizens variously conceived, for example, as argumentation, freedom of speech and assembly, utilitarian calculus, or a will to the common good. Deliberative democracy, in short, is the process wherein authentic deliberation interpreted differently, not the simple act of voting, is the primary source of legitimate democratic culture and action.

2 John Dewey engaged the psychology of moral "deliberation" in democracy. An important phase of deliberation is imagination or what Dewey also termed "dramatic rehearsal". He was concerned with the way we went about deliberating in problematic situations not a prescriptive set of procedures we ought to follow. Problematic situations necessitate inquiry, imagination and artful communication. Democracy emerges as more than voting but rather it is at its core "primarily a mode of associational living and conjoint communicated experience." See, John Dewey, *Democracy and Education: An Introduction to the Philosophy of Education* (New York: The Macmillan Company, 1916), 93.

1

An examination of the colonial and early American "reading revolution" in historical geography, however, uncovers a set of socio-cultural and intellectual taproots back into the Tudor period, with its earlier ideal and praxis—*a moral imagination of an "informed citizenry"* of gentlemen. Literacy catalyzed many new aims, interests, and aesthetic processes involving suitable communication, learning and vital human association in the period of the War of Independence.[3] The revolution of literacy and evolution of print medium needs to be articulated as an important element in early American deliberative democracy. In the preparation for war, transactions of war and in the period afterward, the occupation, perspective and aesthetic-moral-intellectual field of the American patriot printer-journalist arose in full bloom.

The rise of patriotic feeling and emotion during war and the emergence, timing, and geography of the American occupation of the printer-journalist are together a major focus of the work, for example, in Chapter 4 concerned with John Dunlap the newspaperman, and printer of the original copies of the 1776 Declaration of Independence. A few hundred original copies of the Declaration were authored and printed in Philadelphia. They were immediately distributed across the rebelling colonies by fast horse and performed ritualistically and orally to assembled local audiences. Dunlap like others was a "patriot" printer-journalist. The richer possibilities in a new vocation of printer-journalist and possibilities of the text were intimately related to the greater dimensions of deliberative democracy as (i) human association (ii) conjoint expanding spheres and networks of communication, and (iii) learning.

In the War of Independence in the United States, an interest in print communication emerged as something experimental, hybrid and rich. It was a means of obtaining accurate information in war and then peace yet ca-

---

3   Richard. D. Brown, *The Strength of a People: The Idea of an Informed Citizenry in America* (Chapel Hill: University of North Carolina Press. 1996), Brown in his important work describes what he calls the "ideology" (xiii) or "idea" (xiv, 26-118) of an "informed citizenry" in the early republic. The term '"ideology" is particularly misleading in this otherwise extremely valuable text. I reconstruct Brown's probative phrasing with my own term and reference *"the moral imagination of an informed citizenry"* (in the title and used throughout the work). Moral imagination is a more accurate term in describing a seminal process in deliberative democracy in the end supporting the franchise of those deemed legitimate in the community in democracy, but also open to further inclusion in the contingency and continuity of aspiration and struggle in the democratic civil sphere.

pable of inspiring rhetoric in the call to war in 1776 or 1812 no less in supporting rituals of healing and performance after the war. The printed word could empower the struggle of minority voices, or counter publics, or it could project the desires of the majority through power communication across space. It connected the present and the absent in time and space through representation, imagination and transmission.[4] Through it all, the spoken word could challenge the authority of the text.

Integral human communicative experience, as one model, consists of (i) ritual communication, vital local, day-to-day face-to-face action, and inquiry, (ii) transmissions across space. In communication, there is the potential of an "indefinite perfectibility," a term used by Alexis de Tocqueville referencing the moral imagination of an informed citizenry in the inquiry (experimentation) and artful communication of democracy. Tocqueville saw this dynamic of what can be termed deliberative democracy related specifically to the explosion of newspaper production, transmission, and consumption. One way to frame Tocqueville's view, after the fact, is to say he discerned a moral imagination of indefinite perfectibility of an informed citizenry in early American worlds of print. What Tocqueville saw in the 1820s in America was then unique in the world. There was an increasing intensity in small business newspaper startups and turnovers by the 1820s aligned with social, political and business interests across considerable and growing distance. There was government support through policy of the transmission of newspapers, improvements in coach travel and delivery, albeit at first over very bumpy roads. Tocqueville's American Grand Tour exposed him to the results of institutional experimentation with the founding of the Post Office in the United States Constitution, the enormous impact of the Post Office Act of 1793, entrepreneurialism, deeply layered support for freedom of the press, and more.

---

4 The work barely scratches the surface of the thousands of pamphlets, declarations, constitutions, books, newspapers, broadsides, and other vehicles of print (and writing) that need to be folded into a much larger study of early American culture, print and freemasonry. That regional project can be profitably artitulated in ongoing comparative and global studies of the close interrelationship of worlds of print and Freemasonry in the 18th century and before down to the present. Kent Logan Walgren, *Freemasonry, Anti-Masonry and Illuminism in the United States: A Bibliography, 1734-1850*. 2 vols. (Worcester: American Antiquarian Society, 2003); Larissa P. Watkins, ed., *American Masonic Periodicals 1811-2001* (New Castle, DE: Oak Knoll Press, 2003); and, Watkins ed., *International Masonic Periodicals 1738-2005* (New Castle, DE: Oak Knoll Press, 2005).

The moral imagination of an informed citizenry was shaped through the print culture of the newspaper and its consequence of metaphorically shrinking distance in early America. Distances grew far greater but the length of time of transmission diminished with regularity.

At the same time books were coming into America from London. Many were classical texts such as the works of Cato on republican virtue or not to be overlooked the *Book of Constitutions of the Free-Masons* from London in 1723 but re-printed in the colonies in 1734 by Benjamin Franklin. British freemasonry had a considerable influence on American fraternity. The classical texts like that of Cato's collection of letters had a formidable impact on the American social imaginary, while technologies of printing were improving. Technological advances in steam power production coming into practical use in London by 1820 for newspapers, then the rolling press invented in America in 1840, and the proliferation of job-printing contracts with special printing machines were formidable techniques. Road, rail and water-way building—and the growing number of readers—were shifting the global center of gravity in printing capacity. The new geographic core region and system of cities straddling the early American north-east and mid-Atlantic seaboard underlay what was the most intensive printing network in the world by the 1840s and 1850s as hinted in Figure 1. America labored hard to become the world's leading producer of books up against often pirated editions from Ireland or Scotland of inexpensive books flooding in from London.

Transmission can spark less insularity in local solidarity provide orientation in habit correction, seek out opportunity, extend learning, and in these ways expand the boundaries of local communication. Or transmission can be tested in the values and meaning of local communities. Transmission no less can attenuate local solidarities.[5] In the work, I draw attention to the emplaced yet geographically expanding worlds of print in early America and the communication, deliberative democracy, and networked set of occupations that print made possible. Oral/aural habits of discourse with other habits of local life were being replaced with new habits of reading, which increased the role of printers, journalists, distributors and salesmen of the texts and publishers. Freemasonry encouraged the transmission of different vehicles of print in networks of local communities.

---

5   See Zohar Kadmon Sella, "The Journey of Ritual Communication," *Studies in Communication Studies* 7, no 1 (2007): 103-124.

Freemasonry, at first, as a young civic association promoted the celebration of ritual, oratory, an openness of thought, and moral imagination of an informed citizenry via worlds of print in deliberative democracy. It was highly representative of the opening of wider civil society, and advocated or supported new experimental, or more traditional, efforts in education at all levels, and phases of life. Illustrations are given of the masonic lodge conceived as a life-long place of learning among equals, flourishing, and place of resistance by subaltern groups in focusing on a women's lodge of freemasons in Boston, an African-American lodge in the same city with both lodges on the north end, and the freemasonry of a chief of a First Nation and his son.

Chapter 2 examines specific texts of freemasonry printed in 18th century Georgian London. The chapter offers a glimpse at Palladianism as an architectural, cultural, and philosophic movement with earlier encompassing "British" aspirational roots in 17th century England evident in the work of the architect Inigo Jones. The chapter begins a study of the emerging modern "occupation" of printer, engraver, or printer-writers with concomitant networks and briefly references how the printed text assisted the transmission of Palladianism from Italy across the Alps by the architect and master of the masque theater, Jones. The chapter helps to initially explicate the nature of freemasonry and the individual freemason and sets the stage for study of the transmission of freemasonry to the American colonies.

The four texts examined in the chapter set the scene for consideration of (a) freemasonry as reflective of wider processes of civil society, including human ritual and transmission functions (meaningful, embodied and purposive semiotics) of communication in place and across networks of places; (b) an opening discussion of the widespread debates across all civil society, including in freemasonry, of the tension between the merits and practices of ancient and modern learning. The debate on the merits of ancient and modern learning in both temporal flow and discontinuity occurred in both the Italian Renaissance and then the Europe discourse in a very long 18th century on a myriad of topics including the place of Christianity, the ideas of Plato and Aristotle, Renaissance hermetic, neo-Platonic, alchemical and kabalistic studies and emerging experimentation of the new science of Isaac Newton. Ancient and modern disputes in America continued to exist in political debates about the optimum geographic size of a republic, or the place of Roman rhetoric in public deliberation in fashioning a republic. Ancient and modern worldviews were not hollow terms but orientations, geographies and positions of value and transmission in inquiry, moral imagination and deliberation.

Chapter 3 concerns the transmission function of communication in the prioritizing of the post office, the building of a transmission infrastructure, and the creation of vertically integrated print networks, by the printer-journalist, entrepreneur, citizen, and freemason Benjamin Franklin. Franklin instinctively held that communicative action, including print culture, was a condition of possibility for agency and success of an entertained, virtuous, and informed individual and citizenry. His vertical and horizontal integrated networks of industry and social life were imitated by others.

Reading habits were modifying oral-aural habits. Print culture naturalized speech and became an important connective tissue in community life and a network of communities within the growing circumference of distinct print vehicles such as the pamphlet or newspaper. Print culture facilitated new methods in communication and apposite learning locally in place for the imaginative reader in privacy or more publicly at the local reading society or front-porch of the local store. Print culture by its nature sparked imagination of places near and far, and times absent and present in the early American reading revolution and geographically extensive republic. Worlds of print buttressed by economic growth also fostered expanding networks along the original Atlantic coast colonies then soon-to-be union of states. Worlds of print facilitated the individual and communities moving inland along man-made and natural routes.

Franklin has been rightly called the father of American worlds of print, as he helped considerably in fashioning necessary networked infrastructure both institutional and geographic for print culture, the ideals of modern journalism and the professional occupation of journalist. However, Franklin also wrestled with the not unrelated questions and pedagogy of what the proper subject matter is, and processes are, of formal education in what became an increasingly literate America. His efforts to start the future University of Pennsylvania, an effort to advance the use of vernacular in public education and not Classic Greek or Latin, and building institutions of communication and learning in civil society such as the Junto with its associated members library, the separate Library Company of

Philadelphia, or his vision of freemasonry as a ritualized place of learning albeit with limitations, serve as examples. Through it all Franklin was concerned with the pragmatic affairs of everyday life at the origins of modern American civil society. Franklin in so many ways presages the American pragmatism and qualitative (integral, affective embodied) thought of the later American great public intellectual John Dewey.

Chapter 4 engages the ritual and transmission functions of communication, human agency, and uses of the printed texts of the patriot, freemason, and printer-journalist John Dunlap in Philadelphia. The chapter examines the different print vehicles of (a) lectures or other communications printed as pamphlets, (b) the Declaration of Independence, and (c) a newspaper report on General George Washington, the freemasons, army, militia, and citizenry at a strategic gathering in Philadelphia during the annual ceremony of St. John observed by freemasons. *The gathering was the first recorded public appearance of Washington as a freemason.* Each of the examples is taken from Dunlap's printed work. They each individually and taken together illustrate the goals, moral imagination and the strategy and tactics of the patriot printer-journalist John Dunlap. The moral imagination, thought and action looked toward a healthy leadership role, at first, for a few in freemasonry in an American War of Independence and in a wider civil society to come after the war, and certainly no less a strong intention to win the war.

Reports from the war period are complemented in newspaper reports after the war by Dunlap, presented in Chapter 6, on the freemasons involved in key ritual performances of the cornerstone ceremonies in the building of the nation's capital, Washington, DC. This latter peacetime reporting and printing work engaged directly (i) the importance of well performed ritual processes in place making, (ii) the planned transmission of printed communication across the colonies for publicity about freemasonry and in nation-building, and (iii) the telling references to abstract surveying intertwined with commercial interests. The republic and its animated geography built upon inheritance, the present situation and imagined future possibilities with well-fitting technique.

Chapter 5 examines the narrative of progress in early America, the moral imagination of an informed citizenry, and the promise of egalitarian education. Indefinite perfectibility, a term taken from *philosophes* like Tocqueville, was evident as not only the thoughtful reorganizing and fashioning of new habits, but also the aspirational, contingent and agonistic struggle of major publics and counter publics in a deliberative democracy. There is an examination of the deep habits and code of inclusion and exclusion, for example, in the unequal possibilities of education or freedom afforded to African-American slaves, First Nations, or women. The ideal of indefinite perfectibility was visible as the thoughtful reorganizing and fashioning of new habits, but also of inspirational, contingent and agonistic struggle of major public interest and the formation of counter publics and their interest in deliberative democracy. The indefinite perfectibility of deliberative democracy included the narrative of enhanced and equal opportunity in education, entailing literacy among an informed citizenry, and possibilities of upward social mobility.

Chapter 6 examines the *gendered* cornerstone ceremonies of the freemasons, specifically in the federal district taking shape in the City of Washington, and Territory of Columbia. *The District was specifically mandated in the United States Constitution as a ritualistic and administrative place as was the United States Post Office for effective transmission.* Each of the cornerstone ceremonies in Washington DC were reported by Dunlap in Philadelphia in his attempts at building the social imaginary and solidarity of the nation.

Each heartfelt foundation ceremony followed by celebration at day's end acted as the aesthetic-moral starting point for abstract land surveys (surveying had economic and state salience in nation-building), in what became urban and national space in the building of buildings and monuments. In turn, the survey located the actual geographic starting point for cornerstone ritual performance. The ritual ceremony for the public formation of the geography of the federal district was situated against celestial measurements, the lay of the wetlands, the rise of slope and direction of the rising sun. The President's House and the national Capitol building were oriented toward the four cardinal directions of space anchored in the daily movement of the sun in east and west directions and its rising in the physical and for the freemasons symbolic or spiritual east, the place of dawn light. The East for the freemason, precisely as for the human being in anthropological time, is the *"place of light"* in an often troubling, or dark, yet sometimes bounteous earth. National reporting involving networked newspaper, including Dunlap's paper focusing on the ceremonies, helped imagine and build the republic.

B. THE ARGUMENT

I argue that freemasonry and freemasons were representatives at the founding of the American republic of other civic associations and wider civil society through their involvement with worlds of print, egalitarian ideals in education, experimentation, and specific moral imagination of an informed citizenry in deliberative democracy. Print culture is vital in both local (temporal) place and in networks of places across space in early America. Print culture provides a valuable access point into the study both of freemasonry and wider civil society in early American cultural and geographic landscapes. Freemasonry provides a demarcated area of study that helps engage the embodied drama of human agency in a mode of conjoint associate living (nascent democracy) and different logics, or semiotics, of communication present at the origins of American civil society. Freemasonry foregrounds for study the place of moral imagination in early American deliberative democracy.

A few freemasons held a considerable leadership role in the movement toward war, the war itself, and with increasing numbers in the formative period after the war. They did this in part through their emerging, professional occupations in printing-journalism, publication and circulation, and the strategic use of print in their political and military lives. The impact of freemasonry, and freemasons, through ritual and transmission functions of communication was larger than the small numbers indicated and powerfully affected their place in the American social imaginary, both in fact but also the play of the imaginary and fantasy. They would go on, at least until the 1820s, to have a disproportionate presence in government and the public sphere at all scales and an important presence in the architecture, signs and monuments of governance. After a downturn in the 1820s (a scandal occurred discussed later) freemasonry within decades became a prominent and contributing American civic association once again. Worlds of print were a force multiplier in human association and conjoint communicative experience and freemasons could enact complementary popular civic drama as in parades.

The freemasons aspired commercially in the economy. They were well positioned for upward social mobility but also worked towards charity and community. American freemasons also emerged as leaders in supporting public education and higher education as a vision of the American republic. The focus on higher education and freemasonry practices is exemplified well in the considerable impact of the fraternity in establishing the University of Michigan, the greatest experiment in public education of its time in the world.[6] This focus on the need for an informed citizenry and need for egalitarian possibilities in education at all levels and the ideal of experimentation was in some considerable part a vital legacy of the War of Independence with human needs exposed and opportunity for the individual and group imagined.

The printed text of the United States Constitution proposed an expanding geographic area of governance, association, and procedure on a scale never before believed possible in prior political theory or praxis. There was to be an "extensive republic."[7] Important transmission technologies and techniques, or technics, emerged as central to the practice of deliberative democracy in the new American republic. This included the horse, the post office, military intelligence and dispatch, fast coach, tight schedule and the policy instrument of tax incentives for the geographic movement of newspaper editions between editors.

The face-to-face communication of ancient Athens was in sharp contrast to the needs of continental America. In Europe, philosophers who were also freemasons like Montesquieu, were concerned with the geographic moment of democratic experience and problems encountered at large geographic scales, as were non-freemasons such as Jean Jacques Rousseau. The seaboard cities were initially the cultural hearth of the nation-state and the origin of American civil society. Alexis de Tocqueville recognized this quality in the New England small town face-to-face-environments at the American founding, but he was able to identify the extraordinary rise, proliferation and transmission of newspapers across the wide expanses of civil society in America.[8] Tocqueville had been accul-

6 Masons migrating often across Lake Erie from New York to Detroit contributed more than substantially to the founding of the University of Michigan; see James Fairbairn Smith, *Michigan Masonic Tracing Board, 1764 to 1976: A Panorama of Masonic History* (n.p.: Sesquicentennial of the Grand Lodge of Free and Accepted Masons of Michigan, 1976), 17.

7 Robert A. Gross and Marky Kelly, eds. *A History of the Book in America: An Extensive Republic: Print, Culture, and Society in the New Nation, 1790s-1840*, vol. 2 (Chapel Hill: University of North Carolina Press, 2010).

8 Alexis de Tocqueville, *Democracy in America*, trans. Harvey C. Mansfield and Delba Winthrop (Chicago: University Of Chicago Press, 2011); George Wilson Pierson,

turated in an aristocratic world of books and print in France. He sensed something different in America, including the obvious wide reaches of its fast-growing steam-boat, commerce and road system cutting through varied geographic landscapes.

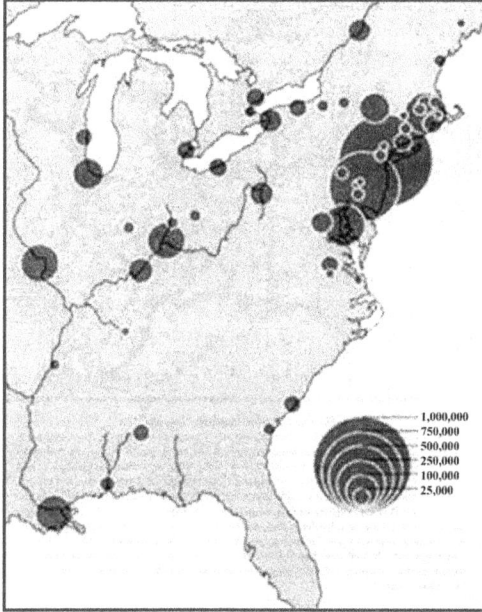

Figure 1. The Population and Pattern of Cities in the Mid-Nineteenth Century Union of States in 1860. (Courtesy Yale University Press)[9]

The networked geography of print worlds in America's national geographic core region depicted in this work held outliers in Savannah and Charleston along the coast, and later moved powerfully along natural and man-made transmission lines inland as with the building of the Erie Canal along the Ohio River, as can be seen in Figure 1. The same agglomeration and transmission effect appeared in New Orleans and Cincinnati with Tocqueville well aware of the landscapes. Tocqueville saw important parts of this print network and community building on his American Grand Tour and recorded his observations for French, American, English and international reading audiences.

Tocqueville in America (London and Baltimore: The Johns Hopkins University Press, 1996), 588-592.

9 See also, Allan Pred, *Urban Growth and the Circulation of Information: The United States System of Cities, 1790-1840* (Cambridge: Harvard University Press, 1973), 8.

In the early 18th century, the networked locales of the American colonies had a population of less than 400,000, with people thinly dispersed relative to some smaller regions in Europe, yet compact. Benedict Anderson noted that "The original Thirteen Colonies comprised an area smaller than Venezuela and one third the size of Argentina. Flocked geographically together, their market-centers in Boston, New York, and Philadelphia were readily accessible to one another and their populations were relatively linked by print as well as commerce. The United States could gradually multiply in numbers over the next 183 years as old and new populations moved westward out of the old east coast core."[10]

The daily, weekly, or bi-weekly ceremonial or ritual consumption was performed "in silent privacy in the lair of the skull ... (yet paradoxically) ... each communicant is well aware that the ceremony he performs is being replicated simultaneously by thousands (or millions) of others whose existence he is confident, yet whose identity he has not the slightest notion."[11] The reader's interest and imagination thrives in the overlap between accessible and inaccessible places and imagined distant places and space, no less imagined distant times, past and future.

The North American landscape was defined by a system of cities and great variety of "wild lands" in what became a new union of states. The social, cultural, and economic milieu supported a diversity of careers, fraternities, associations, occupations, and identities in America. These associations occurred all across bustling cities like Baltimore, Worcester, Philadelphia, New Orleans, and Boston, and no less along routes and sites through the hinterlands.

French was spoken in significant areas of what is today New England and German in parts of Pennsylvania. In what is today North Carolina, there was a substantial Scots Gaelic speaking settlement that survived into the early 20th century. In addition, there were African languages, notably Kimbundu and Kikongo of Central Africa. A diversity of languages could be heard everywhere and they contributed substantially to the geographical nomenclature, and some rhetorical styles, which remains with us. In many regards, the linguistic environment was more diverse and divisive

---

10 Benedict Anderson, *Imagined Communities: Reflections on the Origin and Spread of Nationalism* (London: Verso, 2006), 63-65.

11 Ibid., 35.

than today. However, a broadening reading public was cultivating new shared reading habits among the literate elites.

The European and later American freemasons ultimately printed rituals, or used rituals printed by those who were not freemasons, for internal purposes of memorizing, forming of new habits, and ultimately texts to aid contemplation and discussion. Early American freemasons used the press, often using members of the fraternity who were themselves printer-journalists, publishers, and booksellers to produce and distribute the constitutions of their fraternity. They used print with the very clear intention of spreading the geographic reach of the fraternity in local place and transmission across space and, in the process, making freemasonry better known among the public. Techniques, such as a suite of emerging print vehicles and changing method of production, helped fashion different habits, new interests, follow-on actions, and education of the body-mind in networked places. There was a literacy revolution underway in early America, with its own new set of habits, necessary habit correction, and conduct.

Printed media could be used in coordinated media strategies to advance freemasonry. Freemasons used newspaper to invite local and travelling masons to attend public happenings with freemasonic trappings or to extend an invitation to regularly scheduled or ad hoc private lodge meetings. Freemasons used newspapers for a variety of non-masonic purposes. This included disseminating important information on trade, business advertisements, education, legal matters, as well as increasing reportage on political happenings and contests. A sense of public service as well as personal and economic advancement in the study and praxis of print vehicles existed for the freemason and non-freemasons which involved a variety of print vehicles, including almanacs, books, declarations, constitutions, newspapers, and more.

The openness of early American freemasonry in worlds of print and its valuing of new habits of literacy combined with the actions of some freemason printer-journalists proved important for the wide acceptance of the fraternity that was held in the revolutionary period. In contrast some, such as Thomas Jefferson, held what can now be seen as a prescient concern about freemasonry in its capacity as an exclusive and secret society. Jefferson, who was not a mason, had many close friends with diverse talents who were freemasons with whom he engaged in substantive discussion and visited masonic lodges.[12] Everything changed for the freemasons in 1826, when a group of rogue freemasons kidnapped and likely murdered, perhaps by accident, a freemason and bricklayer in upstate New York named William Morgan, for presuming to publish the secret rituals of freemasonry. Ironically, publication of masonic materials was given legitimacy by freemasons in Europe and America through their growing recourse to publish for internal and external purposes.

The Morgan incident engendered a significant anti-masonry movement, which changed the public image of freemasonry in America and altered the initial cosmopolitan spirit in American freemasonry. Public consensus was that masons had committed a crime, and that high-ranking masonic officials were concealing the truth. According to public view, the freemasons had co-opted the state to have a bad effect for the republic. A strong group response was needed. The response involved the use of the printing technology at-hand. Printing technology was heavily worked as the heart and muscle of the anti-masonry movement diffusing out of central New York along with unabated evangelical oratory and sometimes paranoid imagination of a conspiracy that needed to be exposed.

The anti-masonry movement lasted at its greatest intensity for only a decade but persisted among elements of civil society much longer. Freemasonry did recover its reputation by the mid-19th century considerably through male public performance such as horse-mounted Templar parades and went on to be a major force in what came to be called the golden age of fraternalism in American history running through much of the latter 19th century into the early 20th century. Conspiracy theories have existed since the inception of freemasonry in Europe. Anti-masonry and often related conspiracy theories remain a difficult topic of study with no final conclusion as to their place in the American psyche and in other cultures. A potential antidote is the moral imagination of an informed citizenry which includes support for a strong, free inquiring press and standards of professionalization. The Morgan affair did involve kidnapping but the possible crime of homicide remains unresolved as a legal matter. The Morgan affair is an instance where the ritual solidarity of community can move at least to an epistemological fence and worse to a hostile di-

---

12 Cécile Révauger, "Thomas Jefferson." in Cécile Révauger & Charles Porset, eds., *Le monde maçonnique des Lumières: l'Europe, l'Amérique et de ses colonies, prosopographique Dictionnaire.* (Paris: Champion, 2014), 1522-1525.

vide and violence between the insider and outsider. In such a case transmission, the free flow of information can deconstruct too tightly drawn narrow cultural boundaries.

CHAPTER 2

CRITICAL TEXTS IN LONDON FREEMASONRY

Afterthe publication and circulation in 1723 of the *Book of Constitutions of the Free-masons*, drawing on oral, written, syncretism, and antiquarian traditions, no less Scottish Guilds and offering a glimpse of the new science, a few independent lodges of freemasons in London moved into a new era. The production and transmission of print media became integrally related to the ritual life, interest, and public projection of the new organization. Hard and fast disciplinary areas of study did not exist in this period, as witnessed in the diversity of interests humming around the *Book of Constitutions of the Free-Masons*. Four illustrative texts published in London in this period help summarize the admixture of the meaning-making, valuing, producing of symbols and praxis of the printed text in modern British freemasonry, and in gauging the transmission of freemasonry to America. These texts are the (a) 1723 *Book of Constitutions of the Free-masons*; (b) 1753 *Ahiman Rezon*, the constitution of the ancient freemasons compiled by William Dermott, (c) the 1762 anonymous ritualistic exposure entitled *Jachin and Boaz*, and (d) the *Illustrations of Freemasonry* by William Preston in 1772. In addition, an image of cosmopolitan 18th century freemasons, Figure 5, can be accurately read as a sophisticated theory of the sign already in the 18th century and more specifically a graphical representation of embodied ritual and transmission semiotics communication in modern deliberation.

A. ENGLISH (LONDON) FREEMASONRY

Modern philosophical freemasonry began in the early 18th century in London, Scotland and other sites including France. Men assembled for social fraternity and clubbing, but also for diverse, and imaginative studies.[13] The range of studies included history, philosophy, hermetic studies, and sophisticated expressions of Christian mysticism, antiquarianism. This at first involved the fashioning of temporary places such as a rearranged coffee house interior for actual experimental work in new science.

---

13 Paul Eliot and Stephen Daniels, "The 'School of True, Useful and Universal Science': Freemasonry, Natural Philosophy and Scientific Culture in Eighteenth-Century England," *British Journal of the History of Science* 39, no 2 (2006): 207-229.

An illustration of the trans-disciplinary individual and milieu is Isaac Newton (not a freemason), who was interested in antiquarianism, the new science, alchemy, and the assumed sacred proportions of Solomon's temple. John Brewer has demonstrated that English artists, amateurs, early entrepreneurs, and the public audience developed a deeply imaginative culture still admired in different ways today, from its physical landscapes to wit, intellectual life and drama.[14]

There were diverse historical imaginations in 18th century London, and prior to that in Scotland, when men assembled drawn to the solidarities and places of the stonemason guilds, and other guilds, and even archaeological sites such as Stonehenge where some held mythopoeic beliefs of ancient wisdom. Other views and practices of freemasonry existed in this period, for example, clubbing. Freemasonry was interpreted variously in private and public worlds such as environs fit for clubbing, a secret society out to control the powers of the world or a cosmopolitan institution of learning and charity.

John Macky speaks of London in the 1720s as possessing infinite clubs or societies for the improvement of learning and keeping up with good humor and mirth.[15] Putting clubbing to the side, the masonic lodge internalized moral custom, cultivated an aesthetic-moral habitus of sociability and service and valorized learning. Image, symbol, word, and metaphor deepened communication shaping habits, postures and intellectual positions. Virtue and inquiry were anchored through signs as embodied ritual, communication, and social performance—deliberation widely interpreted alongside the real values and power of transmission.

The number of civic associations or voluntary associations appears to have been less in North American cities through much of the 18th century, although the American numbers were rapidly increasing, ultimately stunning observers like de Tocqueville with their importance in deliberative democracy in local place and their speedy, efficient linkages through print across short and great distances. In Philadelphia, Benjamin Franklin was imagining and instinctively building new voluntary as-

---

14 See, John Brewer, *The Pleasures of the Imagination: English Culture in the 18th Century* (New York: Farrar Straus Giroux. 2007).

15 Peter Clark, *British Clubs and Societies 1580-1800: The Origins of an Associational World* (Oxford: Oxford University Press, 2000), 1.

sociations (public formations and public interest) to address the public and its problems or advance learning throughout his life, for example the Junto a philosophical society. His actions, to a significant degree were local place based, while aware of wider landscapes such as those he experienced in his travels to London or around the eastern littoral as Postmaster General, as shall be seen. Freemasonry was one of the first civil associations he joined, and led. Other examples of his handiwork were the Library Company, akin to a non-profit corporation, and the Philosophical Society. Franklin lived, worked, and played at the cusp of the inherited European apprentice system and modern occupation. He was situated in the overlap between the guilds, trades of print, the modern professions, associations, and their networks that were emerging such as printing-journalism, and in this period and place the patriot printer-journalist.

The masonic lodge emerged to play its own part in the history of education, ultimately in diverse cultures around the world. The developing 18th century ritual space of the lodge in a number of European sites, America, and geographically more widely, was a symbolic and geometric cosmos intended as a place of learning. The ritual place of learning arose in the tension between an imagined ancient sacred place (each lodge symbolized the Temple of Solomon) and modern more secular space. To some extent as men gathered across class boundaries it was also its own type of economic space held together briefly in time for a few hours of meeting. For a period, the idea of architecture and freemasonry in London influenced the wider built environment and vice versa that would alter in the latter years of the 18th century and start of the 19th century to include some impact on schools of architecture.[16] The origins and diffusion of modern philosophical or speculative freemasonry out of Georgian (and Palladian) London and into North America (as well diffusion from Scotland and Ireland in large part) occurred at a time when commerce and associational life increased in London's coffee houses, ale houses, apartments, hotels, print shops, guild halls, and formal educational institutions. Freemasonry was one of the most successful, early, expansive, and largest of the civic or voluntary associations. Freemasonry and the wider civil sphere were apposite processes of communication, learning,

---

16 Lawrence Snezna, "Geometry of Architecture and Freemasonry in 19th-Century England" (doctoral dissertation, Open University, 2002).

and association in a range of cultural and material environments. Early freemasonry is highly representative of the modern civil sphere at its origins, including overlap with the economic sphere and additionally with the state.

Freemasons were governed in the first half of the 18th century by the mandates, rules or practices established in the 1723 *Book of Constitutions of the Free-Masons*, which was an essential part of the transmission and governance of a growing number of symbolic lodges that banded together at first in the London metropolis, proximately for utilitarian purposes.[17] The *Book of Constitutions* has been interpreted by some to a variant extent a synthesis of older constitutions and new ideas. The older so-called Gothic Constitutions, or Ancient Charges, survive from a very different but related form of freemasonry before the 18th century.[18] To a degree, some of these early so-called Gothic Constitutions are printed artifacts that point to an early oral tradition in freemasonry. The earliest surviving Constitution for example is a poem that was likely read to the new mason upon his induction into freemasonry.[19] The poem may well have been a significant part of an oral tradition of transmission.

Andrew Prescott, the founding Director of the Centre for Research into Freemasonry and Fraternalism at the University of Sheffield, pointed out the fundamental starting point for investigations into the early history of the premier Grand Lodge of London and Westminster is the 1723 *Book of Constitutions of the Free-Masons* and he begins by reiterating the "well-known fact" that the Scottish Presbyterian clergyman was its compiler and author.[20] Prescott, nevertheless, moves swiftly beyond accepted wisdom stating that Anderson's involvement would not have been readily apparent to the 1723 reading audience.

---

17 James Anderson, *Book of Constitutions of the Free-Masons* (London, 1723).

18 Henry H. Coil, "Gothic Constitutions," *Masonic Encyclopedia*. (Richmond: Macoy Publishing and Masonic Supply Company, 1995), 292-297.

19 James Orchard Halliwell, "A Poem on the Constitutions of Masonry" (unpublished translation of *The Regius Poem* or, *The Halliwell Manuscript*, c. 1390, from the original manuscript in the King's Library of the British Museum, London, 1840), http://www.pagrandlodge.org/district37/D37_Pdfs/TheRegiusPoem.PDF, retrieved October 10, 2014.

20 Andrew Prescott, "The Productions of the English Books of Constitutions in the Eighteenth Century" (paper, ronde table, *Le Monde Maçonnique*, University of Sorbonne, Paris, 2005), 1.

Figure 2. John Pine, frontispiece of the 1723 *Book of Constitutions of the Free-Masons*: The 2nd Duke of Montagu presents the *Roll of Constitutions* and the compasses to Philip, Duke of Wharton. The Newtonian Desaguliers is presumed on the far right. (Courtesy of the Library of the Grand Lodge of Iowa.)

Anderson is not described as the author on the title page of the *Book of Constitutions of the Free-masons,* or in the dedication, but he is listed in the original text. His name is recorded as master of a lodge; with others on a list of lodges. Prescott argues, correctly, that the names that anyone purchasing the *Book of Constitutions* in 1723 would have noticed were the publishers John Senex and John Hooke listed on the title page: "Printed by William Hunter, for John Senex, at the Globe, and John Hooke at the Flower-de-luce over against St. Dunstan's Church." They would notice the freemason and engraver of the frontispiece "Engraved by John Pine in Aldersgate Street London."[21]

The textual evidence makes clear the book's publishing and finance by Senex and Hooke. Prescott argues that if the emerging Grand Lodge of London or any other person had made investment for the printing, this would have certainly been affirmed in the indentation, similar to the case that was recorded in the Irish *Constitutions* of 1730 published by a Dublin

21 Ibid., 3.

21

bookseller Joseph Watts for John Pennel, the Grand Secretary of the Irish Grand Lodge, a fact recorded in the imprint. Prescott points out that "A very large number of copies of the *Constitutions* survive suggesting Senex and Hooke kept the book in print for a number of years and that reprints were made."[22] The success of the sales may have further attracted, or deepened, the already attentive Anderson, who worked to support himself over the course of his maturing life in publishing.

Senex began his working life as an apprentice printer at the London Stationers' Company. He was in constant proximity to the printed materials in new thought (the new science) and the entirety of material that flowed in and out of London. By law, all printed materials entering England had to move through the geographic location of Stationer's Company, situated near the earlier lodges of freemasonry in the Westminster area and local milieu of St. Paul's Cathedral. Prescott affirms that among the book buying audience in 1723 the "appearance of the names of Senex on the title page and Desaguliers, a prominent Newtonian, at the end of the dedication in the *Book of Constitutions* inextricably linked it with the new scientific thought." [23]

It is often thought that the figure in the dark in the lowermost right hand corner is a depiction of Desaguliers. As often pointed out by Margaret Jacob, Newtonianism had a significant impact on the fashioning of modern freemasonry, even though Newton himself was not a freemason.[24] Prescott concludes that Grand Lodge freemasonry through its *Book of Constitutions* and the enthusiasm of its instrument makers, mapmakers, and engravers was responsible for moving the Scientific Revolution to the European Enlightenment.[25]

Rick Berman points out modern freemasonry did not simply evolve from the mediaeval guilds and religious orders that existed earlier. It was re-

---

22 Loc. cit.

23 See Audrey T. Carpenter, *John Theophilus Desaguliers: A Natural Philosopher, Engineer and Freemason in Newtonian England* (London and New York: Continuum, 2011). Desaguliers was a prominent Newtonian and experimenter arrived in London from Oxford. He was a friend of Senex while nominating him for membership in the Royal Society, all the while a confidant of Newton.

24 *Margaret Jacob, Living the Enlightenment: Freemasonry and Politics in Eighteenth-Century Europe (Oxford: Oxford University Press, 1991).*

25 Prescott, 4.

constructed radically by a self-appointed inner core of freemasons.[26] That inner core is still not entirely known with certainty and the whole set of transactions remain unclear. The modern fraternity from its origins in 1717 to 1723 was shaped as a vehicle for the expression and transmission of an elite group's political, philosophical, and Newton's new science views. They followed loosely assembled meeting places that grew into more robust lodges of ritual performance with buildings dedicated to the work of the lodges and owned by them.

The frontispiece would have had an impact at first sight, on the American Newtonian Franklin in his travels to London. He was seminal in bringing freemasonry into America with his reprint in 1734 of the *Book of Constitutions of the Free-Masons*, the first masonic publication in America.[27] The impact of the text on an already existing freemasonry of autonomous lodges, of varying sorts, perhaps even a prior Grand Lodge in some crude form, was enormous. The growing geographic and imagined arc of transmission, home and movement, followed publication and distribution of the *Constitutions* from the London metropolis across, provinces, regions, and colonies with other texts. Ritual performance was situated itself within a transmission network of ritually constructed, symbolic material places. Local places with densely layered connections and face-to-face embodied communication anchored more dispersed and abstract networks. The lodge was a real place and situated the body-mind and group in ritual, habit correction, and transmission (the embodied individual in feeling, willing, and thinking in a civic association).

Hooke himself had a range of interests including continental philosophy, surveying, geometry and measurement. Euclid and Pythagoras were often highly honored in Ancient Charges or "Constitutions" of the stonemasons that preceded the 1723 text of the *Book of Constitutions of the Free-Masons*. The body-subject and space of the lodge gave an honored place to geometry as the queen of the liberal arts. The inner core of men already mentioned that radicalized and remade the inherited system of induction in the 18th century were on more than one occasion emergent in the formulation of modern science.

---

26 Ric Berman, *The Foundations of Modern Freemasonry: The Grand Architects - Political Change and the Scientific Enlightenment* (East Sussex: Sussex Press, 2012).

27 However, the frontispiece was removed in the American edition, perhaps because of insufficient engraving skills in America at the time, or cost, or a reason yet to be ascertained.

There was a partnership of business and shared interests between Senex and Hooke. For his part, Hooke published Samuel Wyld's pragmatic guide to field measurement entitled *The Practical Surveyor* and as a master of detail and precision resonant with the practices of a man skilled hard fast in typographical work and new thought, he produced the gauge used to standardize French and English units of measurement. His work on the gauge moved across the Channel to waiting officials in France. The surveyor, gauge maker, architect in the Gutenberg galaxy and printer-publisher lived in ocular-centric worlds, within the demands of a precise and ordered transmission epistemology of communication. In this situation, as shall be seen, scientific representation, or the printed report of the practical time-schedule of lodge meetings in London, was intended to mirror perfectly a world of certainty "out there."

In addition to the mutual interests in surveying, broad learning, printing as an ancient and honored position, publishing, and the new science, Senex and Hooke served as brother masons and wardens in felt ritual place, qualitative inhabited space, and abstract geometry of a local masonic lodge. In each lodge, the symbolism and work of Euclidean and Pythagorean geometry held an important, honored place and in some lodges, and lodges meeting in coffee houses, Newtonian physics and newer forms of mathematics were becoming topics of discussion. Geometry was considered a divine art and science a discipline to be closely studied. The path breaking work by Prescott on Senex and Hooke opens important new perspectives on the origins of modern freemasonry in London and an inaugural moment in the spatial studies of freemasonry.

After his apprenticeship in the printing district, Senex rose to become a bookseller and very prominent publisher of the new science at the Globe in Salisbury Court. Within a short time, he printed a translation done by Edmund Halley's distinguished work establishing the periodicity of comets. Senex had earned equal distinction as one of the most prominent map and globe-makers of the period. The geography of the local civil sphere of the lodge for Senex, and many substantive colleagues, was not only simultaneous to the geography of an international Republic of Letters but also intersected the machinations of a global empire.[28] In the penultimate chapter, a map by Senex is depicted as representing the expanding arc of interests of the British Empire. Senex became a Fellow of the Royal Soci-

---

28 See Figure 8, Chapter 6, 181.

ety in 1728, as did his co-publisher Hooke. Hooke's membership in the Royal Society offers the possibility he held Newtonian thought in some deep measure of regard. Senex initiated a business of selling globes, charts, maps, and mathematical tools and went on to produce an extended series of fine publications drawing together his keen interest in the production of maps with the latest scientific discoveries.

Senex in the totality of his work in his masonic lodge, printers shop, publishing, and perhaps the finest globe maker in the world, labored in the overlap between the places and space of near and far, home and movement, primary and secondary experience, ritual and transmission functions (logics or semiotics) of communication, with habit correction. He exemplifies what David Hansen has called the cosmopolitan possibilities of learning, communication and association "in between"—*what is termed in this work as the overlap between*—the near and far of home and movement, embodied, felt place and more abstract spaces of transmission.[29]

Something more is to be said about Desaguliers depicted in the 1723 frontispiece. He was among the many, and certainly the most successful Newtonian demonstrators, experimenters, and lecturers that emerged in the expanding London public lecture circuits. That circuit became better known through the printed flyer or newspaper and increased the sale of books on Newtonianism. In the London milieu, science and commerce were mutually reinforcing. Aims, methods, and interests did not concern vague speculation but rigors of experimental science. Desaguliers helped set a course for others who began to argue business success was not alien to applied natural philosophy in developing engineering solutions to pragmatic commercial problems. Public experiments (in public places), sometimes in masonic lodges or coffee houses, and the work of the Royal Society were part of the commercialization of science. New interest evolved, new occupations were anchored in incipient ways in experimental sites or places of inquiry, action, and communication.

The original *Book of Constitutions* was a work of (neo) Palladian propaganda in its important depiction of the frontispiece of landscape architecture and entire thrust. The costumes of the figures resonate well with the landscape architecture, including the five architectural orders depicted in the

---

29 David Hansen, "Dewey and Cosmopolitanism," in A.G. Rudd, Jay Garrison, and Linda Stone, eds., *John Dewey at 150: Reflections for a New Century* (West Lafayette: Purdue University Press, 2009), 104-116.

stage architecture of the *mis-en-scène*. Sandra Rosenbaum, a specialist in textiles and posture at the Los Angeles County Museum of Modern Art, sees the image as a strong Renaissance perspective grid with large-scale figures in the foreground.[30] The powerful dynamics of perspective pushes the figural grouping forward.

Importantly, the men in the foreground group are not dressed in clothing contemporary with a 1723 date. Rosenbaum views their combined dress as an amalgam of taste ranging back through the 17th century and Renaissance. They are invoking a Palladian but also Renaissance past in an act, a "masque" of theater, the shaping of an English national identity, and *mis-en-scène*.[31] The image as a strong Renaissance perspective grid with large-scale figures in the foreground and a sharply raked single point perspective as ground are fashioned out of arches depicting the five orders of architecture inherited from the Renaissance and the earlier expressions of the classical period of Greece. The five orders link the single background point of perspective and the foreground of the masque. In an important sense, the image presents a tension of ancient and modern worlds, which was a significant tension in late 17th century Paris and London and part of the birthing of 18th century freemasonry.

Palladian architecture is a European style designed from the design of the Italian architect Andrea Palladio (1508-1580), himself drawing on the Classical work of ancient Vitruvius. The term "Palladian" refers to the establishment of buildings inspired by Palladio's own work. Palladianism focused on harmonic proportion found in mathematics, while using design and structural elements such as porticos, Roman decoration, windows and columns, and simplicity as well depicting the assumed respectability

---

30 Sandra Rosenbaum (email communication, March 17, 2007).

31 What is the "masque" understood in the period and place of the seminal 17th century architect, student of dramaturgy and artisan Inigo Jones with his Palladian style? Later in the eighteenth century London experienced a revival of interest in Jones. It was another demonstration of the creative tension of the ancient and modern ideals of learning in which modern civil society was born. As to a definition of masque, it was a performance like an opera but quite hybrid. Words, theater, dance, scenery, and costumes made the masque a particularly hard form to define. When Jones created a scene in a play it could be a scape representing a range of elements in the built environment including parts of temples, theaters, broken columns, bases, and cornices with statuary with the whole invoking some great city of the ancient Romans or Britons. Joseph M. Levin, *Between the Ancients and Moderns: Baroque Culture in Restoration England* (New Haven and London: Yale University Press, 1999), 132-133.

of well-to-do individuals. Palladianism is revisited in Chapter 6 in examining the building of the American President's House (the White House), originally fashioned in a neo-Palladian style by freemasons who were also stonemasons from Ireland and Scotland in considerable part. In this latter instance, they were perhaps drawing on antecedent Palladian elements in Ireland, for example, the Irish House of Parliament built in 1739 and the first parliament in the world with two separate chambers.

The Palladian arrival in England and ultimately wider Europe, and America, cannot be understood without some attention to Inigo Jones. Through intense study and imagination, the remarkable English architect Jones (1573-1652) reconceived the intellectual position of architecture, its orientation, and the crafted space of his own persona as architect, on the public stage (in the public sphere) in England. His work was influential in the attempted fashioning of an intended national space of England, Scotland, and Ireland. Jones fashioned his identity and considerably the identity and "occupation" of architect in England and beyond. Jones' self-creation, his identity and interest, as an architect was a reflection and simultaneously artificer of his architectural designs and crafted spaces of the early Stuart period. Jones drew upon Palladio, and a range of other sources, especially other Italian Renaissance and indigenous English sources.[32] The rebirth of the work of Jones was of importance in the first moments of 18th century freemasonry as evidenced in the earlier discussion of the frontispiece of the 1723 *Book of Constitutions of the Free-masons*. Later, Palladio and Jones influenced the thinking of others such as Goethe the German freemason, artist, and scientist in the *Bildung* traditions in the provinces of Germany. The German term *Bildung* references education, formation and addresses self-cultivation. The German tradition of education and philosophy are intertwined in a way that acknowledges the processes of both individual and group maturation.

Daniel Purdy, in his insightful *The Building in Bildung: Goethe, Palladio, and the Architectural Media,* describes the vital information transmission by Jones, of text and architectural images out of Italy over the Alps.[33] There was movement back and forth across the Alps by tourists, participants in

---

32 *Christy Anderson, Inigo Jones and the Classical Tradition (Cambridge: Cambridge University Press, 2010), 1-20.*

33 Daniel Purdy, "The Building in *Bildung*: Goethe, Palladio, and the Architectural Media," *Goethe Yearbook* (2008): 57-73.

the Grand Tour and pilgrims. In the case of Jones, Purdy describes the
great migration of architectural text, and printed images, in a trans-Al-
pine diffusion. Jones was the original font of the diffusion of Palladianism; at first into Northern Europe, with subsequent architects engaging
the perspective from diverse regions in Europe through generation after
generation. Palladianism was also present for a period in early America.
Architectural processes were often first inspired by the images of Palladio, then subsequently revisiting original sites and buildings in Italy on
a Grand Tour to re-inspire in their own light the work re-incarnated by
Jones. Palladio integrated classical restraint with creative ongoing inven-
tiveness, the tension of the new and old, habit and imagination. Overall,
he bequeathed a profoundly sensual environment and arguably the most
influential series of buildings in art history.[34]

Prescott points to books that were influenced by Jones and (neo) Palladianism listed at the close of the *Book of Constitutions*. He emphasizes
that they refer to the work of architecture inclusive of two luxuriously im-
printed folios: (i) John James's translation who is deemed as a member
of Greenwich Masonic Lodge of Andrea Posso's *Rules and Examples of
Perspective Proper for Painters and Architects*; and the second was recorded
to be Claude Perrault's translation *Treatise of the Five Orders of Columns
in Architecture*. The aforementioned volumes were preliminary texts for
an inquirer interested in better understanding Palladian architecture. The
stipulation of the Palladian handbooks was regarded as the essential history of architect, art and aesthetics by Prescott fundamentally catering
the story of the loss of the secrets of classical architecture secrets, their
rediscovery in the 17th century and possibly revival in the 18th century. [35]
However, the architectural spaces were thought by some to hold a peren-
nial philosophy of integral art, ethics, cosmology and reason. A second
motivation was the fashioning of a national identity conspicuous in the
masques and architecture of Jones.[36] This heady brew was re-animated in
the early eighteenth century of Georgian London woven together by a
simple and growing love in the work of Jones.

As noted by Walter Ong, the print medium, its space and its enclosures,

---

34 James S. Ackerman, *Palladio* (New York and London: Penguin, 1996), 19.

35 Prescott, 4.

36 Kenneth Olwig, *Landscape, Nature, and the Body Politic: From Britain's Renaissance to
Americas New World* (Madison: University of Wisconsin Press, 2002).

needs to be studied together in the historical continuity of the aural/oral transition to literacy in human communicative and sensorimotor experience. "Print embedded the word in space more definitely [than the prior medium of the illuminated then written manuscript with its closer affiliations with oral-aural culture]."[37] Each artful medium has its own logic and builds on affect and transaction. Media are in transaction, one with the other. The printed text of the word made possible new habits of literacy, but the printed images of architectural drawing was also an important condition of possibility in the transmission and practice of the attempted Palladian renaissance in architecture and newly imagined national identity hinted at overall in the frontispiece of the 1723 *Book of Constitutions of the Free-Masons.*

The transmission or geographic diffusion of Palladianism out of Italy into diverse parts of Europe helps set the scene and tell the story. The ancient discipline and modern occupation of architect depends on transmission across space and time of information but also the funded richness of tradition or accumulation of experience that is in local culture. Something of the same process has been true since the development of early alphabets and geometries, to the latest coding in cyberspace. In all periods and places, the mnemonics, semiotics and transmission of knowledge has been reliant on the dominant technologies, technique, or techniques, of each period and place. Mario Carpo demonstrated how communication media used by Western architects from classical times through the Renaissance to the modern period is intimately related to unique forms of architectural thought and expression.[38]

The important symbol and metaphor of the "lost-word" in modern freemasonry is first mentioned in history in Pritchard's *Masonry Dissected,* an exposure that appeared in 1730 in London and is discussed shortly. There are earlier historical references to the "mason's word" in Scotland apparently not yet "lost." In that earlier period the mason's word was used as a means of one mason identifying another at home or when travelling to foreign cities and regions (transmission and pilgrimage as an

---

37 Walter J. Ong, *Orality and Literacy: The Technology of the Word* (London and New York: Routledge, 2006), 121.

38 Mario Carpo, *Architecture in the Age of Printing: Orality, Writing, Typography, and Printed Images in the History of Architectural Theory,* trans. Sarah Besnson (Cambridge and London: MIT Press, 2001).

opportunity to learn) to work as an operative stone mason. The search for ancient wisdom and the 'living word' evoked a sense of mythos, a sophisticated Christian mysticism, mystery of sacred human origins, and a sense of self and journey. In another reading, it references the idea of deferred meaning using a metaphor of place and space, or perhaps of equal accuracy real psychological and physical displacement at the origins of modernity. The "lost word" also can signify a sophisticated early theory of the sign and tension of presence and absence in artful human imagination and action.

This marks a major period of social transition. Alberto Pérez-Gómez has shown that between the later years of the Renaissance and opening years of the 19th century, the perceived valued ancient arts of architecture were under radical transformation, specifically within the context of the scientific revolution of Galileo, Newton, and others with their own spatial demands.[39] Joseph Rykwert, throughout his work in the *First Moderns: the Architecture of the Eighteenth Century*, addresses the same historical narrative. Rykwert is keenly aware of the work of the 17th century scholar Charles Perrault and his groundbreaking and fulsome comparison of the ancients and moderns in the arts and sciences, including his significant commentary on architecture and architectural history.[40] Rykwert, engaging Perrault, states:

> ... The ancients so ... [thought Perrault as he states in opening his book] believed with reason that the rules of proportion which give beauty to buildings were taken from the human body, and that as nature formed solid bodies adapted to labor, and those who should be adroit and agile in a lighter mould, so there are different rules in the art of building ... those different proportions ac-

---

39 Alberto Pérez-Gómez, *Architecture and the Crisis of Modern Science* (Cambridge and London: Cambridge University Press, 1992).

40 Charles Perrault, *Parallele des anciens et des modernes en ce qui regarde les arts et les sciences: Dialogues*, 4 vols, (Paris: Jean-Baptiste Coignard. 1692-1697); Charles Perrault & Paul Bonnefon, *Mémoires de ma vie* (Paris: Renouard, 1669). Perrault (12 January 1628-16May 1703) was a French author and member of the Académie française. He was an influential figure in the 17th century French world of letters and leader of the modern faction during the arguments of the ancients and moderns in literature. He also engages the topic of architecture in his century.

companied by the ornaments which suit them make the
different orders of architecture.[41]

The juxtaposition or resonance of the body and the architectural orders
is worth noting. There emerged a sense of the architect divine, charged
with the deepest significance in pursuit of the embodied and philosophic good life for himself and the group. That is not to say the relationship
between the body and built environment could not be lost in different
periods and places.

Gomez says that throughout this period, the mystical and numerological
foundation in architecture and built environment gave way to functional
and technical uses in theory and practice. He states:

> This functionalization of architectural theory implies its
> transformation into a set of operational rules, into a tool
> of exclusively technological character. Its main concern
> becomes how to build in an efficient and economic man-
> ner, while avoiding questions related to why one builds
> and whether such activity is justified in the existential
> context.[42]

It seems the *Book of Constitutions* concerned, at first, a very few men in
love with learning; perhaps both in their printer's art and in their understanding and refashioning of the ancient inherited traditions, customs,
and habits, of guild freemasonry and re-imagining of the Renaissance and
Medieval architect.

The central Grail mystery of philosophy in the fraternity across its syncretism became the search for the lost word. Yet, the search for the polyvalent lost word in the 18th century historical semantics of freemasonry
marked consciously for a select few and unconsciously for the majority
of the transition from the habits, aesthetics, and communal possibilities
of aurality and orality to the refashioned habits and somatic spaces of literacy, and a functional architectural space, in human experience. In the
reformulated abstract space the centrality of the lived body and its environment the good life could be lost. But the loss perhaps could lead to
rediscovery in lived experience at a higher level of the spiral.

---

41 Joseph Rykwert, *The First Moderns: The Architects of the Eighteenth-Century* (Cambridge: MIT Press, 1980), 34.

42 Pérez-Gómez, 4.

The pedagogical concern involved men and perhaps some women in serious philosophic search for perceived lost cannons of geometric proportion, ancient wisdom, and the living word in emplaced human experience and movement (reconstructed experience). Stated differently, the living word is reconstructed experience, integral aesthetic-moral primary experience and secondary (representational and epistemic) experience, not dualistic. The period was marked by a wrestling with the emergence of the abstractions and experimentation of new science and its contrast with ancient learning. Ancient concepts of space, for example, collided against new concepts of space with no one outcome certain. There was a parallel growing secularism in civil society and new forms of public space such as the London coffee house and its makeshift masonic lodge that emerged from an anterior moral theology and sacred cosmos.

Originally it is important to note the "word" *not lost* was a means of identification among traveling operative builders (a network of builders) in the medieval period where they could recognize each other as masons by ritual signs, gestures and words. But that real word in the development of 18th century ritual and symbolism was reworked by someone, or group, unknown as "the lost word." A more mundane but accurate interpretation of the sign of the lost word in the eighteenth century dramaturgy of freemasonry is its institution in mystery as the alluring mechanism and draw of show business for gaining new adherents to freemasonry. Mystery is essential as one aspect of dramaturgy as vital communication, the magic, and drama of presence and absence for child and adult: consider children's game of peek-a-boo. Mystery is in short a beautiful phenomenon. We are attracted to it. The imagination is a moth to a flame or to flights in darkness set around.

Senex and Hooke in their intellectual reach and in occupations as printers and members of the Stationer's Company were significant representatives of the origin of modern freemasonry with Desaguliers. The initial role of Anderson in the founding moments of modern speculative freemasonry was not of singular importance as sometimes portrayed in masonic accounts yet he was significant.[43]

---

43 David Stevenson, "James Anderson," Eds. Cécile Révauger & Charles Porset, 89-96.

B. COSMOPOLITAN FREEMASONS' INTEREST IN RITUAL, QUALITATIVE PLACE, AND TRANSMISSION

Figure 3 is from the encyclopedic work *Cérémonies et coutumes réligieus-es de tous les peuples du monde,* published in 1736.[44] The original image was accompanied by a small commentary. The very brief commentary contains a reference to the masonic exposure *Masonry Dissected,* which already had been published in 1730. The earlier text detailed the ritual working of what in recent time at a point unknown had become the basic three degrees of the freemasons. The reader of the larger volume was presented (as seen in Figure 3) firstly with (a) an exercise in visualization of cosmopolitan place and (often imperial) network emanating from London, and (b) an image of social performance either shortly before the commencement of a masonic ritual or afterward. Things were moving in time and shifting in place and action was underway in a network of places. Secondly, the ritual work itself was described in *Masonry Dissected,* as mentioned in the *Cérémonies et coutumes réligieuses de tous les peuples du monde.* It was possible, therefore, that the body-staging of the three degrees as represented on the floor and practiced in other lodges around the expanding metropolis and ever widening networks outward bound and back (home and movement) could be imagined by the reader non-mason or mason. There would have been an allure an enlivening curiosity in the aforementioned process. And it was excellent scholarship.

The three degrees of the freemasons are briefly summarized as follows: At the heart of the system is an imagined and ritualistically constructed Solomon's Temple. The site serving as the lodge space whether an apartment, or coffee house and including the first few dedicated lodges, became Solomon's Temple through integral embodied, rotating and emplaced sign systems and speech acts of the individual and group. The symbolic edifice of the temple, the masonic lodge of the 18th century, was both a sacred and secular space fashioned by a divine artificer perhaps like Plato's great architect. The ceremonies with modifications have survived until today.

To enter the ritual construction and imagination of the place of the lodge is to work for the world, and facilitate different methods of inquiry and

---

44 The engraving is a collaboration of Fabritious Du Bourg and John Faber. See Bernard Picart & Jean Frederic Bernard, eds., *Cérémonies et coutumes réligieuses de tous les peuples du monde,* 7 vols. (Amsterdam: J. F Bernard, 1723-1737), Figure 3, 38.

Figure 3. Bernard Picart & Jean Frederic Bernard, eds., *Grand Lodge of London 1735, une image de la franc-maçonnerie cosmopolites, Cérémonies et coutumes réligieuses de tous les peuples du monde,* 1723-46, engraving (Getty Open Content Internet Archive).

construction out from the foundational pillars of wisdom, strength, beauty and building upon the light of nature and man. The pillars are critical elements of the metaphorical and real structure of the lodge and symbolism of the individual and group. The spatial structures and inhabited place of early African-American freemasonry in one reading is a space of otherness and can be a space of resistance. In addition, the lodge is an archaeological layering of graded spaces, with each new ritual space of a higher-degree swiftly opening a greater complexity because of additional strata over earlier constructed places. The symbolic language of added complexity and sophistication, in one reading, is an exercise in the pursuit or moral imagination of freedom, and positioning, or orientation in action, as well parallel responsibility in the cultural experience of a civic habitus. Culture is freedom seeking in the elaboration of symbol making and embodied felt action or experience of the individual and group in an environment.[45]

---

45 Ernst Cassirer, *The Philosophy of Symbolic Forms,* 3 vols. (New Haven: Yale University

The profane enters the closed space of the temple and goes through trials and therein becomes an "entered apprentice", which is the first ritualistic degree of freemasonry enacted in a place of ritual performance. At times, there can be a stunning and dramatic changes and tests in the dramatic yet scripted scenes unfolding in the lodge. There is a hazing and disorienting of the candidate in situated place as he proceeds on his journey of inquiry, mystery, and adventure. To experience the drama of the ritual and its closing speech act is to achieve the rank of entered apprentice.[46] The grade or degree of apprentice exists with its own symbolic challenges, images, somatic signs, and symbolic and sometimes real tasks of stone making and habit correction of the inductee in temporal place. After working on a symbolic and sometimes a real stone the mason is advanced to the place, position, and standing of a "fellow of the craft" in a subsequent ceremony.

To experience this second ritual in due and proper form and through the imputed power of the spoken word and assembled group of masons is to become a fellow-craft freemason. The fellow craft began to perfect the living "stone" of the self and action both inside and outside the lodge. In the incremental process of experiencing the rituals the mason gradually acquires a civic habitus.[47] The interrelated rituals take place amid the initiate's band of brothers and with due preparation and resolve.

In time, the initiate is advanced across a play of cultural and material signs and through doors, steps, and floors that pass him through the second

---

Press, 1953), 1-67.

46 At a point in the mounting tension of the ritual, the master of the lodge constitutes or makes a mason through a speech-act. The phrasing with accompanying gestures deeply en-cultured in place and inheritance can be something like "By the power invested in me by this worshipful lodge of masons, etc., I constitute you an entered apprentice." The accompanying gestures becomes a "deed." A physical action and new set of relations, semiotics and functions are constituted through artful and meaningful communication. The communication in "making" a mason or advancing him through the degrees is involved precisely with making, or constituting in affective place and not mirroring phenomena although the abstract coordinates of space are at hand, for example, the cardinal direction of east as the place of the rising sun. Yet the "speech-act" is as a tin drum without felt embodied habit and deep cultural habitus. A speech act in the philosophy of language is an utterance that has performative function in language and communication. The ritual roots of a speech-act goes all the way down in qualitative place, temporal flow and context.

47 Kristianne K. Hasselmann, "Performing Freemasonry: The Practical-Symbolic Constitution of a *Civic Habitus* in Eighteenth-Century England," *Journal for Research into Freemasonry and Fraternalism* 1, no 2 (2010): 184-194.

degree called fellow of the craft and ultimately through the portal of death and rebirth discovered in the third degree of freemasonry, the degree of master mason. In this plateau degree, he is immersed in the dramaturgy centered on courage, sacrifice, and death of an ancient ancestor and great builder in freemasonry, Hiram Abiff, who some argue skillfully labored in building the Temple of Solomon under hire to King Solomon. In the aesthetic-moral experience, intellectual inquiry, and drama of the third degree, the shortly-to-be master is guided onto the center of the lodge floor and lost in immersion in the embodied, re-told, and reenacted story of the slaying of Hiram Abiff.

Abiff was slain holding firm to the secret mason's word of the master builder, not giving it to ruffian fellows of the craft who demanded it, as the word can be given only to those duly prepared in the peculiar moral science, not the undeserving. There is a great valuing of the spoken word in the myth, coding of sacred and profane, and narrative in freemasonry. There is a rebirth in the self-identification by the initiate of the re-invoked sacrifice where the master builder gave up his life, rather than give the mason word to the unworthy, to those who had not worked for it. In the action spaces of murder and mythopoeic invocation of ancestors the fellow craft mason precipitates the identity, interest, position, and place of the master mason(s) before him, with him, and yet to come. In a dramatic moment of self-identification in an unfolding drama and positioning of the body by others he becomes the ancient ancestor, Hiram, and he is slain on the lodge floor in reenactment. He is born anew in the degree of master mason and its ritual space with no woman present. The drama and reality unfold in mythopoeic space constructed in thought, word, and ritual. There is a simultaneous doing, feeling and thinking in a qualitative situation.

In the ritual performance, the new mason is told through story that with the murder of the ancient one, the word had been lost because it would not be divulged to those who demanded it crudely and did not deserve it. The new master mason must journey and labor to find that word, and he is properly fit to seek the word in the expanses of the world. He is fit to build in the lodge, just as he is equally fit to be an artificer in the wider world. The mason is a learned man in ancient and modern ways, having gone through the instruction, habit correction, and lived experience of the three degrees. In a modern sense, a balancing of communitarian and individualistic perspectives exists to that which is near and far in time and in geographic home and wider networks of transmission.

Each grade or degree of freemasonry is constituted of a place and so-cio-symbolic structure in which creative patterns for living are fashioned in habit. Feeling and thought are fused through the embodied, brave ac-tion and habituation of the body-mind of Hiram Abiff (now the new mas-ter mason) in a meaningful and felt qualitative place. His moral courage and the fusing of identities of Hiram Abiff and the new master mason animates a profound civic habitus in and outside the lodge. The symbol-ism of King Solomon's Temple was appropriated. At one level of interpre-tation, the metaphors of journey, seeking-light, and building combined with the moral imagination of geometry as the queen of the liberal arts to help fashion the neural-environmental sense and rule-intensive signifi-cation and praxis of freemasonry. In addition, there were resultant new occupations accruing on Newtonian space in a post-Euclidean and post Pythagorean world. It was a moment in time and space of embodiment, yet greater abstraction in the late 17th and early 18th century. Life is co-equal with the place, material, and time it inhabits.

The house of the temple was and remains a presentation of universal truth and moral stance, for example, geometry in the liberal arts was used to shape the body-mind in aesthetic, ethical, and abstract ways mediated by habit and habit correction. As a simple illustration, the mason is made to stand upright (literally) and to square his actions toward others and to be on the level. The developing embodied habit and performativity of differ-ent gestures and acts is intended to inculcate cardinal virtues such as pru-dence, modern virtues of tolerance, or theological virtues in Anglophone freemasonry of faith, hope, and charity. The habits and performativity of ethics and learning, habit and habit correction, is the "will"—the doing or action—of the mason's new life. The symbolism of the temple is adopted from Jewish tradition and then compounded with the considerable flair of 18th century imagination and aesthetic quality in the breadth and depth of a perceived universal science with many disciplines, and syncretism of traditions, involved. Agency as the transactional self and learning process is constituted and constituting in the layering and creative meanings of embodied place and space, an array of habit and habit correction in the spaces, times, interest, and medium between the near and far. This is hint-ed at in the engraved imagery of both Figure 2 and Figure 3.

The costumes worn by the assembly of freemasons in Figure 3 are of the "international style" of French fashion that dominated since the death of Louis XIV and would have been worn by gentlemen whether in Paris, Amsterdam, or London. The clothing in the scene presents a true cosmopolitan look with stylizing roots in Paris. Paris as a design center had both the aesthetic drama or ritualized and cultural performance space and the transmission infrastructure of an emerging international industry. The personal tastes of the culture industry, a type of success, involving occupations, were born alongside the rise of modern capitalism and the structural transformation of the public sphere. The public sphere, which is the court of public opinion, is not simple rational discourse in an ideal typical sense nor attack politics alone, but style and artfulness to good and bad ends.

The voluminous skirts holding out the jacket bottoms shown in the imagery of Figure 3 were a shaping element of the artful communication and style; the taste, success, and performativity of gentlemen. The skirts express fashioned and fashioning tastes of the time. They could be held out variously through paper inserts, starch, or whalebone. Rosenbaum sees in the scene desire by the designer of the engraving to show authenticity and experience of the felt qualitative immediacy of the moment. This authenticity is a hallmark of the tastes and demands of an emerging, fast changing modern civil society. This is why we see the men with their backs to us, interprets Rosenbaum, as part of the relaxed yet dignified movement in dramaturgical space. We are eyewitnesses in a virtual reality to the felt qualitative immediacy (of place) of the authentic real-thing as it happens. Beneath the felt qualitative immediacy of the gesture, moment and moving of ritual performance, is the pre-reflective intentionality of interdependent and interpenetrating habits in an environment. The atmospherics are gentlemanly and intellectual.

The constituent parts of the framing of Figure 3 include the horizontal and vertical spatial referents, which are distinct but aesthetically unified in a three dimensional volume, something of a rectangular cube, in the relation of parts and volumes. Individual lodges represented on the vertical backboard are displayed in quantitative, ordinal rank. In the ranking these are measure-intensive and, as such, symbols. They are indices pointing to ritual performance occurring in action space and felt qualitative geographic place. More accurately, they are pointing to (a symbolic representation of) a network of places around metropolitan London and ultimately beyond. *The image-text is a stunning expression of the ritual and transmission semiotics of human association and conjoint communications anchored and mediated in felt, embodied temporal place and networks of place.*

In the symbols and indices of the backboard, there is imagined a transmission of information across a network of places. The background action of the transmission function in the scene, and ritual performance on the lodge floor, are mutually interdependent as seen by the engraver of the image and his imagined audience. Embodied habit fuses the quality and feeling of embodied ritual place with abstractions and there is intellectual reflection all around on any proposed subject matter, what the American pragmatist Dewey called qualitative thought.[48] Without embodied habit there is no ritual, without embodied habit there is no occupation of printer, no embodied habits of literacy, no transmission of text and lodge across the metropolis and beyond, no qualitative thought. Quality, feeling, cognition and embodied habit and then imagination draw the whole together.

In Figure 3, all work proceeds beneath the gravitas and habitus of Grand Master of the Grand Lodge of London here indicated by the height and centrality of the coat of arms of Lord Weymouth, then the Grand Master of the Grand Lodge of London, and a powerful symbol of the relationship that would grow between London freemasonry and British imperialism.[49] Yet, beneath the sign of imperial expansion using freemasonry, which was of particular interest to Weymouth, there is a powerful representation of Richard Steele, an Irishman, a supporter of the arts, and man of letters, in important early English strivings at civil society.

This aesthetic and artful depiction of the ritual space in Figure 3 of habit and performativity, the self-presentation and self-creation of the group of freemasons, is far different from the much "stiffer" Palladian theater and masque invoked only a decade earlier in the Renaissance masque of

---

48 Steven Stankiewicz, "Qualitative Thought, Thinking Through the Body, and Embodied Thinking: Dewey and His Successors," in Larry A. Hickman, Matthew Caleb Flamm, Krzysztof Piotr Skowronski, and Jennifer A. Rea, eds., *The Continuing Relevance of John Dewey: Reflections on Aesthetics, Morality, Science, and Society* (Amsterdam and New York: Rodopi, 2011), 101-118.

49 Jessica H. Jacobs, *Builders of Empire: Freemasons and British Imperialism* (Chapel Hill: University of North-Carolina Press, 2007).

the frontispiece of the 1723 *Book of Constitutions,* as seen in Figure 2. In Figure 4, there is a loosening of the tight habitus of aristocratic and royal ritual performance, and oration, with the more fluid aesthetic-moral tone of an aspiring, embodied, cosmopolitan individual and civil society, even with Dutch censorship of freemasonry underway at different moments. The civil self is born in resistance, not in imagined harmony. The midpoint between the two figures, the earlier formal one, and the later "authentic" performance depicts the actual point of emergence of modern civil society in a sacred but also secular space, something akin to a gendered civil religion. It is a token moment early in the work of the moral imagination and birth of civil society and the public sphere in modernity.

The image of the freemasons in Figure 3 shows some delight in the fresh nature of Dutch cosmopolitanism, while invoking the stiffer habitus of English legitimacy through the vehicle of freemasonry. At the same time, Sandra Rosenbaum has pointed to the gendered nature of Figure 3. She notes that the men stand in postures "have been trained to display their lower leg/calves to advantage. Men of the upper classes and wannabes were taught how to stand and move with grace and elegance by dancing masters, when they were children. Movement was based on basic ballet positions. Men's legs were admired as women's breasts are today."[50] Habits were developed. Finally, returning to Figure 3, on the ends of the largest table there are two books, possibly referencing *Masonry Dissected* as a ritual handbook, or perhaps lodge minutes, a book of philosophy, science or the arts, the Bible, or the 1723 *Book of Constitutions.*

In a central and high place of authority on the backboard are representations of Richard Steele and Lord Weymouth, with a coat of arms representing the office and person of Weymouth. These two are signified at the top of the vertical board immediately above the Master of the lodge on the lodge floor, giving them a powerful presence in the image text. One of Lord Weymouth's strongest interest was in seeing the freemasonry moving overseas and out of London. The image in this context with its spiraling representational backboard followed the empire building wishes of the Grand Master. Freemasonry began to follow the course of the English Empire, but there were manifestations of the fraternity outside this English circumference proper. The Grand Master was certainly aware of the engraved image. The identity of Steele as a freemason is not certain,

---

50 Sandra Rosenbaum (personal communication, to John Slifko on March, 19, 2007).

but given the reputable and accurate nature of the image as a whole, including the strong imprimatur of Lord Weymouth, it is likely to believe that the Irish born Steele was a freemason in London, and a perceived important one.[51]

C. THE TATTLER

Who was Richard Steele that he should be so highly placed beneath Lord Weymouth in the engraving by the Dutch artisans Dubourg and Faber, who produced the image? Richard Steele (1672-1729) was an Irish writer, member of Parliament and Hanoverian, often remembered as co-founder, with his friend Joseph Addison, of the magazine *The Spectator*.[52] It is interesting to speculate on a possible Irish freemason valued so highly in position in the earliest days of London Grand Lodge freemasonry. It goes against the grain of English ethnic disdain of the Irish in this period and place. In any event, a stated goal of the *Spectator* was to animate morality through wit and to temper wit with morality; an embodied moral-aesthetics, or aesthetic moral habitus, a new civic habitus. It was in part an idea to bring philosophy out of the closeted libraries, homes, schools, and places of learning, to different public places and societies. One function was the provision to readers of educated, timely talking points to use in public in a polite manner.

The daily circulation was not large, perhaps around three-thousand copies; however, it was consumed such that as many as 60,000 Londoners likely had access by reading at local coffee houses and other sites. Sixty-thousand Londoners represented about a tenth of the capital's population at the time. Importantly, the reading public came from nearly all classes and stations in civil society. That having been said, the focus was on the emerging middle-class, which included merchants, artisans and

---

51 Rae Blanchard, "Was Sir Richard Steele a Freemason?," *Publications of the Modern Language Association of America* 63, no 3 (September, 1948): 903-917.

52 Joseph Addison and Sir Richard Steele, *The Spectator* (London: J. and R. Tonson, 1726). *The Tattler*, Steele's first journal, first came out on April 12, 1709, and ran three times a week. Following the demise of *The Tattler*, the two men, Addison and Steele, founded *The Spectator* and the *Guardian*. The *Spectator* ran from 1711 to 1712, and revived again for six months in 1714, but without Steele. Each printing, or "number", was composed around 2,500 words in length. There were 555 numbers collected into seven volumes and as such published repeatedly for many decades afterwards. The 1714 revival was collected into the eighth volume.

traders working at many scales. All the while, the earlier *Tattler* and later *Spectator* advanced the argument that participation of women in politics (even in political dialogues) was simply and straightforwardly ludicrous. The actual coffee houses did have women present.

Jürgen Habermas, in his important *Structural Transformation of the Public Sphere,* sees *The Spectator* as instrumental in the structural transformation of the public life and stage occurring in England, and Western European urban centers and freemasonry as representative if not the actual origins of modern civil society. Freemasonry, states Habermas quoting Lessing, was just as old as bourgeois society "if indeed bourgeois society is not the offspring of Freemasonry."[53] This period is defined here in an ideal typical sense, as the cosmopolitan century, holding the cosmopolitan ideal of apposite communication, learning, and association in home and movement, ritual, and transmission.[54] Habermas's argument is that transformation came about through the communicative actions of the emerging middle-class, the emergence of different print vehicles, and the rise of an early capitalism in urban centers in western and northern Europe. Although *The Spectator* declared itself politically neutral, it was widely understood as promoting Whig values and interests. The bound volumes of *The Spectator* went on to be widely read as late as the 19th century. It was an attractive marriage of fine prose, the depiction of communication through polite gesture in company, qualitative thought, and morality. It was overall an aesthetic-moral brew, and text related performative and civic habitus, of sociability that attracted solid readership.

D. AHIMAN REZON: IRISH ANTI-IMPERIAL ACCENTS

The most robust challenge to the legitimacy of the premier grand lodge in England arose from Irish masons living in the London metropolis. A considerable number of the Irish immigrants in London were masons, artisans, merchants, and other working members who came from the lower classes. Part of their perceived "otherness" was their Irish ethnic identity.

---

53 Quoted in Jürgen Habermas, *The Structural Transformation of the Public Sphere: An Inquiry into a Category of Bourgeois Society,* trans. Thomas Burger and Frederick Lawrence (Cambridge: The MIT Press, 1991), 35.

54 Thomas J. Schlereth, *The Cosmopolitan Ideal in Enlightenment Thought: Its Form and Function in the Ideas of Franklin, Hume, and Voltaire, 1694-1790* (Notre Dame and London: University of Notre Dame Press, 1977), xiii.

The practical effect was often rejected when Irish masons petitioned to affiliate with a London lodge for membership, or when non-mason Irishmen living in the English metropolis pursued induction (what would be termed today initiation). Then, in 1751, Irish immigrants (the subaltern rejecting the authority of those who, in short, were rejecting them) organized their own grand lodge. Some had been masons in Ireland. This new institution was "The Most Honorable Society of Free and Accepted Masons according to the Old Institutions." Soon, the name The Ancient Grand Lodge of England would be attached to them, largely perhaps through their own doing in publicity. (Note the spelling could be antient and ancient, both were used and acceptable.)

The foremost Irish leader of the new association of masons was Lawrence Dermott (1720-1791), initiated in 1740, aged 20, into Lodge No. 26, Dublin, Irish constitution, and "exalted" in the Royal Arch in No. 26, Dublin, in 1746. It was some time after Dermott moved to London where he became the Second Grand Secretary and later Deputy Grand Master of the Grand Lodge of the Ancients Grand Lodge. The exact date of the formation of this Grand Lodge perhaps may never be known, much beyond the basic recording of a meeting held on July 17, 1751 and the election of Robert Turner as Grand Master on December 5, 1753.

The meeting in 1751 was an assembly of masters from five lodges meeting at the Turk's Head Tavern in Greek Street, Soho. Dermott asserted, along with others, that the first grand lodge had moved into grave error in drifting away from ancient ritual, procedure, learning, and traditions. Above all else, these ancient traditions needed to be preserved. By appealing to the mythic dimension of an ancient lineage, all the while speaking pejoratively about the limited and increasingly wayward practices of the modern premier Grand Lodge, he outmaneuvered the older (modern) grand lodge in masonic and public appeal. "Anciency" defined here as a romantic appeal to ancient worlds and experience, as shall be seen throughout the research project, has mythic and imaginative attraction in freemasonry and in human experience generally around the world. In the meantime, Dermott was introducing his own changes, sometimes borrowing from the "moderns."

Dermott compiled the first book of constitutions for the ancients, which was issued by the Ancient Grand Lodge of England in 1756 with the obscure title *Ahiman Rezon*; the definition of which remains opaque, at best;

but is often accepted as meaning "Help to a Brother," perhaps with its origins in a distorted reading of Hebrew.[55] Little is known of his education and Dermott may have been self-taught in different areas including studies in Hebrew, Latin, and Greek. Dermott's *Ahiman Rezon* was a compilation from numerous sources, including the 1738 edition of the *Book of Constitutions* of the premier Grand Lodge of London. It had considerable impact and roughly between the 1750s and 1850s there were over 40 editions, with nine in England, 21 in Ireland, and 14 in America.

The ritual performances with emotional appeal to "Anciency," a romanticism of times long ago, and presiding constitutional text, were enormously influential in establishing a hybrid space (in this case, an ethnic place of Irish resistance) distinct from the English system of lodges. Iterative changes of ritual and text are observable in the development of freemasonry. In this sense, ritual and text preserve cultural traditions in a conservative manner, yet can in some situations, open the conditions of possibility of renewal and innovation in an emerging cultural form.

E. The Jachin and Boaz Exposure

The development of the craft degrees may have occurred as an interrelated symbolic system worked at some point in three degrees in the first three decades of the 18th century marked by the publication of the first masonic exposure *Masonry Dissected*.[56] There were subsequent exposures in the 18th century that help present a picture of the ritual life and work of freemasonry in this formative period.[57] Pritchard's *Masonry Dissected* in 1730 likely signifies the end of a one or two-degree system inherited from the guild traditions and the beginning of movement into a system (spatial palimpsest in the masonic lodge) of three degrees; that is to say, ritually constructed spaces and sites of graded initiations. These were then, and

---

55 Laurence Dermot, *Ahiman Rezon; or, A help to a brother; shewing the excellency of secrecy, and the first cause, or motive, of the institution of free-masonry, &c. Followed by a choice selection of songs* (London, 1756).

56 Samuel Pritchard, *Masonry Dissected* (London: J. Wilford, 1730). The first three and basic degrees of freemasonry hold marked similarities to their equivalents in symbolic freemasonry today with variations across the world.

57 M-O-V-N, *Three Distinct Knocks* (London: H. Serjeant without Temple Bar, 1756); A Gentleman from the Lodge of Jerusalem, *Jachin and Boaz, or, An Authentic Key to the Door of Free-Masonry Both Antient and Modern. Calculated Not Only for the Instruction of every New-Made Mason, but also for the Information of All who intend to become Brethren*

remain, the degrees of entered apprentice, fellow craft, and master mason, with different terms used occasionally. This text was discussed earlier in this chapter with some description of the three degrees of freemasonry. Other exposures were soon to follow including *Three Distinct Knocks* and *Jachin and Boaz*. *Jachin and Boaz* is important because of its wholeness and overall quality presenting an early trigradal ritual. The publishers had committed to the idea and practice of advertising to increase sales.

The first edition of *Jachin and Boaz* was pre-announced in the *Public Advertiser*, London, on Saturday, March 20, 1762. An initial advertisement contained the following text: *Jachin and Boaz; or An Authentic Key to the Door of Free-Masonry Both Antient and Modern* .... It also stated "London. Printed for W. Nicoll, at the Paper-Mill, St. Paul's Churchyard. MDC-CLXII." A second advertisement for what would be a 56-page pamphlet occurred on March 22nd in the *Advertiser* with the pamphlet, as stated in the advertisement, published that very same day. Additional commercial notice occurred for the new publication on March 23 and 26, 1762 in the *Advertiser*. A similar entry appeared in the issue dated March 22-24, in the printer W. Nicholl's own newspaper, *Lloyd's Evening Post and British Chronicle*.

News of availability similarly appeared in publication in Newcastle and York in the same year; and a second edition of the pamphlet was advertised two more times in both the *Public Advertiser* and Lloyd's *Evening Post* in London between October 20 and October 24, 1762. The book in its drama and transmission experienced enormous success from its first appearance. An estimated 34 editions appeared up until 1800, including imprints in Dublin, New York, Philadelphia, Albany, and Boston.[58]

It was a very significant English 18th century text used by masons and the learning public for their edification. It demonstrates perfectly the mediation of print in the origins of modern freemasonry as it is known today. The well thought-out public advertising put together for this *Constitution* appears far more aggressive than decades earlier with the initial publication of the 1723 *Book of Constitutions of the Free-Masons*. The power of advertising in a newspaper for freemasonry in different ways, and publica-

---

(London: W. Nicoll, 1790).

58 Harry Carr, ed., *Three Distinct Knocks, and Jachin and Boaz* (Bloomington: Masonic Book Club, 1981, first published 1756, and 1762), 177-178.

tions of the actual subject matter and rituals of freemasonry, had become evident as it would through experience in America.

The initial exposés of ritual that came soon after the publication of the Constitutions of the Free-Masons was *Masonry Dissected* in 1730. It was the first known to represent a three degree system, but some thought the pamphlet was incomplete containing errors and to be read with discretion. On the other hand, the denunciation could have been from freemasonry in a type of misinformation campaign to hide the fact that *Masonry Dissected* was quite accurate. The exposures did improve in quality and thoroughness (perhaps better-termed revisions and extensions in slow iteration of performative habitus) through the course of the 18th century. The 1762 imprint of *Jachin and Boaz* was quite significant in what was becoming increasingly popular freemasonry. The book was a valuable means of proliferating ritual and encouraging or hoping for ritual publication by masons. There were masons who wanted to do their best in learning the ritual and to advertise freemasonry publicly. The book was a seminal influence in Thomas Smith Webb's (1771-1819) working, which became the standard of ritual work in America. [59] As with the latter publication by Webb, *Jachin and Boaz* provided steadiness-of-hand in the geographic transmission of the ritual and symbolism of freemasonry out of England to America.[60]

Beginning in the 1720s and moving forward in the English-speaking world, a small handful of prominent freemasons could occasionally deliver lectures or orations in their lodges. The lectures for the most part were designed to give some hint at the nature, principles, and desired qualities of character and intellect for the freemason or inquiring public. In that period, nothing of any significance had been printed explaining or illustrating the ritual and still sparse symbolism. New materials are now being gathered and collected that may help greatly in clarifying this topic.[61] Harry Carr sees a new phase of Anglophone freemasonry starting

---

59 Thomas Smith Webb, *The Freemason's Monitor, or, Illustrations of Masonry* (Albany: Fry and Southwick, 1797).

60 There were other geographic areas in Europe from which masons migrated to America, for example Scotland, France, the Netherlands, and Ireland.

61 Cécile *Révauger, Jan Snoek, and Jack Peter,* eds., *British Freemasonry, 1717-1813, A Five-Volume Primary-Source Edition* (Oxford: Taylor & Frances / Routledge, forthcoming).

in 1772 with William Preston's *Illustrations of Masonry,* concerned with the pedagogy and content of the fraternity.[62] Similarly, Carr places William Hutchinson's *Spirit of Freemasonry* in 1775 in this new phase.[63] It may happen that future research work opens up the years between the *Book of Constitutions* and Preston's work in England as richer than anticipated by Carr in speculative discourse about neo-Platonism, Aristotle, Renaissance, French and German. Preston's quite important *Illustrations* achieved 12 editions in his lifetime, and several more after his death. There also appeared two American editions, and the book appeared in two German editions in 1776 and 1780.[64]

F. WILLIAM PRESTON'S *ILLUSTRATIONS OF MASONRY*

Preston's *Illustrations of Masonry* built upon the constitutions and experience of the modern freemasons, while incorporating the working of the ancient members of the fraternity. The influential publication was the product of intense inquiry and artful communication by Preston although it was not absent mistakes of various historical, theoretical practical or philosophical perspectives, for example, Preston believed that through learning as that practiced in the masonic lodge society could achieve perfection, (with a final telos), a point of view open to severe historical disputation and in observations of the difficult world all around us in the current moment. Preston benefited from some measure of formal education. He was considerably self-educated through work as an apprentice printer, later printer, editor, and author as with Senex and others who are examined. Preston had face-to-face contact with London masons and communication with masons and others not masons outside the metropolis. *Illustrations* was crafted to complement a series of orations devised by Preston and intended to be delivered regularly to lodges in closed ritual space as an integral part of the ritual performance, inquiry, transmission and educational system. It was assumed by Preston that lectures would become central in the learning experience of masons who, likely, he presumed, valued all learning.

---

62 William Preston, *Illustrations of Masonry: By William Preston, Past Master of the Lodge of Antiquity Acting by Immemorial Constitution (London: 1792).*

63 William Hutchinson, *The Spirit of Masonry in Moral and Elucidatory Lectures: By Wm Hutchinson (Boston: J. Wilkie and W. Goldsmith, 1775).*

64 Carr, 181.

Preston was born in Edinburgh in 1742 and died in London in 1818. Rising from the rank of apprentice printer, over the course of his life he was a successful printer, editor, author, newspaperman, and an accomplished freemason. It is unknown when he was initiated in the fraternity, but is often thought to have entered in 1762 or 1763 in London and from that point forward became a zealous student of freemasonry. The young teenager, taken out of an endowed school after the death of his classically educated father moved into employment as secretary for Thomas Rudiman, a prominent classicist and linguist of the period, as well librarian and printer (with a partner) of an Edinburgh newspaper—*The Caledonian Mercury*, followed by the unexpected death of Thomas Rudiman, Preston at the age of twelve was apprenticed as a printer to Walter Rudiman, the brother of the linguist and printer. With permission of his printing master in Scotland, he decided to set upon a journey to London, carrying an important letter of reference addressed to William Strahan, the King's Printer.

It was with Strahan that he found near life-long employment, with responsibilities including assistance in preparing texts for publication. A relationship developed between Strahan and Benjamin Franklin in the years ahead. Preston's creative and professional work, his occupation, put him into personal contact with a diversity of prominent writers of the day. Preston also edited the London *Chronicle*, which is known as the newspaper of a family belonging to Georgian London. It published the paper thrice in a week and enclosed world and national news, as well covered inventive, literary, scientific, and events taking place in London.

Colin Dyer gives two foci to Preston's work in this period: firstly, the preparation of his basic lecture system, promulgated in 1772 and 1774 with the consequent production of his companion volume, *Illustrations of Freemasonry*.[65] This important text first appeared in 1772 with a second considerably revised version in 1775, which was the basis for later editions. Secondly, he was employed from 1768 to 1777 as assistant to the Grand Secretary of the Grand Lodge. His particular responsibility in that regard was preparing updates of the historical supplement included in the periodical revisions of the *Book of Constitutions*. He studied vigorously, as best he could, in preparation of the supplement. Preston's work had considerable impact in the American experience of freemasonry,

---

65 Colin Dyer, *William Preston and His Work* (London: Lewis Masonic, 1987), ix-x.

once transmitted. Webb's *Monitor of Freemasonry,* a foundational classic in the American fraternity, was written with Preston's work close at hand on Webb's desk wherever he might be writing.

G. SUMMARY AND CONCLUSIONS

The 1723 *Book of Constitutions of the Free-Masons* valorized both ancient and modern knowledge, or tradition and renewal, in the experience of freemasonry, as well as increasing awareness of worlds of print as significant in processes of ritual in "place making" and the transmission and authority of the fraternity across space. Printing on its own was emerging as a force of learning across civil society, inside as well outside freemasonry. The frontispiece of the *Book of Constitution* portrayed an aesthetic, moral, and intellectual position and posture, which reflects the contents of the book. In addition, the frontispiece contained allusions to Newtonian science with the possible representation of Desaguliers. In totality, the frontispiece as an invocation of an earlier Renaissance masque, and philosophy reimagining the architect in the 18th century was something different from clubbing, or emerging middle-class socializing. That is not to say clubbing and a place of learning were mutually exclusive things in eighteenth century London coffeehouses, rented halls, or alehouses. The *Constitutions* as an art object, or aesthetic form that changes with its changing interpreting audience, has endured through time and space in diverse a range socio-cultural formations and with diverse audiences.

Figure 2 was juxtaposed with Figure 3 in a vital part of the analysis of the chapter. Figure 3, an image of the cosmopolitan freemasons, pictures the complementarities of ritual and transmission logics of communication in the story and history of the sign in the 18th century. The ritual function of communication is seen unfolding on the floor of the makeshift lodge, while the transmission function of communication is immediately clear in the ordinal ranking of a growing transmission network of lodges on the backboard in the image, with indices pointing to actual physical lodges and the time and place of their ritual meetings.

The image illustrates the gendered nature of embodied habit and practiced civic habitus in freemasonry. Of equal importance, the image is in stark contrast to the actions, habits, and performativity indicated in the frontispiece of the *Book of Constitutions* published only a few years earlier. The image depicts a transition from the habitus and ideals of moral theology and both royal and aristocratic formality to the idea of authentic performance and a polite manner, a new personal and upwardly successful style, a different aesthetic. The depiction represents the new aesthetic-moral civil sphere of polite sociability and intellectual reflection. There is visible in the contrast of images a new transactional awareness between Aristotle's aristoi and demos on the precise cusp of ancient and modern worlds in the 17th and 18th centuries.

Ahiman Rezon the second important book of constitutions of the ancient freemasons depicts the valuing of ancient and modern learning in freemasonry, as does the constitutions of the moderns, but also marks the ethnic and class tensions of Irish, Scottish, and English populations. Ritual, perhaps even more so than language, can mark the boundaries of what is inside and outside the group. Ritual could be said to express an ontology of being and subtly but potently, and in a primordial way, rituals sets the groundwork for the epistemology of the fence that divides that which is within and that which is without. Ritual, as shall be seen, can be the profound strength and place of community or contribute to its death through suffocation and incestuous practices. Exposures such as *Jachin and Boaz* or *Masonry Dissected* assist recovery of actual ritual work of 18th century freemasonry, as they would be performed in the 18th and 19th centuries.

The *Book of Illustrations* by Preston presents the aspect of freemasonry that valorized learning, intellectual inquiry, but also aesthetic-moral virtue in human experience. Freemasonry, through his eyes, was the aesthetic-moral habitus and performativity of internalized and embodied virtue, masculine performance, and a particular view of learning. Learning had an end point. In the perfecting and perfection of society there is a parallel in the rough ashlar worked into the perfect stone practically and symbolically in freemasonry. So thought Preston in his world view and pedagogy. Preston also begins the rise to his life's work through printing and journalism and is a portent of things to come among an important number of freemasons in America in this exact regard, as well pointing early to a vital thread throughout this work.

CHAPTER 3

EARLY AMERICAN FREEMASONRY, WIDER CIVIL SOCIETY, AND RITUAL AND TRANSMISSION LOGICS OF THE PRINTED TEXT

In the years before 1720, roughly at the time of Benjamin Franklin's birth in Boston, the performative habitus of loyalty to the Crown, establishment churches, and colonial authorities were unquestioned tradition and expressed core values among the provincials. However, reading habits and interest for different types of materials moved on within the course of Franklin's lifetime. Slow metamorphosis to a civic habitus in proto-democratic action paralleled a range of evolving print vehicles, including newspapers with changing content, pamphlets, maps, school readers, and texts on elocution. Pamphlets, as an illustration, were increasingly secular over the course of the 18th century, in contrast to earlier published sermons. The texts, habits, and hierarchical habitus of another era had grown stale, bureaucratic and inadequate to the new day. There came a growing moral imagination in freemasonry and among the wider citizenry of the need for an informed citizenry. The sense and need was magnified in the approach and experience of war and its aftermath. It was imagined there would be open ended deliberation, progress, precision and artfulness anchored in worlds of print in place and across networks. Experimentation and egalitarian possibilities in learning and education also were imagined as necessary to the dream of the white male demos in the imagined and now material republic.

In the midst of powerful commercial and civic change, Franklin emphasized what he termed the art of virtue. The art shaped new habits of learning, leading to personal success and the moral imagination of informed, educated, and upwardly mobile citizenry. The occupation of postmaster, a job held by Franklin, was in fast transition and was of vital importance in an emergent civil society and nation, yet Franklin understood affect and home life in worlds of print witness *Poor Richard's Almanac*. Drama, aesthetics, and entertainment value were not absent in Franklin's writing. Franklin may be used as a model to emphasize the moral imagination of an informed citizenry and both the transmission and ritual logics of communication and its advocates in early America.

Newspapers and other vehicles of print began to circulate in high levels of intensity of manufacture, distribution and consumption. Transmission multiplied between emplaced nodes, and at great distance on new roads, in the early America republic. Ultimately Americans would attempt to build an American system of manufacture for printed material in contrast to imports of books, for example, from London. Ritual and transmission transactions in human experience simultaneously involved embodied, emplaced, and networked communication. Deliberation was a vital phase of moral conduct and to understanding and evaluating the problematic environment, but imagination was essential to exploring the possibilities and potential of that contingent situation.

A. Philadelphia

During the period of the American Revolution, Philadelphia became the largest commercial center in English-speaking America. The city, in its central geographic position situated richly as it was in the overlap between New York and the fecund Chesapeake regions, as well as inland resources, hamlets and land in Pennsylvania, became the center of American industry, commerce, government, science and culture. It was a crossroads as well as an early Cosmopolis with a hinterland of its own. Beginning with the moral imagination, actions, and conceptual positions promulgated in William Penn's liberal immigration policy, the course of natural population growth among immigrants in Pennsylvania as a whole had moved upward from 2,200 in the early 1700s to 19,000 in 1760, with an upward climb to about 30,000 as the War of Independence moved near to ignition in 1775.[66] The population curve was steep and cultural and material transactions of all sorts greatly increased. Networks were condensed and expanded within and between towns, the provinces, and the early frontier, for example the wilderness territory of Detroit, Michigan and overseas.

During this growth, the merchants and shopkeepers of Philadelphia were the topic of local legend. Numerous merchants had their names etched within the landscape in street names or associated with survey plots and land-speculation in the emergence of commercial society alongside civil society. Reaching inland from sites like Philadelphia tapping First Nation

---

66   Gary Nash, *First City: Philadelphia and the Forging of Historical Memory* (Philadelphia: University of Pennsylvania Press, 2002), 31.

furs, rich soil, and open to Atlantic trade, fortunes were made by transporting agricultural products, timber (often for British ships-of-war), and products of hunting in the hinterland to sites throughout the British Empire. While barter was common at the very first stirrings of the city, transactions grew more complex in the early 1700s, requiring new vehicles of print mediation such as letters of credit and bills of exchange.

An important innovation supplanting specie and coin was the printing of paper money (a print vehicle, transmission, and cultural product), which was first issued in Philadelphia, Pennsylvania in 1723 as a policy response to an early recession.[67] Later, stamps were impressed on the paper utilized in newspapers and other vehicles of print across the colonies. The transactional medium, and concomitant cultural and material semiotics, of these stamps were intended to provide a central means of taxation by the British military, Empire, and Crown. Proceeds were used for proper but also questionable ends, for example to fund overseas military and imperial activities, including in the colonies. Printed money was increasingly central in human transactions and the circuitry of power in a socio semiotics that communicated in local place and across networks in space.[68] Printed money involves indices of transactional life experienced in a network of places.

The import, values, and interpretation of stamped paper used for a range of print vehicles ultimately helped spark the harsh armed and bloody rebellion and bio-semiotics of the American Revolution. There were "negative externalities," unintended consequences and technologies of the Crown igniting, through communicative action, the formation of new post-colonial publics, then nation-state. The formation of a public or public interest in response to the unintended or intended consequences of the actions of the King and British Parliament is a view of how the civil sphere or public, and counter publics, are formed in the classical American pragmatism of John Dewey.[69] That is to say, public formation, sometimes emerging as a singular public interest for a moment, is a real response and communica-

---

67   Ibid., 45.

68   Mark Gottdiener, *Postmodern Semiotics: Material Culture and theForms of Postmodern Life* (Oxford: Blackwell, 1995), 25-29. Mark Gottdiener drawing on C. S Peirce, uses the term socio-semiotics to describe a material or embodied system of signs in opposition to the untethered sign making of postmodernism.

69   John Dewey, *The Public and Its Problems* (New York: H. Holt and Company, 1927), 47-48.

tive action to a real problem, not abstract theory. With the upheaval and uncertainty of war, the newspaper, pamphlet, and broadside, and other vehicles of print emerged in cities such as Philadelphia, New York, and Boston as important media of communication in the dramaturgy and transactions of geographic place, and networks of place.

In the *Social Life of Information,* John Seely Brown and Paul Duguid point out that with massive increases and transmission of information, it is possible to overlook the fact that individuals, the group, and information are situated in place.[70] An illustration is the printing and journalistic agglomeration of talent, institutions, and skill that constituted Philadelphia. Information processes into knowledge and wisdom when it embodies objects in ritual, artful and communitarian behavior.

B. THE MORAL IMAGINATION OF AN INFORMED CITIZENRY[71]

In his lifetime, Franklin was significant in shaping the printing and publishing networks, pubic reading habits, and moral imagination of an informed citizenry in young republic. The moral imagination of an informed citizenry in early America enhanced democratic possibilities in diverse processes of deliberation. Deliberation was imbricate in the growth of literacy, and the perceived emerging necessity of egalitarian education, and experimentation, in a new environment. Deliberation is experimental—and a dramatic rehearsal—in examining options. The experiment is carried out in dramatic and tentative rehearsals in thought then deed. Experiment and moral imagination are situated in anticipation of the future while engaging the emplaced present needs and problems of the moment and drawing on the past. Franklin was a seminal figure in efforts at deliberative democracy as experimentation, inquiry, habit correction and imaginative acts of the spoken and written word in his personal and public life. Franklin grew towards more egalitarian views as a central need in a republic. In the imaginative communication of his values and

---

70   John Brown Seely & Paul Duguid, *The Social Life of Information* (Boston: Harvard Business School Press, 2000), 45.

71   For extended and insightful discussion concerning imagination as dramatic rehearsal (and the qualitative thought in process aesthetics) in deliberation, see Steven Fesmire, *John Dewey and Moral Imagination: Pragmatism in Ethics* (Bloomington: Indiana University Press, 2003); Fesmire, *Dewey* (London: Rouledge: 2014), 130-136; Thomas M. Alexander, *The Human Eros: Eco-Ontology and the Aesthetics of Existence,* (New York: Fordham University Press, 2013), 180-206.

ideas before the war, he established a transmission network of printers across the colonies among men he judged of good habit and character.[72] His practiced and studied networking for transmission before, during, and then again later after the war, was intended to fulfill various functions such as economic investment and return, political force, intelligence networks, honest inquiry, and instrumental mechanisms for the growth of the press. Much was possible set upon the glue of personal bonding and trust in place then across networks.

For the man, and professional, Franklin, there were numerous iterative moments of completion or consummation (a process aesthetics) in the instrumental and aesthetic experience of completed cycles of a print-job or weekly edition of a newspaper, or almanac, if they were well done. The fulfillment of one edition led to the imagination—dramatic rehearsal—potential completion and enrichment of the next. He had a strong interest in his occupation and its fulfilling moments and enrichments as he simultaneously helped create that same modern networked profession in pursuing a news story. In a similar way the communicative transmission, deliberation and performance of Thomas Paine's *Common Sense* a remarkably potent pamphlet helped spark the deliberations and then authorship of the moral imagination of the Declaration of Independence.

A newspaper report on freemasonry in Philadelphia could lead to the first American printing of the original 1734 *Book of Constitutions of the Free-Masons*. Another newspaper report could point to a problematic situation in need of repair at the portside in economic matters or going inland. Tocqueville later would work to grasp this dynamic in his phrasing of the American press in particular as participating in *processes* of "endless perfectibility". In the post-revolutionary period, Franklin became an important cultural focus of rhetorical and educational efforts by associations of printers, themselves working to affirm and honor the contribution of the press, and of Franklin the individual, to the revolutionary movements in culture, moral imagination and politics.[73]

---

72   Dewey, *Democracy and Education*, 3. The full quotation reads: "Society exists through a process of transmission quite as much as biological life. This transmission occurs by means of communication of habits of doing, thinking and feeling from the older to the younger. Without this communication of ideals, hopes, expectations, standards, opinions, from those member of society who are passing out of the group life to those who are coming into it, social life could not survive."

73   Stephen Botein. "Printers and the American Revolution," in, Bernard Bailyn and John

Printers who were masons and non-masons each contributed to the revolutionary cause. It cannot be forgotten that there were printers, and freemasons, making their stand among loyalists to the Crown and who, at the same time, lost a great deal in taking sides with British interests. Among the patriots, Franklin became the central symbol of a new identity and subjectivity that printers imagined for themselves and the future. [74] In the printing profession and more widely it was a building of the *self* with new habits of self-control, action, and performativity in print culture in civil society in the emerging republic.

Within this early American context, a variety of print vehicles including newspapers, constitutions and pamphlets, could be instrumental in the fulfillments of associational life. A fine illustration is Franklin's entrance into freemasonry. In 1731 after courting attention from freemasons in Philadelphia by publishing news of the existence of the fraternity in Pennsylvania in his newspaper, Franklin was invited to be initiated into the perceived elite solidarity of freemasons. It was not long afterward that he was initiated in the first degree of freemasonry (entered apprentice), passed to the second degree (fellow craft), and rose to the third degree (master mason) of the symbolic lodge.

In the course of his rapid rise in freemasonry in Pennsylvania, he reprinted in America, in 1734, the 1723 *Book of Constitutions of the Free-masons,*

B. Hench, eds., *The Press and the American Revolution* (Boston: Northeast University Press, 1981), 13.

74 There are far reaching implications in the human sciences and praxis concerning imagination as a phase, perhaps the most vital phase, in deliberation, including moral deliberation in democracy. Imagination as engaged by Dewey in a strong, even radical form of deliberative democracy becomes a starting point in opening new vistas in communication and experimentation in institution and tool making. Imagination as a starting point in political philosophy and democratic praxis involving dynamic and situated doing, thinking and feeling (qualitative thought) is in stark contrast, for example, to a purified trajectory or abstract stance by John Rawls as an "original position." (Steven Fesmire, email exchange with Steven Fesmire on December 08, 2014.) The moral self for Dewey "cannot be conceived as some absolutely isolated, or unchanging entity, a source of propositional attitudes, free actions, emotive ejaculation, or rational commands. It is a process of growth ecologically connected with its biological and cultural world." Moral life cannot be summarized by examination of an act, or an absolute, nor human essence without change. "Still Dewey can agree with Aristotle that acts establish the habitual basis for character, and established habits become the conditions whereby future acts tend to be generated. From this process the self arises" .... "The nature of moral conduct is analogous to a process of artistic creation." Alexander, *The Human Eros*, 200.

originally published in London. This text first became the foundation stone of freemasonry in the modern period. Its influence has continued into the 20th century around the world, while often enduring as blind-superstition bound to the dead letter. There has so far been an inexact knowledge of the text and its actual early 18th century contexts, historical semantics, and meaning for freemasonry. There have grown powerful forces for sacred inclusion and profane exclusion, initially based on interpretations of the rules of the *Book of Constitutions* by at first a few discussed in Chapter 2 and subsequent traditions with changes in reading and interpretation of the ritual that evolved.

Franklin published the *Constitutions of the Free-masons* in America after visiting London without the Palladian aesthetic-moral frontispiece.[75] As a Newtonian, publisher, printer-journalist, and a bit more, Franklin was among a small group in the colonies capable of recognizing the names of Senex and Hooke appearing on the frontispiece as strong English advocates of the new science and perhaps a likeness of Newton's disciple and friend Desaguliers. Senex and Hooke were important original factors in the publishing of the *Book of Constitutions* and likely part of overlapping core networks, some of which were responsible for the evolution then launch of the modern freemasonry of three degrees. Franklin, as a Newtonian, would have been immediately attracted to the book and the imagined London milieu of its action figures such as Senex and Desaguliers. Franklin when in London very much wanted to meet Newton but circumstances did not work out.

Over decades, newspapers books and other print vehicles in America illustrated social, economic, and cultural changes underway. The formation of new habits and vicarious, shared drama of stories moved to bind an imagined community of civil society and mythopoeic nation By 1776, there were increasing signs of critical social inquiry and need for the accurate, stable transmission of information, among newspapermen and some women publishers as well the reading audience. The newspaper as transmission had both (a) a dramatic and embodied ritual function sparking imagination (the drama of Lexington and Concord), and (b) mirroring

---

75   James Anderson and Benjamin Franklin, *The Constitutions of the Free-Masons*, Facsimile, 1734, Paul Royster, ed. (Lincoln: Faculty Publications, of the University of Nebraska-Lincoln, 2015), accessed July 1, 2015, http://digitalcommons.unl.edu/library science/25/.

function (facts about the fighting) in communication as a technology, or technique. The newspaper was a tool, stabilized by the habits of a learned vocation and need for accurate information, as well a shared and imagined "ritualized" solidarity set in the material and cultural soil of local place and across networks of place. In the colonies, the engagement with manifold problems and rise of emotion, especially with the British, came to mean the desire and then actively perceived need for an informed American citizenry. Emotion, desire, and quality hold a situation together as integral experience and moving process, and then imagination or dramatic rehearsal potentially coheres with the action in authentic deliberation. The newspaper as communication and transmission fashioned dramas of the included and the other.

In earlier England, the arguments of Dissenters and Radical Whigs had appeared in print. These English groups accepted social stratification but in general it was believed says Richard Brown:

> ... that inequalities should be based more on merit than preferment, and there was a willingness to criticize the status quo. In this view, an informed citizenry ought to be more comprehensive and comprise more than just liberally educated gentlemen.[76]

Brown asserts:

> Just as critical inquiry was vital for establishing religious and scientific truths, from their ... [the English] perspective a politically informed citizenry, one that was equipped to evaluate public policy, ... [deliberation] was vital for the well-being of the state and the liberty of its people. By mid-century, this viewpoint, which valued a politically informed citizenry over a realm populated by subjects indoctrinated in [the channeled habits of] religious and political conformity was part of the Anglo-America discussion, even turning up occasionally in such respected British periodicals as Addison and Steele's often-reprinted *Spectator* and Bolingbrokes's *Craftsman*.[77]

---

76   Richard Brown, *The Strength of a People: The Idea of an Informed Citizenry in America, 1650-1870* (Chapel Hill and London: University of North Carolina Press, 1996), 38.

77   Loc. cit.

America was England, but with a difference, with growing differences. A budding narrative of progress underwent a dramatization, and a reality check, just prior to the crisis of the American War of Independence. The notion of an informed citizenry had been advocated rarely, or ethereally, in the mid-18th century colonies. Newspapers, for their part in England, were often interested in, with reading habits of, foreign warfare and movements of court and Parliament. In the colonies, there were contests and newly crafted or habituated intellectual positions in print concerning the frontier and its resources, information on urban commercial transactions, patronage, partisanship, and sectarian issues. What then emerged, in an important measure as already stipulated, was the moral imagination of an informed citizenry. Brown states:

> Between 1763 and 1775, the idea [moral imagination] of an informed citizenry was activated. The catalyst was a series of parliamentary acts and administrative policies the British initiated in their efforts to reform the imperial system. The new British measures, which effected overseas trade, imported consumer goods, western lands, and newspapers, and all legal transactions, aroused repeated protests from the elite political classes in the colonies. Planters and merchants were joined by almost everyone with a college degree or a claim to gentry's status as well as master tradesmen like shipbuilders, printers, and iron masters. When these self-styled gentlemen sought to mobilize opposition to the measures via legislative resolutions, public meetings, newspapers, and pamphlets, they discovered the importance of the idea of an informed citizenry. They seized and elevated to prominence a concept that had hitherto lain inert in the background of Whig thought. What had been merely a last resort of liberty in Radical Whig doctrine was suddenly of central practical as well as theoretical importance.[78]

The dynamics involved doing and undergoing, the centrifugal and centripetal forces of habits of the body-mind and environment, the optimally inquiring and artfully communicating citizen in a new extensive republic connecting the near and far. Imagination, muscle, and resources moved

---

78   Ibid., 52.

toward solution and new, more instrumental and felicitous habits—small and large in geographic and temporal scale—in an infinite myriad of problematic or nurturing situations imbricated in overlapping spheres of the state, economy and artful living (culture) of civil society. Empathetic projection of the individual and group in proto democratic experience and later deliberative democracy and efforts at expanding the franchise made possible creatively tapping a situations possibilities whether in nurturing experiences or the colloquy of problematic cultural and material landscapes.[79]

C. Franklin and the Transmission of Information in Civil Society

Franklin in Philadelphia and William Hunter in Williamsburg, both postmasters, were appointed Joint Postmasters General for the Crown in the 1750s. In preparation for the colonial restructuring, Franklin studied England first hand, and, in addition, set out on extended geographic tours to inspect post offices in northern colonies and as far south as Virginia. Under Franklin, new geographic surveys were conducted, milestones arranged on principal roads, and new and shorter routes were also trotted out. Post riders were assigned to carry mail day and night between Philadelphia and New York, where traveling time was abridged by nearly half over some years of work and planning. The Philadelphia and New York set of roads were the central communication axis in North America. Then, in 1760, Franklin offered the British Postmaster General a surplus, which was initially the postal service in North America. It was an end that consummated prior work, with internal critique, and made possible further instrumental aesthetic consummations.

The interrelationship of post office, printing, and publishing goes to the very beginnings of American journalism, and development of commerce, transportation, and communication. The postmasters established most early newspapers. Richard Kielbowicz has stated:

> In fact, many of the postal laws enacted in the 1790s simply codified customs that had evolved during the colonial period. In 1758, Benjamin Franklin and William Hunter, Deputy Postmasters General, adopted the first

---

79 Fesmire, *Dewey*, 130-136.

formal policy governing the circulation of the news in the mails. They permitted post riders to deliver newspapers to subscribers for nine pence per year for every fifty miles transported by post. Franklin and Hunter also allowed printers to exchange copies of their papers among one another without charge as a means of acquiring news. Postage-free printers' exchanges, recognized in the first United States postal laws, remained the principal method of newsgathering until the invention of the telegraph and the development of press associations in the mid-1800s.[80]

By the time Franklin left his office as Deputy Joint Post Master General for the colonies, post roads etched out from Maine to Florida and from New York to Canada, and mail between the colonies and the mother country operated on time with a regular printed schedule that the public could read. Franklin and Hunter had achieved over time regulation of the post offices which included audit accounts. In 1772 the position of geographic surveyor was created by Franklin. This position became the precursor of today's Postal Inspection Service. The formation of the public and the more slow-moving "state" grew out of a problematic situation, not an abstraction of social contract theory, or postulated primitive natural state of man which some thought manifest before there was language.

By 1774, however, the colonists had begun to view the royal post office with suspicion, and the Crown dismissed Franklin because he was perceived as taking actions sympathetic to the cause of the colonies. Within a short period, William Goddard, a printer and newspaper publisher, set up a Constitutional Post for the delivery of mail between the colonies-states.[81] The colonies funded the operation through subscriptions, and any profits were used to improve the postal service, rather than returned to subscribers. When the Continental Congress met at Philadelphia in 1775 on the eve of armed revolution, Goddard's colonial postal system was flour-

---

80 Richard Kielbowicz, "The Press, Post Office, and Flow of News in the Early Republic," *Journal of the Early Republic* 3, no 3 (1983): 250.

81 William Goddard's daughter inherited his printing business while residing in Baltimore. It was she that produced, with a strong sense of the value of women in society, and the emerging nation, the second printing of the *Declaration of Independence*. Women were sometimes permitted by the community to own property and work in worlds of print. There was often backlash.

ishing with 30 post offices operating between Portsmouth, New Hampshire, and Williamsburg, Virginia. The communication network, which involved people known to each other, was used by some as an early part of the knowledge and material base of later intelligence networks (inquiry and artful communication in their own manner) of the American War of Independence. Individuals and core groups in communication networks in Boston were aware of activities and specific personalities in Philadelphia and the same was true the other way around. New York and the city of Baltimore also nurtured personal and professional intra-and intercity transmission and socially integrated networks. These were instances of socio-cultural bonds and wide transmission networking consanguine in a new geography of the American union.

Franklin assisted, materially and spiritually, the young apprentice printer John Dunlap and his father (with the younger ultimately the official printer of Congress) who was responsible for printing the original copies of the *Declaration of Independence* (perhaps 200 or more), the *Articles of Confederation*, and original copies of the *Constitution* used by Congress for debate. Franklin likely helped to raise Dunlap and his father to achieve success in the business of print.[82] Franklin aided others while selling them materials to his personal benefit. These were distribution networks and supply chains where both the consumer and provider benefited. Franklin hoped for others the same economic growth and opportunities for learning he had experienced in the upward social mobility of his own life; and he was interested in the benefits of virtue and increasingly of egalitarian education for the individual and group. The ideal of an informed citizenry was a catalyst, an imagination, of individual self-development and the simultaneous growth of the community, economic health, and body politics.

Franklin believed that for individuals to behave virtuously a selfish-motive or self-interest would be needed. Otherwise, the individual would not adopt Franklin's plan of self-perfecting, discipline of new habit formation (self-control), public virtue, and taste for learning. Ralph Frasca states Franklin's view that people would defer without the attraction of self-interest. Franklin envisioned material gain as a vital motivating factor. As in *Poor Richard's Almanac* and throughout his writings and planning

82   Ralph Frasca, *Benjamin Franklin's Printing Network: Disseminating Virtue in Early America.* (New York: Columbia University Press, 2006), 179.

he would argue virtues such as industry, steadfastness and frugality were wealth producing.[83]

It was not only assistance to those below on the social rung that held his attention, Franklin in his *Autobiography* observed his reputation and business opportunities increased as he became personally acquainted with "many principle People of the Province" and developed "some very ingenious Acquaintances whose Conversation was of great Advantage to me."[84]

From his youngest years, Franklin was interested in the "art of virtue," how to acquire it and further perfect it. He believed that moral strength was the result of rational deliberation, sincere thrift, labor, and the disciplined behavior of habits. However, there was an imaginative and aesthetic quality to Franklin, not captured in specific terms such as "rational deliberation" and "industrious labor." Franklin, for example, consciously or unconsciously, often used the metaphor of art, to swing his morality and printers' world-view into the semantic field of imagination. The terms art and the artist helped to frame his view of the meaning, purpose, values, and traditions of printing.[85]

Franklin believed that the simple but far-reaching virtues he desired in himself were the result of an acquired art (a developed moral artistry, an act of reaching, conduct building on established habits and habit correction), rather than simply an innate skill. To embrace virtue, people must learn "the Principles of the Art, be shown all the Methods of Working, and how to acquire the *Habits* [emphasis in the original] of using properly all the Instruments; and thus regularly and gradually arrive by Practice at some Perfection in the Art[86]." As working distinctions, Franklin seemed instinctively to move toward the infrastructure of networks ("the transmission metaphor ") and drama ("the metaphor of ritual") as functions,

83   Ibid., 7-21.

84   Benjamin Franklin, *Autobiography* (New York: Dover Publications, 1996), 51, 57.

85   Franklin was the only individual to sign both *The Declaration of Independence* and the *United-States Constitution*. These printed documents remain remarkable cultural pieces. The *Declaration* and *Constitution*, so far, have never been exhausted in their interpreted meaning, value seeking, nor their shifting aesthetic-mroal form. For an in depth view of the shifiting aesthetic form, or "aesthetic field", of an artist, art object, interpretive audience, and performer of the art object through time, see, Arnold Berleant, *The Aesthetic Field: A Phenomenology of Aesthetic Experience* (Springfield: Charles C. Thomas Cybereditions, 1970), 121.

86   Frasca, 17.

or semiotic logics, and habits of communication; for example, the prose, poetry and wide diffusion of *Poor Richard's Almanac*.

Franklin utilized one art (printing) to communicate another (the art of virtue). His imaginative and aesthetic-moral conceptualization of the printer was situated in the received tradition (going back centuries) that printing was an "esteemed ... art, requiring special skills and knowledge beyond the grasp of the ordinary person."[87] Senex and Hooke, the printers and freemasons in London examined in Chapter 2, likely held this view with their involvement in the production of the *Book of Constitutions of the Free-Masons*. Franklin, for his part, constantly moved toward ideas and ideals of egalitarian education; a new set of habits and promising conduct for those lower on the socio-economic scale. There was a transformation and experimentation underway, with ideas and practices pushed and drawn from Tudor England and other sites such as the Dutch republic and Huguenots.

Early American printer-journalists and freemasons such as Isaiah Thomas (discussed later in this chapter) were immersed in "the art which is the preserver of all arts" (referring to printing), a phrase coined by Thomas, one of the founding fathers, along with Franklin, of American worlds of print.[88] Thomas believed the art of printing gave universality to, and helped perpetuate through time, every other art, and social improvement. Franklin used his *Poor Richard's Almanac*, and other vehicles of print such as his *Pennsylvania Gazette*, to provide moral education, entertainment, and to give information to the masses, as well as gather information. There were objections in his time, such as that from Thomas Jefferson, who thought "it unwise" to undertake reform of all of one's neighbors.[89]

In the course of his life, and the development of his art of virtue, and habit correction, Franklin also shows the movement into modern forms of education, learning, communication, and civics contrasted with ancient praxes. Sandra Gustafson points out:

---

87 Loc. cit.

88 Isaiah Thomas, *The History of Printing in America, with a Biography of Printers and an Account of Newspapers* (New York: Weathervane Books. 1973), 3.

89 Thomas Jefferson, *The Papers of Thomas Jefferson*, ed. Julian P. Boyd, Volume 19: January 1791 to March 1791 (Princeton: Princeton University Press, 1974), 252-253.

One principal lesson [to be drawn from Franklin] is that in a modern and increasingly democratic republic the ability to minimize the self is an essential component of self-making. In sharp contrast with Cicero, who earned a lasting reputation for self-promotion, the aspiring new man of the early republic had to disguise his agency while trusting others to credit his efforts. Franklin's emphasis on self-effacement was tied to his preferred modes of expression: he criticized the use of classical languages [for example, in pedagogy], which he saw as promoting hubris, and he never tried to imitate the eloquence of his Roman predecessors, choosing instead to exercise influence principally through [the underlying habits and quality of] print and conversation. Nevertheless Franklin was a frequent presence in the elocution manuals designed to train young Americans to speak effectively and participate in civic life.[90]

As Franklin trained many early journalists, he also helped establish a distinctively American character and habitus of public service for the American press. This public-service ideology (more accurately an aesthetic-moral imagination, habit formation, and conceptual working) elevated the printer-publishers from tradesmen of modest social status to recognition as a class of prominent and respected leaders of public opinion, similar to the esteemed status of the printer in the 16th and 17th centuries. In all of this, Franklin was a harbinger of press professionalization, production, and performativity. Stated differently, the press, as aesthetically rough and primitive as it was in early America, was a creative tension of prose, information gathering, artfulness and poetry in American letters.

The transmission networks established by Franklin that lasted from the 1720s to roughly the end of the 18th century helped transform American worlds of print. Franklin understood the need to make the vehicles of print attractive to the public through humor, mystique, and the drama of communication. This artful view is well illustrated in the aesthetic-moral appeal of character he put into play, such as in the almanac *Poor*

---

90 Sandra M. Gustafson, *Imagining Deliberative Democracy in the Early American Republic* (Chicago: University of Chicago Press, 2011), 79.

Richard. He imagined the place of print in people's everyday lives, not as an abstraction, but as people actually, qualitatively lived, just as he also worked to use the press as a means of transmission of information and economic enterprise. Print vehicles and specific editions, in addition to economic possibilities through advertisements and subscription or sales, were imagined as moral-practical affairs and could be intended as problem solving. The semiotics of communication going into war was well grounded in real-world problems and their potential amelioration as well the rhetoric of war.

Franklin's instinctive sense of the place of the "sign" in human experience, and its potential in war, can be examined variously and not only in the public sphere. His mastery of the sign is found as well in his role as one of the founding fathers of American spy networks. He played this role along with other men who also often happened to be freemasons, such as George Washington and Joseph Warren, as well men that offer some evidence of masonic membership, as with John Jay. These men constituted the uppermost level of military intelligence at its beginning in the American nation becoming a state. Communication thrives in all ecologies. Women also became involved in these intelligence networks with their own secret signs and practices, for example the hanging of wash in the yard in certain patterns. African American as house servants keeping a low profile and shrinking demeanor were recruited usefully in the transmission and signing of spy-networks.

Franklin's work and ideas were instrumental in establishing the enduring social importance, aesthetics and habitus of journalism, still present as part of the American collective psyche, and established in political context as freedom of the press in the Bill of Rights. Franklin's views contributed to the idea of the free press as an institution and to the aesthetic-moral imagination of the indefinite perfectibility of the individual's dream of the good life in America with a concomitant necessary egalitarian access to information and education for the group. Habits of learning are at a high-level in an open democracy with inquiry, critique, and ongoing praxis in artful, as well instrumental, logics or functions of communication providing ferment and spark.

D. WILLIAM BENTLEY AND THE UNIVERSAL MOVEMENT OF
INFORMATION IN THE ENLIGHTENED REPUBLIC

As outlined by Richard Brown in his *Knowledge is Power: the Diffusion of Information in Early America*, 1700-1865, the cosmopolite William Bentley (1759-1819) was with Thomas Jefferson, one of the great polymaths of the early republic and concerned with the moral imagination and tasks of diffusing information and fashioning an informed citizenry.[91] Leading American societies recognized his erudition as a graduate of Harvard, enthusiastic freemason, and Unitarian minister. Among civil associations who held him in high respect, was the American Philosophical Society, the American Antiquarian Society, and the Massachusetts Historical Society. It was Jefferson who eagerly sought Bentley to become the founding president of his beloved University of Virginia, and it was Bentley who counted in his circles of association the remarkable activist the African American freemason Prince Hall of Boston, the antiquarian, printer, and publisher Isaiah Thomas, and equally so, Franklin. Bentley's twice weekly summary of world news and international politics for the *Salem Gazette* and *Salem Register* was considered the best brief chronicle on these topics by John Pintard, the learned and enthusiastic New York philanthropist, freemason, advocate for public education, patriot, radical, and Right Reverend.[92]

Bentley's interest in German culture did no less than help inspire the later thinking of American Transcendentalists in the tradition of Ralph Waldo Emerson and Henry David Thoreau. The freemason and minister spoke or could write in 20 languages. As Brown summarizes for breadth and depth of learning, Bentley whose personal library of 4,000 volumes ranked with America's greatest private collections "had few intellectual peers."[93] The Massachusetts Unitarian Bentley was a member of the Essex

---

91   Richard D. Brown, *The Strength of a People: The Idea of an Informed Citizenry in America, 1650-1870* (Chapel Hill: University of North Carolina Press, 1997), 110. See also, Brown, *Knowledge is Power: The Diffusion of Information in Early America, 1700-1865* (New York: Oxford University Press, 1989), 197-217.

92   Pintard was a friend of DeWitt Clinton discussed later in this chapter and his brother in Holland Lodge in New York City. On February 19, 1805 he began the efforts, which became the present free school system in New York among many contributions he made in the civil sphere. He was a descendant of Antoine Pintard, a Huguenot from La Rochelle, France.

93   Brown, *Knowledge is Power*, 197.

Lodge of masons in Massachusetts, and a Royal Arch mason.[94] He was one of the most popular, and published, of all turn-of-the-century Masonic orators and considered a perfect choice by Jefferson to be the first head of the University of Virginia. It was in masonry, and in the pulpit, that Bentley honed his rhetorical skills.

Alongside Bentley's secular accomplishments he, and his close confidants, are interesting participants in the story of the book as gospel and living word and its transmission. Ministers and church organizations of all sects saw clearly how their own interpretation of the word of God could be spread everywhere in England and America through print. In the case of Reverend Bentley, preaching in the emerging American version of the Unitarian Church, this interpretation of the word of the gospel involved a rational epistemology, a naturalist ontology, and Socinian Jesus.[95] Unitarianism left England in the 18th century via the printed text, entering America in Boston. It was then geographically transmitted to Salem, where Bentley came to settle. From that locus, his theology moved widely in transmission. It was in Salem that Bentley practiced on occasion the art of printing, while continuing his prodigious efforts in oratory. Bentley (with colleagues) maintained a potent "system of disseminating Unitarianism by print" out of Massachusetts.[96]

In widely disseminating Unitarian tracts and sermons coming at first from printing establishments in London, a battle of texts was underway in young America involving interpretations of the ostensibly inerrant word of the bible. The infrastructure for that ongoing battle would ultimately be turned on freemasonry in anti-masonry in a fusillade of print in recalling the Morgan affair discussed in Chapter 1.

Brown stated:

> The desire to proselytize shaped the very materiality of
> the works .... Liberal books were generally lengthy ones
> .... Bentley wrote a catechism of an already short effi-

---

94 This is a "higher degree" ritualistic body in freemasonry considered by some a pinnacle.

95 Socianism developed around the time of the Reformation was a form of Nontrinitarianism. The name itself derived from Laelius Soccinus [d. 1562] in Poland.

96 Rixey Ruffin, *A Paradise of Reason: William Bentley and Enlightenment Christianity in the Early Republic* (Oxford and New York: Oxford University Press, 2008), 95.

ciently produced work by J. B. Priestley entitled an *Extract* ... intentionally for the sake of dispersal. These were works meant to be easily and inexpensively reprinted, transported, and distributed en masse. As Bentley told his congregants [as minister and well known mason] ... the new reformation would work only "by making information cheap and easy to the common people."[97]

Moderate liberal Christianity was promulgated in part through a cannonade of published treatises and philosophical and social interpretation. That said, the social library in Salem, with considerable holdings in a liberal Christianity appealing to mercantile and professional elites, worked with entrenched habit, habitus, in holding knowledge from the common people. Bentley, in contrast, argued for the accessibility of printed materials across the union.

Bentley, as he matured, came to oppose the union of church and state; he was suspicious of corruption and conspiracy by insiders, and insisted on a free press and free exchange of ideas. His priorities lay in preserving rights to information, ideas, and enlightenment, which he saw "as the best sureties of the spread of morality and thus human happiness." He continued his collection of books "enough so that by the time he died, his personal library was one of the largest in the country, perhaps second in size behind only Jefferson."[98] Bentley wrote his in his will to bequeath the theological and classical volumes to Allegheny College in Meadville, Pennsylvania. Allegheny College, for reasons not quite clear, became a center of philanthropic activity and interest in education by some freemasons from different corners of the country in this period, as well as non-masons.[99] "The rest [he] dedicated to the [at that time, all-male] American Antiquarian Society in Worcester, Massachusetts, recently formed by his friend [and prominent fellow freemason] Isaiah Thomas."[100]

---

97 Quoted in Ruffin, 96-97.

98 Ruffin, 186.

99 An unexamined history is the many instances in the American experience in different states, cities and territories, including Pennsylvania that freemasons supported all levels of education including higher education. This has occurred more in America in freemasonry than any nation where freemasonry has existed since its inception. An illustration mentioned in the work is the origins of the University of Michigan.

100 Ruffin, 184.

E. Isaiah Thomas and another Printing Network in Worcester à la Franklin

Isaiah Thomas (1749-1831) maintained a lifelong involvement with American worlds of print from his youthful apprenticeship in colonial times beginning at age 6, where he learned to read via the developed habits, and habit correction, of breaking down type through the years before the War of Independence. He ultimately stepped out of the grinding apprentice system inherited from Europe and went on to become the foremost entrepreneurial printer and publisher in his own day, with the possible exception of Mathew Carrey, another freemason publisher and distributor working over wide geographic areas, including the Spanish speaking American southwest as in California, and Mexico. Thomas's contribution, over the course of his life, included the publication of educational textbooks, books, newspapers, music, and literature. In this broad array, he made a significant contribution to the development of American literature and can be studied in that context alone.

Thomas maintained a lifelong aspiration to write on the development of printing and its singular importance in civil society. This hit a high point in 1810 in his important *History of Printing in America, with a Biography of Printers, and an Account of Newspapers.*[101] He believed that printing developed as art out of the mechanic's craft from whence he came, and with the greatest passion spread the view that it had the unique status as "preserver of other arts."[102] However, the art could also be referred as an occupation and is treated in both ways in this work. His most significant accomplishment in the world of letters and philanthropy was the founding in 1812 of the American Antiquarian Society.

His efforts in the printing and publishing trades were undertaken with more than one motivation. Firstly, he was animated by his own economic self-interest and social mobility. This included establishing a collaborative network of apprentices and journeymen printers whom he could trust and assist or partner. In networking in this fashion, he knowingly duplicated the ideas and practices of economic self-help and simultaneous transmission, and altruism, of his elder colleague, Franklin.[103] Like Frank-

---

101 Isaiah Thomas, *The History of Printing in America, with a Biography of Printers, and an Account of Newspapers* (Worcester: Isaiah Thomas, 181.

102 Thomas, 3.

103 Frasca, 205.

lin, he published transmission schedules and other necessary material for the post office system. Secondly, as a self-educated man, not the least of Thomas's interests in print was his valorization of learning. Thirdly, there was the matter of his growing patriotism. He understood and promulgated the use of print and transmission in the American War of Independence. Like other printer-journalists of this period, he viewed the printed word as contributing not only to the commercial success of America, but also to the virtue of a people. Commercial society and the virtues and learning of polite, civil society emerged in tandem. He believed newspapers were an important part of learning in a new republic.

It is not clear where Thomas joined the fraternity of freemasonry, but it may have been at Trinity Lodge during the war in 1778 in Lancaster, Massachusetts where he subsequently became master of the lodge.[104] He did go on to become the charter master of Morning Star Lodge of Worcester, Massachusetts in 1793.[105] He was elected senior Grand Warden of the Grand Lodge of Massachusetts in 1794, and went on to become Grand Master from 1803 to 1805 and then again in 1809. From September 1807 to September 1809, he was Most Excellent High Grand Priest of the Grand Royal Arch, Royal Arch Chapter of Massachusetts.

In 1770, Thomas founded the *Massachusetts Spy*, which, besides its fame as an important voice of American dissent against the British, held the distinction as likely the first American newspaper aimed at middle-class readers. Distribution of newspapers in the colonies could run in the low hundreds in the decades before the war, whereas the *Spy* was initially going out to an approximate 3,500 readers. Others, in turn, read these copies in secondary circulations as they were passed hand-to-hand. In addition, the *Spy* and other papers might be read aloud, orated in simple fashion, in a variety of public places at local stores, newspaper offices, and local establishments served by post-riders; or other public meeting places, even along fences. The contents of *the Spy* were also copied in other newspapers. The best of the newspapers, such as the *Spy* in the period of the war, could convey precise information, yet the *Spy* was at the same

---

104 Thomas Roy Sherrard, *Stalwart Builders: A History of the Grand Lodge of Masons in Massachusetts, 1733-1970* (Boston: The Masonic Education and Charity Trust of the Grand Lodge of Massachusetts, 1971), 40.

105 Annie Russell Marble, *From 'Prentice to Patron': The Life Story of Isaiah Thomas* (New York and London: D. Appleton-Century Company, 1935), 238.

time a dramatic form of communication, when Thomas reported eyewitness accounts of the battles at Lexington and Concord. Lexington and Concord were matters of heart, head, bloody proprioception, and techniques. In an illustrative view the rifle, mind, and body orienting by the index of the gun-sight were matters of life or death, but the story needed to be told and accurately for the rising demos in the republic.

While freemasons could be found as either loyalist or patriot, Thomas' acquaintances within the fraternity increasingly, and early on, involved rebel voices in the American cause such as Paul Revere, Joseph Warren, and John Hancock, each a freemason, and among the first aspirational American Templars, all. A variety of civic and political organizations overlapped in the pre-revolutionary period, for example, the freemasons and the Sons of Liberty. It is in this moment and place that freemasonry imported from England, Ireland, and Scotland (sometimes via military lodges holding patents) began its rise in Boston and Philadelphia. There was an important infusion of ancient Irish freemasonry into America beginning in this period, as well lodges created under Scottish constitutions.

The ancient freemasons tended to come from lower, middle, and upwardly mobile classes such as artisans, master tradesmen, merchants, and mariners. The ancients spoke the loudest about their concerns with perceived British commercial and imperial practices. The freemasons, influenced in some measure by ancients such as Thomas in Boston and Worcester and Dunlap in Philadelphia, no less Scottish patents, prepared the way for the extraordinary popularity of freemasonry in the post-revolutionary period when lodges formed many towns. Symbols and signs of revolution such as the number 13 referring to the original colonies, for a period, were transposed onto ancient freemasonry as part of its symbolism.

Even if Thomas has been largely forgotten, he helped fashion the aesthetic-moral imagination and disposition of the way things were. The Irish ancient freemasons, and Scottish patents, began their American assent in Boston before Thomas began his life in the fraternity. The ancients were also small but significant in Philadelphia as illustrated by circles around Dunlap. After the war, the Americans went their own way, separating from modern freemasonry in England with some states holding elements of the moderns within what became the larger network of ancients in the new union. The American system of grand lodges became a hybrid mix of ancient and modern with the ancient in ascendency and very significant in Pennsylvania.

Thomas was aware of the importance of social drama, raw politics, and the life and death struggle unfolding around him. While likely threatening his own safety, he arranged for special post riders around the colonies to exchange newspapers and materials in transmission networks among citizens sympathetic to the patriots, and quite likely very discreetly moving information valuable to those involved in the stirrings of war. He was considerably involved in setting the transmission infrastructure of the printed word in wartime and peacetime in the northeast, as with Franklin in the greater Philadelphia area and beyond. Thomas interpreted the gravity of his difficult circumstances and finally, on the eve of war, moved his paper out of Boston inland to Charleston and then on to Worcester, Massachusetts. The first issue of the *Spy* after its move out of Boston bore the challenge "Americans, Liberty or Death."[106]

Thomas instinctively understood the tension of social drama and information transmission. He gave accurate eyewitness accounts of the battles of Lexington and Concord fought to the west of Boston. This promulgated accurate news but also vicarious drama, and as such inspired the raw currents, feeling and emotion, of patriotism; the animated body-mind in an environment then imagination of a republic. A number of the men of the Tea Party were activist freemasons, or Sons of Liberty, and others were involved in similar associations such as the Mechanics Society. There were often dual memberships in fast-rising associations. Overlapping networks often were developed as sites of emerging intelligence networks and special military operations, as with the Mechanics Society.

Political performance and very real armed action was heavily influenced by freemasons at their own building the Green Dragon Tavern, which opened its doors to the Sons of Liberty, and others, such as the Mechanics. As reports of the drama from Lexington and Concord were circulated, the *Spy* helped solidify support for the patriots. The days of armed conflict were rapidly unfolding and the written word was an intimate part of the deliberative course of events in America. Existing scarce resources for printing were pushed to their maximum and then beyond.

---

106 Marble, 97.

Thomas became a wealthy man with his considerable business skills. [107] Thomas came to own bookstores in Massachusetts, New Hampshire, New York, and Maryland. In vertical economic integration, he owned a paper mill and printing houses in Boston and Worcester, which together maintained numerous presses. He was instrumental in the development of the turnpike, a matter of transmission, between Boston and Worcester, contributing to the growth of Worcester as an important industrial city. The rapidly growing town sustained a range of merchants, shops, and financial and legal services. There were ubiquitous encouragements of commercial and agriculture advertisements, throughout the printed columns of the *Massachusetts Spy*.[108] An important factor in the development of the region consisted in the efforts of Thomas, and others, in establishing Worcester as a center for post riders in a regional transmission infrastructure connecting towns in Massachusetts, New Hampshire, and Rhode Island.

In 1812, Thomas put his accumulated wealth and personal library to work in founding a civil society, initially all-male, intended to preserve a record of the worlds of print he had labored within so capably all of his life. His civic vision of a society perpetuating the "literature of liberty" became the origin of the American Antiquarian Society. Letters of acceptance for membership in the Society, with its attendant library, in his lifetime included those from Thomas Jefferson, Daniel Webster, and Andrew Jackson, the last a fellow freemason. The project for a new historical society with print materials gathered from across the new states, always maintaining a regional awareness, was intentionally designed to be an inter-regional, national, and budding international resource. He worked within networks of transmission, and over an imagined horizon in time and space, near and far in the medium of print. In the attempt to combine resources strategically, Thomas's *History of Printing in America* was meant to assist actual cataloguing and history required by the new society. The Society is a fitting legacy to Thomas.

The society's founding indicates Thomas' perception of the place of freemasonry in the American civil sphere. The inaugural 217-page catalogue of books of Thomas' collection given to the Society was divided into 17 sections. One of the sections was entitled *Masonic Works*. There

---

107 Ibid., vii.

108 Ibid., 257.

were classifications including *Ancient Books* (before 1700), *Modern Books* (after 1700), *Bibles, Dictionaries,* and *Books in the Indian Language.* Also demarcated were categories of *Books Printed by Isaiah Thomas, Periodical Works,* and *Printing.* Thomas saw in freemasonry the fraternity's potential to foster intellectual study and virtue among its practitioners, just as DeWitt Clinton discussed below and others, consciously or unconsciously, sensed the mutual advantages of the ritual life of freemasonry in local community and the informational aspects of print in wider civil society. The embodied semiotics of transmission and ritual mutually reinforced one another, in shaping lives, in communicative action in place and a network of places.

F. DeWitt Clinton

DeWitt Clinton (1769-1828) graduated from Columbia College in 1786 and was admitted to the bar in 1790.[109] Clinton served as the private secretary to the Governor of New York from 1790 to 1795. This last was a period in which he spoke as a young man on education, learning, freemasonry, virtue, and printing, before the Holland Lodge of freemasons, the lodge in which he was a member, just as he addressed other societies on the importance of egalitarian education. Holland Lodge had an increasing reputation as the most important American masonic lodge in rebuilding freemasonry after the destruction of the Revolutionary War, although it can be said that freemasonry was a very small affair in America before the revolution. The lodge was often associated with intellectual, artistic (for example, the theater life of New York), and philosophic endeavors in its early years. There was an aesthetic, moral, and intellectual range in the life of the lodge as well the power of position. His oration before the lodge in 1793 was subsequently printed as a pamphlet, and some of its contents are discussed below.[110]

He was a unionist also became governor of his state. Clinton became Grand Master of freemasons in New York, the head of the fast growing national Knights Templar, and Royal Arch systems of freemasonry. He paralleled this with activities in civil society as one of the major figures in educational reform at state and national levels and the building of trans-

---

109 Columbia had been closed in 1776 at the outbreak of war.

110 DeWitt Clinton, *An Address Delivered Before Holland Lodge, December 24, 1793* (New York: Francis Childs and John Swaine, 1794).

mission infrastructure, including a major train route, and the Erie Canal, for what would become the Empire State and the wider westerly expanding nation-state.

Clinton held a moral imagination of an informed and virtuous citizenry. His was a dramatic rehearsal of possibilities for an expanding nation. Such a citizenry was increasingly considered essential for the growth of the republic as stated elsewhere. The emergence of print media made instruction possible to all "ranks of people."[111] Literacy rose sharply in the early American republic in a reading revolution in tandem with an elocution revolution.

Clinton stated that with the help of generations exploring religion and philosophy over a long period, equality emerged as mankind's greatest historical discovery. He presented these ideas in public lectures to non-masonic audiences, as well as to his lodge. He asserted that the egalitarian spirit was popularized through print media. Worlds of print were essential to the individual and group in a movement toward liberty, the free flow of information, and virtue. Freemasonry was part of that advance. Clinton was knowingly, or unknowingly, echoing the thoughts, at least for a moment, of the German freemason, Gotthold Ephraim Lessing (1721-1781), cited by Jürgen Habermas in his *Structural Transformation of the Public Sphere*. Lessing was quoted by Habermas saying that freemasonry was as old as civil society "if indeed bourgeois society is not merely an offspring of Freemasonry."[112] Clinton may have had access to a range of texts from continental Europe (and thus perhaps to Lessing's thoughts, and much more) through Holland Lodge in New York, his lodge, and through other print networks and nodes of private and public libraries. Holland Lodge originally worked in Dutch.

Lessing was an accomplished dramatist, aesthetician, librarian, critic, and activist for religious tolerance. He was arguably the main representative of the Enlightenment in Germany, and is often interpreted as the true founder of modern German literature. Habermas, for his part, references Lessing in the context that freemasonry in Europe was initially a secret society but secrecy, at first (at least in continental Europe), helped safeguard the individual and group from the obstructions of police activity and cen-

---

111 Clinton, 3.

112 Habermas, 35.

sorship. Lessing's writings were on more than one occasion banned by authorities.

In the 1790s, Clinton was a leader of freemasonry with a civic-minded spirit situated in temporal place and one of the most significant educational reformers in the cultural and material medium of New York and the union. [113] He became the most accomplished leader of American freemasonry in his generation. In the oration delivered before Holland Lodge, and a similar lecture delivered at other civil societies, he gave an egalitarian *raison d'être* of early American worlds of print, civil society, education, and the ritual life of freemasonry.

Clinton theorized that the impressions, meanings, and values created by the fraternity and impressed upon the passive "mind" in ritual performance were exactly akin to the impressions made on stamped pages of the newspaper or the seal upon hot wax. The dichotomous processes were thought potentially emancipating for humanity and its nations. However, despite the position of Locke, the individual does not first perceive to create a full-scale internal picture, or model, of the world around them, which is then utilized to generate appropriate action in the group and environment. Embodied perception involves rolling sensorimotor experience, a variety of types of habit in stasis and motion, imagination, neural connections and environment.

Expression is not an internal fountain from a transcendental core moving outward through the senses. Expression is part of an aesthetic field involving artful players, audience, art object, and struggle in a medium which is not an exclusive reference to a work of art in a museum. Expression involves artful living: the transactional processes of an "art object", potentially imaginative agency and praxis as embodied subject, new performers of the art object (this is more clear in the model of music, as opposed to sculpture, or in addition, readings of poetry, theater with many other examples that could be given from the practical activities of daily living) and changing audiences through time in the culture of quotidian affairs.[114]

---

113 Clinton came to be known as the Founding Father of the Erie Canal. He saw the canal as a great blessing emerging from the public good and something that would help link a new continental nation and endure through time.

114 Clinton, 14-24.

Clinton held egalitarian views of learning and civic-mindedness. Arguing against elitism in an 1809 oration, Clinton stated:

> This cardinal mistake [elitism in education] is not only to be found in the institutions of the old world and in the condition of its inhabitants, but is to be seen in most of the books which have been written on the subject of education. The celebrated Locke, whose treatises on government and the human understanding have covered him with immortal glory, devoted to the powers of his mighty intellect, to the elucidation of education—but in the very threshold of this book [Two Treatises on Government], we discover this radical error —his treatise is professedly intended to help the children of gentleman. 'If those that rank [says he], are by their education once set right, they will quickly bring all the rest in order', and he appears to consider the education of other children as of little importance. The consequence of this monstrous heresy has been, that ignorance, the prolific parent of every crime and vice, has predominated over the great body of the people, and a corresponding debasement has prevailed.[115]

Clinton accepted Locke's epistemology of knowing, but opposed his elitist views of the task of gentlemanly education. Franklin, as earlier pointed out, evolved toward the same egalitarianism in the generation prior to Clinton. Clinton held firm that the perspective held by Locke was a great flaw of Europe and inadequate to the unfolding human story and American republic and the destiny of mankind overall. His was an emplaced yet cosmopolitan and egalitarian view of learning and indefinite perfectibility.

Over his entire adult life, Clinton focused relentlessly on the moral imagination, instrumental strategizing, and physical tasks of post-war rebuilding in New York, including a sharp focus on education. Inchoate emotion and ambiguity, as in war, were followed by a probing response and shaping new habits. In the unpublished dissertation of Edward Fitzpatrick at Teachers College at Columbia University in 1911, Clinton was described,

---

115 Edgar Augustus Fitzpatrick, *The Educational Views and Influence of DeWitt Clinton* (New York: Teachers College, Columbia University, 1911).

to his honor, as the most adequate spokesman of his generation for the educational implications of the American Revolution.[116]

In Clinton's estimation, the pedagogical inheritance of the war was the articulation of equality in education and experimentation. This included for Clinton the poor, women, African Americans, wayward juveniles, workers, mechanics, and the impaired. These visionary, cosmopolitan efforts concerned with the amelioration of injustices, and pointing toward opportunities, occurred amid great obstacles and reactionary counter-trends in post-revolutionary America. Reactions were contrary to the cosmopolitan imagination and idealism at their pitch in the war and lingering resonance in men like Clinton.[117] The uncertainties, crises, and ambiguities of war as an undetermined situation evoked an instrumental aesthetic and felt response within savaged coordinates of form, habit, and medium. There was a sensibility that something new and different was necessary in education and the citizenry if there was to be a republic and stability.

Steven Bullock gives significance to the 1793 oration by Clinton, which was very similar to that delivered in 1809 to the Public School Society, and other civil societies. The first oration was given upon his installation as master of Holland Lodge in New York. Clinton's life showed an intense overlap of membership and expression of ideals in freemasonry and other civic associations.[118] He argued repeatedly that freemasonry and wider society worked to promote individual and social happiness. At the same time, he emphasized that each of these social formations (freemasonry and the associations of civil society) were deeply imbricated within print media. He believed that print media was not in ultimate conflict with the cultural, oral, also ritual inheritance and learning, of the ancients, especially Rome, and the Classical Greek city-state. Yet, he remained constrained as a philosopher of pedagogy in his acceptance of Locke's epistemology.[119]

---

116 Fitzpatrick, 35.

117 Idealism is the sign of imagination necessarily anchored in the individual and social ordering of embodied, emplaced experience and perception. Imagination while ordering in the moment is concerned with things not present.

118 Kent Logan Walgren. Freemasonry, Anti-Masonry and Illuminism in the United States, 1734-1850: A Bibliography. Steven Bullock, "Preface: Publishing Masonry," lxi-lxxxi, Vol. 1. 2003.

119 Regarding the significant influence of Locke on early American civic speculation and civil society, see Jerome P Huyler. *Locke in America: The Moral Philosophy of the Found-*

Both ancient and modern learning (for example, Plato, Newton, Locke, and Guttenberg) were to be valorized and utilized in the new republic and freemasonry thought Clinton. Nevertheless, Clinton believed that individual liberty was the American ideal and its corollary, the natural equality of humankind. This was assumed a truth hidden from the ancients. Clinton, at age 24, orated that freemasonry had its inception in ancient times. Unlike many, he made efforts to discriminate between the fanciful and the actual possible historical origins of freemasonry, where the fraternity developed with "the arts and sciences" ... "Among ingenious men" and became the means of safe-guarding knowledge in the arts and sciences.[120] This was done in the face of oppressive forms of government, and a church whose leaders had cloistered and inhibited scholarly study of arts and sciences. Education had been seen as only for the privileged few, but now change was at hand in the modern valorization of the accumulation and transmission of information.

Clinton said:

> When the invention of printing had opened the means of instruction to all ranks of people, then the generous cultivators of Masonry communicated with cheerfulness to the world, those secrets of the arts and sciences, which had been transmitted and improved from the foundation of the institution, then our fraternity bent their principal attention to the cultivation of morality; and Masonry may now be defined, a moral institution, intended to promote individual and social happiness ... there are mysteries ... but certain it is that every Mason ought to enrich his mind with knowledge, and not only because it better qualifies him to discharge the duties of character, but because information and virtues are generally to be found in the same society.[121]

The printing and transmission of information occurred across increasing distances of physical space in a decreasing length of time and remained

---

ing Era (Lawrence: University Press of Kansas, 1995).

120 Clinton, 4.

121 Loc cit.

important in the need for accurate information and shared often-vicarious drama in local community life.[122] Ritual performance, elocution, and printing for Clinton as a freemason were parts of the significant life, the good life. Elocution was a significant dimension in Clinton's portfolio of skills: he had been made aware the importance of speaking at Columbia College. He acquired communication skills, as well, in ritual performance and oratory in freemasonry and in public settings and among other associations. He understood the power of the printed text in transmission and the ideal of equal opportunity in the education of a citizenry. He saw print a preserver of both ancient and modern knowledge and perhaps a harbinger of things to come.

G. HEZEKIAH NILES AND THE GENERATION
AFTER THE REVOLUTIONARY WAR

Hezekiah Niles (1777-1839) represents the first generation of American printer-journalists, freemasons, patriots, and publishers born during or just after the Revolutionary War. His death in 1839 and the resultant collapse of the remarkable national and international paper he established as a first high-water mark in the geographic reach of the printer-journalist in America marks an organic closing year for this work.[123] With the accidental death of his father in Wilmington, the young Niles was apprenticed to Benjamin Johnson, a printer, binder, and bookseller in Philadelphia. In the supportive atmosphere (felt quality of the workplace and home) provided by Johnson and within the spirit of the reading revolution underway across early America, Niles was given free access to all of the books in the shop. Norval Neil Luxon described this period in Philadelphia for Niles as working to combine an emerging interest in politics in Niles with a growing commitment to journalism and publishing as a way to express his values and perspectives.[124] Moving into young adulthood, Niles was in search of his public voice, self and identity as an informed citizen and

---

122 As an illustration, revolutionary action is built of dramatic passion but requires precision.

123 Figure 1 depicts the network of cities at the heart of worlds of print later in the antebellum period but this map is consanguine with the trajectory of things as they were developing in 1839.

124 Norval Neil Luxon, *Nile's Weekly Register: News Magazine of the Nineteenth Century* (Baton Rouge: Louisiana State University, 1941), 28.

in the process of finding it moved him and family to a bustling and print intensive Baltimore.[125]

Worlds of print were in transition themselves. After the war, the newspapers relied heavily upon the skills of the printer to keep things above water with many if not most faltering after a period of struggle. With roughly 200 or so newspapers in 1800, only a small number went back to the days of the war, with no paper in the south older than a few decades. Urban density could be important as well the skills of the bold entrepreneur working hard to put out a newspaper as extra income to a job-printing and publishing effort. The advertisements of business were seen alongside paragraphs, postures, and coverage of partisan politics, and a mighty effort at neutral, objective reporting on many issues including anti-masonry.

Niles became an enthusiastic freemason during the War of 1812. He had launched the *Register* in 1811 in the immediate build up to the war after prior failure in Philadelphia and with a short lived earlier failure in Baltimore. The *Register* became the nation's first national newspaper, with each issue at 16 pages and ready on a weekly basis on Saturday. In its pages with its geographically disparate readers, a nation was imagined just as articulated by Anderson in the late 20th century. Niles was a rationalist opposing

---

125 The election of 1832 was unique in that it was the first time parties would convene a national nominating convention for the presidency and implement the building of national "party platforms." Simultaneously, there was the introduction of the first third party in American history, the Anti-Masons. Niles political coverage attempted to be even handed even when speaking on Anti-Masonry in the United States and abroad.. Niles in this effort at neutrality is indicative of the general trend of the other patriot printer-journalists who were freemasons and discussed in this work. Andrew Jackson, a freemason, headed the "democratic" ticket. The Anti-Mason party was led by a former freemason, as well Jackson's main opponent. Freemasonry represents here the growth overall of fraternities and other civic associations in America as the white male electorate. And it can be suggested the new national nominating convention's first appearance indicates the lives of civic associations such as freemasonry were geographically stretching out across the country near and far. The civic associations, and the first real national newspaper—*Nile's Register*—were helping make possible the presence of shared national conversations both hostile and harmonic (Anderson's imagined community) but in the end bespeaking one continuous civil society before and after a presidential election and the exercise of the vote in a national democracy. The great exception came soon in the American Civil War. Newspapers and other reading materials in all cases were a vital part of deliberative democracy in early America among diverse and overlapping civic associations.

superstition in religion and public life. He died in 1839, with the paper continuing until 1849 as a shadow of its former self.[126] The paper lacked advertisements, giving more space for news coverage with numerous primary sources and government documents filling its densely packed columns. America was imagined as the grandest experiment. The paper went out to between 700 and 800 post offices, with more subscribing and the content often reprinted because of its perceived value and sobriety. "Voluminous articles from the London and New York press, including documents, proclamations, treaties, decrees, speeches, and diplomatic correspondences were deftly summarized by the editor."[127]

Niles represents the secular stream in freemasonry as well its celebration of American manhood among a new generation. He was a strong advocate of the War of 1812, in part believing the war could demonstrate the masculinity of his generation, idealizing those men who had gone before in revolution. There was a masculine territoriality in American freemasonry emerging at the state, local, regional and national level, just as there was a territoriality in the *Register* with print the vehicle of conscious nation building and world watching.

The *Register* was the first national weekly newsmagazine, and sustained the largest American circulation for its time perhaps with 1,500, or more, annual subscriptions. Its voice was situated in civil society and ruminated over the economic sphere, history, geography, science, and the tasks of building the nation-state, including reporting in full the rulings of the

---

126 The steam-powered rotary printing press [replacing the flat-bed press], invented in 1843 in the United States by Richard M. Hoe, ultimately permitted production of tens of thousands and then more of copies of a paper page in a single day. Output in the mass production of printed works exploded after the transition to rolled paper and steam power. The presses operated with a continuous feed of paper. In addition, at mid-century, the distinct development of jobbing presses was at hand. These smaller machines churned out new small-format vehicles of print such as billheads, letterheads, business cards, and envelopes. The dynamics of the industry and consumer were in fast revolution in the transmission of information across space and transactional human interest and imagination between home and movement. And the aesthetic form and content of newspapers were changing. The work stops research of worlds of print in early America from 1734 to 1839 with the passing of Hezekiah Niles and the death of his newspaper shortly after.

127 Roy Goodman, "Hezekiah Niles, His Weekly Register, and the Atlantic Revolutionary World," in *Profiles of the Revolutionaries in Atlantic History, 1700-1850*, eds. R. William Weisberger, Dennis P. Hupchick, and David L. Anderson (Boulder: Columbia University Press, 2007), 180.

Supreme Court. The court system in the American experience for its part came to be an institution of civil society and procedural governance.

The American population doubled between 1800 and 1820, with the *Register* founded at the mid-point of growth for the fast-growing Baltimore of 1811 on the eve of the War of 1812. During this period, the number of miles of post roads in the emerging nation increased 21-fold from 1,875 to 44,000, with post-offices increasing 30-fold from 75 to 2,300. The same public goals in the civil sphere and government that funded growing national infrastructure promoted literacy and education. Citizens needed to be informed. Commerce conducted over long distances required proficient readers and calculators. Reading was thought essential in education, the health of the community and principles of nation building.[128]

With clockwork regularity, Niles wrote large parts of the *Register* sitting in a comfortable, large chair, transmitted through a generation from the days of the revolution. Niles illustrates the idea of an imagined nation fashioned in the private reading and public writing and diffusion of newspapers to near and distant geographies delineated by Benedict Anderson and discussed in Chapter 2. He called these regular moments in his life "fire-side-chats" as pointed out by Luxon.[129] This was more than a century before the fire-side-chats of Franklin Delano Roosevelt in his communications with the American people in the crisis of the Great Depression and using the medium of radio.

Fireside chats in Nile's comfortable front-room in his home and his contextual worlds of print, or Roosevelt later at the White House with his radio microphone broadcasting to American living rooms wide and far, catches as a phrase or imagery the fusion of ritual and transmission, home and movement, dimensions of communication grounded in the current research project. Niles died in 1839, which is to some degree the arbitrary terminating year of the period examined. As stipulated in the opening of this section, he represents the first generation of Americans born after the War of Independence and he is important as the editor, journalist, and printer of what can arguably be called the union's first national newspaper—the New York Times of its day—and Anderson's imagined commu-

---

128 Joyce Appleby, *Inheriting the Revolution: The First Generation of Americans* (Cambridge: Belknap Press, 2000), 92.

129 Luxon, 17.

nity in the embodied human, imaginative interest in the overlap between home and movement.

H. SUMMARY AND CONCLUSIONS

The early American reception of freemasonry occurred in two distinct swaths of time: first, during the colonial period beginning in 1734 in the main with Franklin reproducing the *Book of Constitutions of the Free-Masons* while building printing capacity and transportation and communication infrastructure; and second, in a period with much greater levels of expansion, including in worlds of print, during and following the American War of Independence. Franklin also understood the vibrancy of art and aesthetics as a necessary complement to the tasks of prose in print medium. There was some expansion of freemasonry going into the war in specific cities and military encampments led by members of military lodges. In the last quarter of the 18th century, there was increasing involvement of freemasons in worlds of print accelerated by the War of Independence, as shall be seen in Chapter 4, no less Niles in the current chapter on the heels of the War of 1812. Print culture also expanded rapidly across civil society and public sphere in peacetime. Worlds of print were fashioned simultaneously through the transmission of information and ritual solidarity.

Illustrative freemasons involved in the diffusion of information in civil society and the public sphere using the printed word were Franklin, Bentley, Thomas, Clinton, and Niles. In the occupation of postmaster, Franklin understood clearly the need to build a rapidly expanding transportation and information transmission network in a dawning American experience of apposite communication, learning, and association in a young republic. Bentley saw how culture and religion in his time and place were transmitted through worlds of print across greater and greater distances. Clinton thought both ancient and modern learning (for example, Plato, Newton, Locke, and Guttenberg) were to be valorized and utilized in the new republic and freemasonry, yet the ideal of American equality was a truth hidden from the ancients. The printing and transmission of information across increasing distances of physical space in a decreasing length of time was important in the need for accurate information and shared often-vicarious drama in local community life. Ritual performance, elocution, and printing for Clinton as a freemason were essential parts of the good life.

An attempt to theorize ritual and transmission semiotics of communication in human experience in the early American landscape was offered by DeWitt Clinton, who was heavily influenced by the philosophy of Locke. The theory was inadequate to the task in postulating a dualism where both ritual and print as external devices influenced the inner man and mental associations made in a detached, observing mind. Lockean thought did not grasp the reality of a singular rotating process of sensorimotor experience in apposite human communication, learning, and association in an environment, although Locke labored to find the significance of communication and to anchor this physically. As can be seen in retrospect, doing and undergoing of the individual and group in the American founding moments integrated embodied ritual and transmission as continuous looping and habit correction in an environment.

In the generation of patriot printer-journalists who were freemasons after the war, with Niles considered representative of his cohort, there was a growing interest in politics and the individual's public voice combined with a commitment to journalism. There was an ongoing effort by at least a few to build a philosophy and professional standards for an occupation, namely journalism. Niles built from within and without what Anderson would call in the late 20th century the imagined community of a nation. Niles, at the same time, was concerned with the idealized actions of patriots, and freemasons, overseas in a struggle for human emancipation. He could also cover presidential politics such as that with President Jackson, the freemason, running at the time of the anti-Masonic scare because of the Morgan affair. Niles represented the phenomenon of secularity and attempted objective strain, as did others examined in the chapter, in early American freemasonry and worlds of print.

CHAPTER 4

John Dunlap and Early American Worlds of Print

An examination of the printer's occupation and print vehicles produced by the patriot John Dunlap in Philadelphia on Market Street near Independence Hall, including his newspaper the *Pennsylvania Packet,* opens a view on to Dunlap's quality of life, habitus, agency, and symbolic worlds of communication. Print integrated all aspects of daily life for the individual and group. Logically, the stability of acquired habits of the printer-journalist was fundamental to the new levels of skill and overall performativity in worlds of print. The habit and means of the printed text, technique, in the problems and needs of war, and then war's aftermath, were fused with the imagined goals of an informed and virtuous local community and citizenry in networks and nation building. The illustrative texts published by the patriot printer-journalist Dunlap open a view on to the reading, elocutionary, political, spatial, and military revolutions underway.

In this chapter I examine three patriotic publications by Dunlap, namely (a) the printed funeral oration of the soldier, leading freemason, and General, Joseph Warren slain at Bunker's Hill, (b) the ritual performance and transmission of original broadsides of the 1776 American *Declaration of Independence,* and (c) the newspaper edition covering the first known public performance as a freemason of General George Washington. Dunlap's re-printing of the funeral oration of General Warren was to mobilize fellow citizens for war, to sell to consuming publics, as well advance the reputation of freemasonry and the patriotic cause. His printing of the Declaration was by order of the Congress but also with the intent to mobilize a public for war across the rebelling colonies. It was a vital part of the formation of a public. Washington's use of the press, and that of Dunlap, was as a strategic and tactical tool in war, with freemasons heavily intermeshed in the printing network to an extent not yet quantified or examined in the literature. The use of the press was also intended to advance the reputation of freemasonry. Each of the publications together help illustrate how the freemasons using worlds of print and different logics of communication such as ritual performance, oratory, and transmission achieved a greater influence in the rebelling colonies than their small numbers as a civic association indicated. Freemasonry was a cohering influence and emotion in the civil sphere and new public formation before the rise of political parties in America. It was first in temporal order and eventual impact in the fray and social ordering of civic associations, while it overlapped with other more radical civic associations going into war such as the Mechanics Society in Boston and the Sons of Liberty in more than one place and network.

John Dunlap, the future printer-journalist and patriot, was born in 1747 in Tyrone County, Ireland and died in Philadelphia, Pennsylvania on November 2, 1812. He arrived in America in 1757 from Ireland, already apprenticed to learn the printing trade from his uncle William Dunlap. Dunlap managed to raise himself, and his family, to a comfortable living.[130] He became wealthy as publisher of the *Pennsylvania Packet, or General Advertiser,* and official printer to the Continental Congress.[131] As a Philadelphia landlord and through land-speculation in Philadelphia and Kentucky he added to his wealth.[132] He was capable of contributing financially to the beleaguered Continental Army during the war and giving liberally to charities after the war, and did both. He was a sober revolutionary who after the war expressed federalist and later Jeffersonian democratic republican sentiments. It was through his occupation as a job printer, (patriot) printer-journalist, and publisher, that he influenced the American mili-

---

130 Economics is bracketed in this work. For an economic analysis of early American worlds of print, see Rosalind Remer, *Printers and Men of Capital: Philadelphia Book Publishers in the New Republic,* Early American Studies (Philadelphia: University of Pennsylvania Press, 1996).

131 *The Pennsylvania Packet, or the General Advertiser* was founded in 1771 and went on to become a successful paper amid many others that failed. The paper was founded by Dunlap in Philadelphia as a weekly paper in late 1771 later changing its name to the *Pennsylvania Packet and Daily Advertiser,* reflecting the paper's move to daily publication. The paper subsequently underwent additional name changes, dropping the *Pennsylvania Packet* prefix in 1791, and becoming *Dunlap's American Daily Advertiser* [1791-93] with additional changes. On September 21, 1796, of significance, it was the first to publish George Washington's Farewell Address and can be argued as the origins of the *Philadelphia Inquirer.*

132 Kerby A. Miller, Arnold Schrier, Bruce D. Boling, and David N. Doyle, eds., *Irish Immigrants in theLand of Canaan: Letters and Memoirs from Colonial and Revolutionary America, 1775-1815* (Oxford: Oxford University Press, 2003), 87. Kentucky and Tennessee emerged along the Ohio River as particularly attractive sites for land speculation in the early American period.

tary effort and civil society. Dunlap, upon reaching maturity, was initiated into freemasonry at Lodge No. 2, an ancient lodge in Philadelphia.

Dunlap's involvement in the lodge was indicative of a wider transition. The original, modern lodges in Pennsylvania were relatively elite and selective comprised of professionals, such as Franklin the businessman, a number of doctors and lawyers, albeit with a majority membership of upwardly mobile artisans and retailers. The newer ancient lodges were equally selective, yet developing a reputation for egalitarianism in their membership very open to artisans, such as Dunlap, the middle and lower classes and all ranks of the military. These included Irish and Scottish soldiers in Boston and Philadelphia in the British Army, who were sometimes initiated into ancient freemasonry or working with charters from Scotland. Soldiers and military lodges could be found in modern freemasonry as well.

Since their beginning in Pennsylvania in 1734, the modern lodges of that province never constituted more than four lodges in one period before the revolution. In contrast, the budding Ancient Grand Lodge of England, founded in considerable part by Dermott, issued printed lodge warrants with zeal such that from 1758 to 1778, the Ancient Grand Lodge had 31 subordinate lodges in the union in multiple states.[133] A partial list of members of Lodge No. 2 in 1775-1780 shows a strong roster of soldiers with 16 colonels, 10 majors, and 28 captains.[134] Though not universal, a resonance likely was present between the ancient's Scottish and Irish soldiers allied emotionally with colonial ancient freemasons who were espousing the cause of independence with the moderns perhaps more inclined to be loyalist. The freemasons of Scotland and Ireland had seen what could be the harsh treatment of their communities by the English on many occasions. Ere long after the war the moderns disappeared in Pennsylvania. There was often a colonial admiration of ancient civilization ideals, such as that of the Roman Republic, with figures such as Washington fashioned in Roman glory and other resonant iconography. This helped buttress the attraction to a perceived ancient freemasonry by the revolutionary generation now involved in considerable bloodletting in the War of Independence.

---

133 Wayne Huss, *The Master Builders: A History of the Grand Lodge of Free and Accepted Masons of Pennsylvania*, Volume 1 (Philadelphia: The Grand Lodge, 1986), 37.

134 Julius Sachse and Norris F. Barratt, *Freemasonry in Pennsylvania, 1727-1907*, Volume 1 (Lancaster: New Era Printing Company, 1908). xiii.

A. PRINTING NETWORKS

Dunlap and his father were assisted in establishing themselves as printers and publishers on American soil by no less a figure than Franklin, a major architect in what became horizontally and vertically integrated printing, publishing, and bookselling industries.[135] Franklin's bold intention, both before the war and in a second attempt afterward, was to establish networks of printers across expanding American landscapes as a means of economic self-betterment for all concerned, including himself as a supplier of material at the apex of a pyramid. He was also concerned in the promulgation of his transmission networks with the ideal of spreading knowledge and the art of virtue in the colonies and nation.[136] While the precise figure may never be known, some number, small or large, in these printing networks established by Franklin were freemasons.

A veritable reading revolution, an explosion in literacy, was underway and indeed reading had become a necessity of life, practiced pleasure, and often an aesthetic experience.[137] This was more or less true across most layers of society. In Dunlap's specific situation, his printing reveals, among other things, strong business sense, patriotism, and modern sensibilities of the worth of "publicity"—media events. He had a moral imagination of an informed citizenry in the young republic; an ideal that became one part of the drive of what can be termed the printing trade's "vocational ideology" in the early republic.[138] The printing profession grew rapidly, often involving vertically and horizontally networks of suppliers of material for the manufacture of paper, buyers, book salesmen, lecturers, and government or volunteer postal workers in small towns or even smaller communities, but also emerging larger cities such as New York, Boston and in the current chapter Philadelphia. Dunlap had keen economic interests as earlier stipulated.

---

135 Ralph Frasca, *Benjjamin Franklin Printing Networks: Disseminating Virtue in Early America.* (Columbia: Columbia Missouri Press, 2006), 175, 177-185.

136 Frasca, 179.

137 William Gilmore writes comprehensively on the increasing importance of reading; see Gilmore, *Reading Becomes a Necessity of Life: Material and Cultural Life in Rural New England, 1780-1835* (Knoxville: University of Tennessee Press, 1989), 18.

138 Vocational ideology is understood in this instance as the general system of values and beliefs held and advocated by someone in an occupation (such as printing). See Vernon K. Dibble, "Occupations and Ideologies," *American Journal of Sociology* 63 (1962): 22.

B. DUNLAP'S BREADTH OF WORK

Immediately after becoming a master mason, Dunlap became secretary of his lodge.[139] He was called upon in ensuing years to print summons' for the meetings of the lodge, make announcements about meetings in his newspaper targeting local but also travelling freemasons, and report on events supported by the lodge, including events to raise funds for the poor. His occupation may in part explain the growing prominence of his ancient lodge.

An indication of Dunlap's range as a printer-publisher-editor, before the war, in 1773, was his printing of an early and important antislavery pamphlet by prominent reformer and friend Benjamin Rush, *An Address to the Inhabitants of the British Settlements in America upon Slave-Keeping.*[140] In addition there was an important tract by a woman proto-feminist.[141] Patricia Bradley engaged the question of the extent to which the full range of patriot printer-journalists as a group in this period held their level of commitment to engage public discourse robustly concerning the freedom of African American community because of her perception of ambiguity in the print record through time.[142] The term patriot-printer journalist here entails mason and non-mason.

The *Declaration* was an important text produced by Dunlap as printer to the Congress. Dunlap's few hundred original broadsides were often the instrumental means facilitating reprinting of the Declaration in a number of local newspapers, an instrumental aesthetics with one consummation inviting or potentially building toward another. His editions covering many issues were mined and newspaper copies in Philadelphia and across the fledgling republic were sometimes affixed to walls in homes and public sites as at a local store. Two original copies of the Declaration by Dunlap rapidly found their way by military route to London where they survive. These latter transmissions involved the deep reach and need of military intelligence by the British. As shall be seen, the *Declaration* as an

---

139 Sachse and Barrat, xiii.

140 Benjamin Rush, *An Address to the Inhabitants of the British Settlements in America, Upon Slave-keeping* (Philadelphia, 1773).

141 Anonymous, *The Sentiments of an American Woman*, broadside (Philadelphia: John Dunlap, 1780).

142 Patricia Bradley, *Slavery, Propaganda and the American Revolution* (Jackson: University of Mississippi Press, 1988), 77.

art object, transmission of information and profound performance, held the attention of both military and civic audiences and actors with similar but often different habit correction in martial or civil worlds. The civic and military spheres were related but different aesthetic fields regarding the printing, dissemination and performance of the Declaration before different audience participants.

C. THE ANCIENTS AND THE MODERNS

American freemasonry before the war was a smaller institution with outcomes and reputation unclear. A premier ancient Lodge No. 2 in Pennsylvania fell into disarray with the occupation by British Regiments of Philadelphia in 1777 and 1778. As the British approached Philadelphia, Dunlap evacuated his newspaper west to Lancaster. Thomas, examined earlier in Chapter 3, also had evacuated his paper to the west out of Boston to Worcester, with the able-bodied physical assistance of the ancient freemason Joseph Warren, and other significant future, and likely then, freemasons. In the process, he continued to publish dramatic news and accurate (ritual and transmission) accounts on the progress of the war. During the occupation of Philadelphia, British soldiers under General Howe looted Dunlap's Lodge No. 2 "as a spy's nest" while protecting the modern freemasons of Philadelphia.[143] These were actions with implications. The actions of the British very likely were noticed and remembered by the public and furthered the reputation of ancient freemasonry in the social imaginary at first in the approach to war. It was in Lancaster that Dunlap published articles and pamphlets by Thomas Paine. Paine was himself in Lancaster in a tactical retreat from Philadelphia.

It is known that Dunlap became a skilled soldier in the elite 1st Troop of Philadelphia Cavalry constituting Washington's bodyguard at Princeton and Trenton in 1779. During war, in 1780, while publishing the *Packet*, he contributed £4,000 of his own money to supply provisions to the revolutionary army. After the war, as Captain, he commanded the 1st Troop in the deployment ordered by President Washington in the Whiskey Rebellion. There were American freemasons fighting on both sides in the Whiskey Rebellion.

The transition in revolutionary freemasonry, modern to ancient in America, has in large part gone unnoticed by American historians, yet

---

143 Huss, 39.

the transformation is relevant in discerning the social profile of freemasonry, and wider civil society, in the urban seaports of the early American republic and the fraternity's considerable popularity in the American social imaginary. This occurred in some part because of the patriotic resolve of the few ancients before and during the war, and reporting on freemasonry in this regard in the public press and word of mouth. Transactions between ancient and modern freemasons and wider 18th century European and American intellectual currents are complex. It is not yet understood whether ancient and modern debates in American freemasonry were related to wider movements in civil society of the old and new, for example in education, politics, or literature, and to what degree relative to regions in Europe.

Ancient and modern tensions may have first appeared in Europe in literature and philosophy with the migration of the conflict to religion and politics. To illustrate the pervasiveness of the tension of the ideas this time in American poetry, Edgar Allen Poe, writing for as wide an audience as possible, engaged the clash of the ancients and moderns in freemasonry in his *Cask of Amontillado*.[144] His dramatic development of the confrontations of the two with each other is an illustration of the wide public awareness of the two types of freemasonry in early America. It was a known topic, or Poe would not be reaching out to a hoped for reading audience which held an interest in the subject matter. The drama in *the Cask of Amontillado* was the moderns seeking revenge in a macabre fashion against the ancients for their superstitious destruction of the modern tradition of freemasonry.[145]

The political struggle of ancient and moderns within the institutional framework of freemasonry, it need be said, on one level opened on American soil the pre-existent conflict in the United Kingdom. Beginning in London, the ancients in freemasonry indicted the moderns about the latter's presumed reorganization of the ritual in the 1730s and at other times. As Steven Bullock notes, however, change and the problematic tensions

---

144 Edgar Allen Poe, "A Cask of Amontillado," *Godey's Ladies Journal* 33, no 5 (New York, 1846): 216-218.

145 For a discussion of the deep and wide sociocultural context of freemasonry in early America in Poe's *Cask of Amontillado,* including the warfare between the ancients and moderns, see Robert Con Davis-Unidiano, "Poe and the American Affiliation with Freemasonry," *symploke* 7, no 1-2 (1999): 119-138.

of ancient and modern worldviews as a discourse in freemasonry was often merely the outward manifestation of the division. Social, class, and ethnic difference, and deeply channeled habits of feeling and the body-mind, provided the context and underlying passion to the debate about the "true" masonic ritual in both England and America according to Bullock. The Scottish and Irish were not the English. The diverse populations knew how deeply the English had suppressed rebellion in Ireland and Scotland, and therein how much was at stake in the battles to come. However, further research needs to be developed articulating the relationship between worldviews of ancient and modern in emerging civil society and in the specificity of freemasonry as a civic association among others in the new United States.

The American conflicts between ancient and modern masons began in Boston and Philadelphia which were two major urban starting points of the War of Independence, then moved outward in geographic diffusion. New Jersey emerged as the place in which the war was most frequently fought in actual battle on contested landscapes. Among the reasons for New Jersey to emerge as the major battlefield of the war, was that Washington early on realized the British were making strong efforts to capture the loyalties of the populations of New Jersey and there needed to be a counteraction. Both sides began to sense Jersey's central location in the colonies.

Philadelphia culture and newspapers influenced New Jersey, as did newspapers from New York City. Yet, there was a struggle to develop newspapers in New Jersey for ritual and transmission functions of communication on both sides of the war. Washington finally decided to let a printer turned artilleryman named Shepherd Kollock resign and to start publishing his own newspaper, which fast became "a fiery spokesman for the American cause."[146] Kollock might have been a freemason in New Jersey, perhaps in Monmouth County. After the war in close by New York, he published *The constitutions of the Ancient and Honourable Fraternity of Free and Accepted Masons, in the State of New-York.*[147]

---

146 George T. Flemming, "Crossroads of the American Revolution," in *New Jersey and the American Revolution*, ed. B. J. Minick (New Brunswick and London: Rutgers University Press, 2005), 12.

147 Grand Lodge of Freemasons in New York, *The Constitutions of the Ancient and Honorable Fraternity of Free and Accepted Masons in the State of New-York* (New York: Shepherd Kollock, 1805).

The divisions eventually healed between the ancients and moderns in America in the 1790s in different states, and the two sides of freemasonry began to merge in different admixture in different states. Nevertheless, by initially opening freemasonry to different social strata and groups outside elite circles and by maintaining the modern identification of the fraternity with polite cosmopolitan culture, ancient freemasons as alluded to by Bullock formed a civil association of considerable appeal. In addition, there was the patriotism that increasingly became attached in the social imaginary to the ancient freemasons during the war. As one example, the number 13 (referencing the original colonies in rebellion) was more than once associated with ancient freemasonry in the early American social imaginary in and across regions.

D. THE ORATION IN DUNLAP'S PORTFOLIO AND THE PERCEIVED MARTYR JOSEPH WARREN

Joseph Warren (1741–1775) was a leader in agitation against Great Britain from the time of the 1765 Stamp Act. As conflict developed between elements in Boston and the British government, matters were reaching a crescendo between 1773 and 1775. Warren was born locally, educated at Harvard as a doctor, and appointed to the Suffolk Committee of Correspondence. These committees were organized by local and provincial governments across the original 13 colonies for the express purpose of coordinating the transmission of information to others. They increasingly held the capacity to rally forces on common cause in the formation of a public, to help develop a public interest. The small civic groups became the operational core out of which grew the national political union of the United States and at a lesser institutional scale and for an important moment the birthing of the military intelligence transmission network.

Warren, upon receiving information through his cultivated and growing intelligence networks, sent William Dawes and Revere from the North End of Boston riding inland to warn fellow patriots of British movements. The opening communication networks contained intelligence transmission as well special operations. Warren took part as a leader in the follow-on battles of Lexington and Concord, and commanded militia as they harassed British troops returning to Boston from the inland battles. He became president of the Provincial Congress of Massachusetts, perhaps played the central role in organizing the Massachusetts militia, the local major Committee of Correspondence, and intelligence transmissions. He was commissioned as a major general although he served in the rank-and-file as his papers had yet arrived to his safe keeping.

Warren became a mason before the war in September 1761 in St. Andrews lodge, with a patent from the Grand Lodge of Scotland. Warren was elected worshipful master of St. Andrew's lodge on November 30, 1768. Together with three traveling lodges associated with British Army regiments stationed in Boston, he petitioned George, Earl of Dalhousie, Grand Master of Scotland, for the formation of a Provincial Grand Lodge. Warren was commissioned Grand Master of a provincial grand lodge on May 30, 1769, with a proposed operating territorial radius of 100 miles to be centered in Boston. When the Earl of Dumfries succeeded Dalhousie as Grand Master of Scotland, he issued another appointment to Warren, dated March 7, 1772, constituting Warren "Grand Master of Masons for the Continent of America," holding perhaps a side-message to the English that freemasonry existed in Scotland before it existed in England.[148] It may have been a simple outright challenge or done in simple innocence.

Orations, precipitated as pamphlets, or referenced in newspapers, were a vital part of the print output of civic and religious associations, including the civil society of freemasonry, in the colonial, revolutionary, and republican periods. Their content and style changed over time, including movement in a secular direction—for example from pastor to lawyer as author, agent and orator. Rhetoric offered opportunities for newer expressive forms of self-hood, bold flair, and perceived authenticity, legitimacy and consent in the public sphere. Paradoxically, concomitant with self-presentation, the valuing of self-effacement as public virtue became an ideal of the ethos of rhetorical becoming and performance. Rhetoric in word and print, including prose, was important in making claims of moral rightness, authenticity, personal sincerity, and aesthetic value in deliberation. Yet argumentation in deliberation—or deliberative democracy—can involve more than truth or validity claims in the public sphere in consensus building, or a charm offensive to the audience, adherence

---

148 Each of the two commissions perhaps fulfilled a growing desire (perhaps at first small) by Warren to have constitutional authority in freemasonry outside of any derived from freemasonry in the London metropolis and King George's royalty. For more details on Warren, see G. D. Pushee, "Joseph Warren, Martyr of Bunker Hill" (lecture, C. B. Vance Council # 85, Allied Masonic Degrees, Chesapeake, Virginia, 1994).

to rules, or utilitarian calculations. There could be an attempted problem solving, for example, through imaginative dramatic rehearsal of options and experimentation in give and take, inclusive of worlds of print.

The pamphlet, as a category of print vehicle, could illustrate the mutual interdependence of the spoken and printed word, and is an illustration of how orations reached wider local and trans-local reading populations and deliberations in transmission. The circulation of pamphlets, and the feelings, emotions, and desires that the contents stirred then imagined possibilities that came to life became part of American history, fact, and lore. Ritual intertwined with transmission in poetry and prose in the full range of early American democratic deliberation—including word and text.

There was home and movement in the full articulation and consummations of the pamphlet and written word. For example, an instrumental aesthetic and communitarian expression of controlled and responsible rage occurred in the writing and transmission of the pages of the Suffolk Resolves, first drafted by Warren in Massachusetts at a most intense period.[149] The adopted Resolves were dispatched from Massachusetts to the First Continental Congress meeting in Philadelphia and likely had the effect of pushing Congress over the edge toward the deliberations that culminated in the 1776 Declaration and the break with the King and England. New York and Pennsylvania had been pushing for compromise with England but the boldness and timing of the Resolves from Suffolk County and Boston had changed the trajectory of the deliberations. There was a dramatic rehearsal of possibilities.

As war loomed, the pamphlet increasingly became the accepted medium of information transmission with powerful affect and effect. The greater numbers of pamphlets in the revolutionary period were produced in Massachusetts, Pennsylvania, and New York, followed by Connecticut

---

149 The Suffolk Resolves was a declaration on September 9, 1774 by the leadership of Suffolk County surrounding Boston whereby the Massachusetts Government Act was rejected and a resolution made that a boycott of imported goods from Britain be made unless the Intolerable Acts were rescinded. It is often thought the Resolves led to the 1776 Declaration of Independence. Joseph Warren had written the first draft and was a major presence. The First Continental Congress with Peyton Randolph, Grand Master of Freemasons in the Grand Lodge of Virginia in 1774 presiding as the first President of the Congress, endorsed the Resolves on September 17, 1774. Word would travel relatively fast via post riders along already existing postal routes and roads used by Committees of Correspondence formed in each colony to deal with

and Rhode Island. These five colonies accounted for 91% of the total print output in all the years before the war for all of the colonies, with 65% of the total produced in these five colonies in the pre-war period occurring in the three and a half years preceding the Declaration of Independence. "Well over half of the political pamphlets on the question of independence appeared in the two and a half years preceding the Declaration."[150] The Declaration was situated in time and space, and a medium, as an ontological, embodied rhetoric of becoming, an ethos of rhetoric, and printed word.

The leading printers of pamphlets were in Boston, Philadelphia, and New York. At the level of the individual establishment, the Boston firm of Benjamin Edes and John Gill was the leading printing shop in America at the time; "both in number of items printed and probably influence as well." In addition, it can be noted ... "John Dunlap of Philadelphia along with Edes and Gill, were responsible for nearly 10% of the total print output of these years."[151] Philadelphia and Boston emerged as the key centers of civil unrest in the launch to war, and there was a parallel development of print culture albeit with severe limitations of necessary materials

An illustrative printing of an oration with masonic content occurred early in the opening of the war. The pamphlet concerned the re-internment of the remains of the fallen war hero, General Warren, a fellow Ancient freemason with Dunlap, who died at the battle of Bunker Hill.[152] The original oration, printed in Boston by a freemason, then reprinted by Dunlap, and an additional printer-journalist, and member of the Sons of Liberty, in New York, stated the fallen Warren had been Grand Master of freemasons in Massachusetts and that the sermon in death and mourning was delivered by a fellow master mason.[153]

---

the rising tensions through effective communication.

150 Thomas Tanselle, "Statistics on American Printing, 1764-1783," in *The Press and the American Revolution*, 363.

151 Loc. cit.

152 Perez Morton, *An Oration, Delivered at King's Chapel in Boston, April 8, 1776, on the Re-Internment of the Remains of the Late Most Worshipful Grand-Master Warren, Esquire, President of the Late Congress of this Colony, and Major-General of the Massachusetts Forces; Who Was Slain in the Battle of Bunker's Hill* (Philadelphia: John Dunlap, 1775).

153 The oration initially appeared as a pamphlet in Boston and was sold by J. Gill in Queen-Street with a second edition by Gill that year. In addition, there was a reprint

Before his death at Bunker Hill, Warren was influential in speaking at two annual commemorations that evolved out of the Boston Massacre. These events were known to the British. He would have been observed in action by watching military eyes as an important rhetorician, leader, and instigator.

Figure 4. Paul Revere, "The Bloody Massacre in King-Street, March 5, 1770." Boston, 1770. (Courtesy of American Antiquarian Society).

Warren, in his orations at the annual ceremonies on the Boston Commons, evoked the spirit of blood spilled on American, now perceived, sacred soil. The Boston Massacre, as depicted in Figure 4, was the killing of a handful of colonists by British regulars on March 5, 1770. It was an instrumental and consummating moment out from a period of tension then bloodletting in the American colonies. Tensions were mounting since Royal troops first appeared in Massachusetts in the later 1760s to enforce the heavy tax burden (and its negative externalities) imposed by the Townsend Acts and communicated through signs, for example, the

by the radical, and networked, member of the Sons of Liberty, John Holt in New York. Dunlap's imprint in Philadelphia was third.

semiotic of the stamp and its object, money, itself a symbol referring to a measure of work. Each year, the architects and rhetoricians of a civic revolution (the formation of a singular "public interest" in difficult circumstances) performed on Boston commons invoking the spilled blood of citizen martyrs. The roaring vocal demand was the blood of the slain soaked into the earth be given a voice, a lost speaking, now found. It was a powerful dramaturgy. The shared space of the Boston Commons held diverse populations that were often in conflict to some greater or lesser extent but shaped in solidarity in the ritual communication and place of the Commons. Proto democracy at the origins of the American republic was both inspirational and agonistic in conflicted, *shared* places and networks.

Figure 4 depicts a calculated piece of propaganda by Revere the patriot, artisan, member of the Sons of Liberty, the Mechanics (a spy association), and a freemason at St Andrew lodge, the ancient lodge brother of Warren.[154] Revere was also part of Warren's intelligence network and today to what is called special operations. The scene by Revere depicts expansive anger and desire for greater breathing space desired by the citizens. Then, there occurred the centripetal response the bloody Boston Massacre. Revere captures in an image an evolving situation. The illustration by Revere demonstrates the power of an image, and image-text, in social and dramaturgical formation of publics, in the development of a momentary, singular public interest.

---

154 Before the advent of the Revolutionary War, Paul Revere organized the Mechanics, a group of around 30 patriots with their roots in the Sons of Liberty. The Mechanics were an intelligence network following the actions of British forces in Boston. Besides Revere, it is not currently known how many of the Mechanics Society were freemasons or belonged to other civil and quasi-military organizations. Overlapping membership in different civil societies was a common experience in the north end of Boston in this period and meant the mixing of different ethnic, class perspectives, and contending human interests, in shared or overlapping public spaces. There was a contested space which precipitated the singular public interest for a moment in declaring the Suffolk Resolves in Boston and later the Declaration of independence in Philadelphia. When Tocqueville toured America in the 1820s he viewed July 4th celebrations of the Declarations in public space and parades where the initial listing of diverse grievances from 1776 was a part of the text in the ritual performance. He reported ripping waves of emotion moved the crowd as one by one the grievances were read. There came in that place and network of places a "singular" public interest, or the "formation of a public". Each time there was a display of public interest but with a difference. For a study of the importance of apposite human association, learning and conjoint communicative action in "public formation" and the fashioning of public interest, see Dewey, *The Public and Its Problems*.

Warren's subsequent services in the American military following the later major sparking points of Lexington and Concord were brief but extensive. After receiving military intelligence about British troop movements, he sent William Dawes and Revere on their famous "Midnight Ride" on April 18, 1775, as well at least one woman on horseback, to warn assembling militia inland at Lexington and Concord of British raids and then departed to the scene very soon after in the dead of night but with a bright moon. He participated in the battles of Lexington and Concord, and over the next few days coordinated and led militia into guerilla fighting against the lines of the British Army returning to Boston to regroup. Once in Boston, he played an important role in recruiting and organizing soldiers, setting plans, and implementing intelligence lines of transmission in through and out of what became the siege of Boston by the British. The Massachusetts Provincial Congress appointed him Major General on June 14, 1775. Warren was the original George Washington.

His commission had not taken effect three days later, when the Battle of Bunker Hill occurred and he chose to serve as a volunteer private, in self-effacement (his written commission had not yet arrived), against the wishes of commanding officers. Fighting on the front lines, rallying troops to the final assault by the British, he was killed by a musket ball fired into his head by a British officer who may have recognized him, perhaps from his prior orations on the Boston commons. He had chosen to fight as a foot soldier, and he was slain in the act. His remains were hastily buried by the British, with no dignity afforded. The body was exhumed later and his fraternal brother in freemasonry, Revere, identified him through artificial teeth he had placed in the jaw, along with identification by Warren's biological brother. He was then reburied, which resulted in the printed pamphlets of the funeral oration produced and circulated by Dunlap.

The Siege of Boston lasted 11 months, from 19 April 1775 to 17 March 1776, when American militia managed to contain British troops within Boston. The American, or Provincial armed forces, were initially called the New England Army gathered from militia who were forming since Bunker Hill. They became part of the Continental Army when it was established in June 1775. General Washington arrived on the scene on Boston's perimeter and took commander the death of Warren. This is perhaps the first place he saw the true depth of the undisciplined and unorganized militia.

Washington could imagine the future consequences of disjointed habits and resultant conduct of the fighting units. Yet, there was a strong awareness by Washington of possibilities in strategy and tactics demonstrated by the militias that had been very effective in ending the siege of Boston through victory as the British forces began to withdraw in order to fight another day. Effective war is driven by precision but also a dramatic rehearsal of possibilities and alternatives with life and death consequences.

E. The Ritual and Transmission Logics of the Declaration of Independence in the Formation of a Public

After the adoption of the Declaration of Independence by Congress on July 2nd, the draft was rapidly dispatched to the nearby printing shop of John Dunlap and over the next days some few hundred original copies were produced as broadsides (Appendix A). The exact number of the original production run is not known, but of the original number, 25, have survived and are known as "Dunlap broadsides." Dunlap's shop was responding to the order by the Continental Congress that the "declaration be authenticated and printed ... and that copies of the declaration ... be sent to the several assemblies, convention's committees, or councils of safety, and to the several commanding officers [so] that it is proclaimed in the United States."[155] The Declaration of Independence is a remarkable illustration of the transactional, embodied relationship of the ritual and transmission function, or logics, of communication in a medium and environment. At the same time there could be conflict and struggle for solidarity in local place and across networks in deliberative democracy.

Competing groups, identities and alliances of groups could be co-present in overlapping or shared public spaces or networks in the heated, rhythmic performance of the American Declaration of Independence before diversely assembled crowds, or the annual rhetorical invocation of the Boston Massacre. Much of this occurred within the active heterogeneity of audiences in the shared public space of Boston Commons.[156] In the

---

155 Jay Fliegelman, *Declaring Independence: Jefferson, Natural Language, and the Culture of Performance* (Stanford: Stanford University Press, 1993), 24.

156 For a discussion of conflicted, shared space as a condition of possibility in the formation of a public in a learning democracy, see Daniel London, *Building the Great Community: John Dewey and the Public Spaces of Social Democracy* (unpublished man-

parliamentary hall and debates of the United States Congress deliberative democracy including the development by Jefferson and committee of the Declaration involved reason's discourse, passionate rhetoric drawing on ideas of the Classical world, and a dramatic rehearsal of possibilities.[157] Embodied communication was animated in ritual and transmission functions of communication in local places and across networks. The clashes and valuing of the (proto) demos are evident from this period in the amalgam and protection of interests of the informed citizenry as detailed in the 1st Amendment of the Bill of Rights.

The 1st Amendment specifically delineates: (i) a *rule* for the ideal of freedom of religion which lays the groundwork in communicative action to "open" inherited ritual practice to freedom of moral choice and worship for the individual and group, (ii) the right to address grievances to the government, stated differently, a process for the individual and group to engage the "externalities," unintended consequences of others, or direct belligerence--problematic situations--at the moment outside the control of the individual and group, (iii) the valorization and guarantee of freedom of speech and (iv) closely related to open avenues of speech the freedom of assembly, (these latter two are united in one reading as the "ritual function" of communication), and (v) freedom of press, or freedom enhanced in the "transmission function" of communication. The rule making and subsequent communicative action made possible in the civil sphere by the 1st Amendment was anchored in the moral imagination of an informed citizenry in an environment and animated the ritual and transmission logics of communication of the printed word, perceived sacred words, spoken word, and gesture in place and across a network of places.[158] The civil sphere (embodied, emplace colloquy) opened in the articulation of the 1st Amendment was conducive to a democratic mode of human association and conjoint communicative action.

---

uscript, New York University, 2010).

157 Classical theoretical treatises on rhetoric enjoyed wide authority both in college curricula and in popular treatments of the art. Classical orators were imitated as models of republican virtue and oratorical style.

158 *The Constitution of the United States*, Amendment I states: "Congress shall make no law respecting an establishment of religion, or prohibiting the free exercise thereof; or abridging the freedom of speech, or of the press; or the right of the people peaceably to assemble, and to petition the government for a redress of grievances". Retrieved on May 10, 2014.

The major inaugural public event for the ritual performance of the Declaration was from an observatory built in 1760 at the state house to witness the sacred-secular transit of Venus. The observatory was constituted and constituting, as were all other relations and parts in the public square on the day of July 6th. There were diverse groups of people assembled, rhetoricians, holders of office, and patriot augurs of the sky. The Declaration as a concentrated *object d'art*, integrated the local populations in an aesthetic-moral field and wider humanity over the horizon as additional audience. The moral imagination of intended local and global audiences influenced the writing of the Declaration as did the influence of music and different oral traditions, for example, from parliamentarian traditions, evangelical flourishing, and others, cast in a crucible of cultures in early America. An augur was one of a group of ancient Roman officials charged with observing and interpreting omens for guidance in public affairs. On July 6th, all assembled were augurs concerning the portent of earth and sky in symbolic alignment made possible in the discernment of Enlightenment rationality and the underlying eternal return of mythos—the mythopoeic—in human experience, the head, soma, and heart.

Jay Fliegelman interpreted the dramatized event as providing a naturalized metaphor for America's political revolution—a new order of ages, *Novus Ordo Saeclorum*. The demos, yet to be grasped with the aesthetic-moral imagination, served as an ominous symbolic light, a sign, a new constellation appearing in the night sky.[159] The motto *Novus Ordo Saeclorum* is translated as "A new order of the ages." The bright spots of the stars were set against the black of space in one more play of light and darkness in human experience in an environment. It was proposed by Charles Thompson, a patriot savant of Latin involved in the design of the Great Seal of the United States. The phrase signifies the beginning of the new American era and was sparked in part through the sheer power of the performance of the Declaration of Independence. There is no solid evidence that the Great Seal despite popular American legend and lore was a fabrication of the freemasons, although there are some minority voices that contend as much.

Fliegelman observed an organic need for re-alignment of ritual and the depth of myth as the individual and group broke from King and country. In this case, there was a mythopoeic earthly drama of an imagined light

159 Fliegelman, 24.

Figure 5. The Declaration of Independence was first officially performed for the public on July 6, 1776 at high noon. A perceived natural cycle in freemasonry and much wider culture and emerging civil societies, at the Old Statehouse yard from an observatory built earlier onto the roof of the building for astronomical observation. (Permission granted by USHistory.org)

in the sky. There was "rightness in placing".[160] The earthly landmark, the observatory, marked a point of origin of a new political and civic union and state, a new home, rightness in placing. The practiced habits of the orator, and different habits of the fence of soldiers on the square below, show the efficacy of habit and emotion but channeled in different media and process. The whole of the parts lends a quality to the pictured place. In Philadelphia at the Declaration's civic performance, bells rang through day and evening, bonfires were lit, and windows illuminated by candles. The nighttime ritual of a burning candle in the window was performed in

---

160 "Rightness in placing" is a term of art drawn from the work of Dewey. Its intended meaning is the momentary balancing in in a situation of contending processes—doing and undergoing, or centripetal and centrifugal habits—of the felt body-mind and environment. Dewey, *Art as Experience* (New York: Minton, Balch & Company, 1934), 216-221.

earlier years to celebrate the newborn body of the King on his birthday. Habermas believes that in those traditional societies holding a King before the advent of modern civil society and public sphere in late 17th and early 18th century deliberation and worlds of print the body of the King or his representation constituted the only public. His argument is that to be before the King, or his representation in this period (the candle in the window), was to be in public.[161] This changed with the emergence of a new sense of self, sensation, and authenticity in the declaring of independence. The candle in the window represented a new public imagined in the deliberations and performance of the 1776 Declaration and its aftermath.

The original copies of the Declaration moved outward from Philadelphia to Eaton, Pennsylvania that, at the time, was an important county seat to the north in Pennsylvania, and in New Jersey to Trenton and New Brunswick (key transmission nodes between New York and Philadelphia), and onward to more geographically distant places with riders moving out of the City of Brotherly Love to the south as well. After the express rider arrived at a location, *mis-en-scène*, the Declaration was rhetorically enacted and reprinted, very often by designated leaders with varying oratorical skills. The express rider worked along pre-planned routes with developed stable habits of transmission. The post-rider system developed at first in the regularity of schedules and support. The duplicates of the Declaration drafted by Jefferson and printed by Dunlap were instrumental circulation and its meaning and values artistically performed as well shaped before active audiences in a medium in aesthetic-moral-intellectual experience.

Figure 6, placed by the Jersey Blue Chapter of the Daughters of the American Revolution in 1913, remains indicative of both the geographic transmission of the Declaration and its emplaced performance. The plaque commemorates the place in New Brunswick, New Jersey where upon the arrival of the rider the Declaration "was acclaimed by all loyal citizens on July 9, 1776, the third town in which the document was read" according to the plaque. New Brunswick, as stipulated above, was an important transmission node in northern New Jersey sitting astride King's Highway connecting New York and Philadelphia. The major route between New York City and Philadelphia was very well traveled and could be transit-

---

161 Habermas, 1-26.

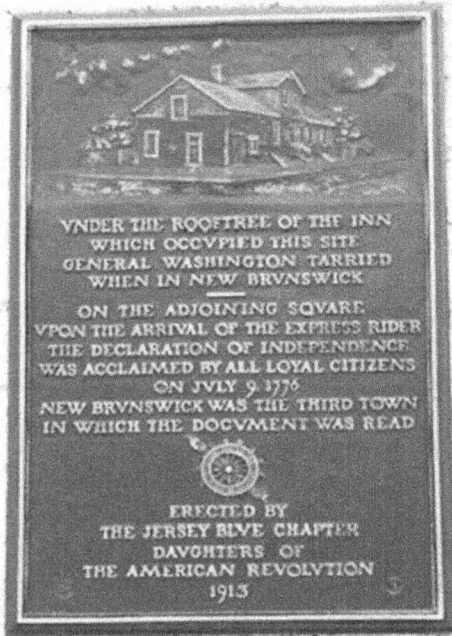

Figure 6. Photo by Michael Curry, UCLA Department of Geography
(Courtesy of Michael Curry)

ed in one day by an express rider, and soon to be fast coach, because of planned and ongoing improvements in the geo-semiotics and material infrastructure of transmission. The route overwhelmed the life, networked places, and usage of an older Native-American trail.

At an earlier point, after the authorization by Congress to assemble an army in 1775, Washington moved north along King's Highway toward New York, with a hand full of officers, and keen on scouting geographic terrain for possibilities of future military advantage as fighting seemed inevitable.[162] This was roughly or exactly the same route that would be traveled by the post-rider with original copies of the Declaration on its northeastern arc. After arriving in New York, Washington moved on the Old Post Road toward Boston on the road, of course, built originally for postal delivery.

After a period spent for reconnoiter, gathering supplies, establishing personal relations, perhaps developing rudiments or holding vague intima-

---

162 The King's Highway had been laid much earlier by command of King Charles II.

tions of a spy network, and building his army, Washington turned and moved southward to what he believed was the strategic site of New York, adjacent to centrally placed New Jersey and its terrain and resources. For example, in New Jersey, a type of "bog iron" was available for the manufacture of musket balls. The Congress, for its part, sitting in Massachusetts in 1776 (and spurred by the earlier battles at Lexington and Concord) headed to New York and then on King's Highway to Philadelphia, gathering civilian support and an increasing escort of militia along the way. Once in Philadelphia the Declaration was debated by the Continental Congress and adopted at Independence Hall. At that point, Dunlap was asked immediately to commence his printer's art.

An original Dunlap broadside was delivered in Worcester Massachusetts by a post rider on July 15, and a few days later to Boston. Thomas delayed the broadside in Worcester on its way to Boston, knowing very well the timing and spacing of the circulation of the post-rider system, a transmission system that he helped to establish. After acquiring the Declaration from the horseman, he watched an assembling crowd or milling about of people and beckoned them perhaps to a nearby porch. It was in a scene such as this he publicly proclaimed the Declaration of Independence. There would be an additional public reading in the town shortly after, as something had been initially planned. Thomas took great pride in stepping in and being the first to declare the document in the Massachusetts Commonwealth, before the Boston performance. The Dunlap broadsides reached all the colonies and their provincial assemblies within July and August.

An additional illustration can be given illustrating the power of place and networking. With Portsmouth, the capital of New Hampshire under British rule, the provincial leaders transferred their capital, earlier, inland to Exeter. In 1775, both Houses of the provincial government meeting in the new provincial capital of Exeter united in instructing their delegates to the Continental Congress through deepening communication links to join with other provinces in declaring the United Colonies free and independent States.[163] After that decision made in more than one colony attention was focused on the actions, and enactments, the Continental Congress might take. It was on July 16th, 1776, that the courier from Congress rode into Exeter, where he headed straight away to the Court House,

---

163   Charles H. Bell, *History of Exeter, New Hampshire* (Boston: J. E. Farwell & Co. Press, 1888), 91-93.

and something of a public square, for a public reading of the Declaration. The Continental Congress had acted in part on the heels of the Suffolk Resolves.

The daily life of a New Hampshire farmer in New England was not too distant from Exeter is revealing. Brown mentions Mathew Patten, an Irish immigrant in his fifties who had settled as a young man in what became Bedford, a small town on no significant transportation route inland in New Hampshire. He made tools, buckets, gunstocks, built and sold furniture, surveyed land, and drafted legal forms of substantial worth to less literate locals. In that very agility, and neighborhood, he had in place in his community, a measure of self-reliance to control his life in exchanges with others in face-to-face community. Patten matured as a young man on the farm, which, as for nearly everyone across the colonies was a family enterprise. It was a felt, tangible, cultural, empowering, and material landscape, but often dangerous or ambiguous.

By the 1760s, Pattern was a leading man in Bedford, having become its first selectman as well town clerk, fence inspector, and appraiser of damages.[164] Largely, Patten was involved in daily routines, face-to-face encounters, and word-of mouth communications in his community, yet he was informed on major wider events such as the Stamp Act. The American War of Independence interrupted Patten's daily experience and custom regarding the flow of information and spoken word.

The very recent battles of Lexington and Concord caused news to move more swiftly by word of mouth than print, but unreliable oral reports aroused a hunger, then need, for the fuller accounts that newspapers could provide. This produced copy for the resource starved press (type, paper and ink), while stimulating a wider audience for the newspapers columns.[165] The battles of Lexington and Concord were extraordinary events in sparking the demand side for American newspapers and reporting. It was a matter of shared drama as well life-and-death, and a growing desire for accurate transmission; the intertwining once again of often integral ritual and transmission functions of communication. After news of Lexington and Concord arrived in Bedford, Patten became heavily in-

---

164 Brown, 252.

165 Ibid, 145.

volved in consulting the town. It followed after the revolution newspapers became more available across New Hampshire, and the other colonies, there was enough interest to sustain the growing markets sought after local and extra-local news and commercial information. His sons had enlisted in the patriot army and moved off to Boston. One of his sons was tragically killed in a battle. Regarding the political ferment then underway, "In July 1776 it was not good enough for him [Patten] to simply know by word-of-mouth the fact that the United States had declared independence." Perhaps that was why Patten bought a printed copy of the Declaration of Independence at Exeter, following a meeting of the Committee of Safety, of which he had become a member after Lexington and Concord. "People would ask Patten what exactly was going on when he returned to his district and he would have the text to show them and to read publicly."[166] Patten might have purchased an extra copy of the Dunlap broadside delivered by express rider and carried in his saddlebag, or it might have been a reprint made on July 16, or very soon after, as the front page of the local newspaper, *The Extraordinary New Hampshire Gazette or, Exeter Morning Chronicle*. In any event, the death of his son was likely with Mathew Patten each day that passed.

F. MILITARY HABIT, QUALITY, AND MASCULINE FORMATION OF THE STATE

It was by direct order of John Hancock, President of the Continental Congress, a freemason that a copy of the Declaration be dispatched up King's Highway firstly to General George Washington (a freemason) at the head of the military for purposes of the Declaration's performance before troops and officers stationed in New York. On July 9, the Declaration was in hand at Washington's military camp. The General ordered officers of the several Continental Army Brigades stationed in New York City to pick up copies of the Declaration prepared and left at the Adjutant General's Office.

Then, with the British "constantly in view upon and at Staten Island," as one participant recalled, the brigades were formed in hollow squares on their respective parades, where they could hear the Declaration read as the General had specified, "with an audible voice." Washington wanted

---

166 Brown, 145.

the event to "serve as a free incentive to every officer, and soldier, to act with Fidelity and Courage ... knowing that now the peace and safety of his Country depends, under God, solely on the success of our arms; And that he is now in the service of a State, possessed of sufficient power to reward his merit, and advance him to the highest honors of a free Country."[167]

Washington, in mustering his forces, was spacing and positioning them with the breathing room necessary between the forming brigades and the counter position and quality of British forces well positioned and outfitted for war. For a moment in time, in the performance of the Declaration before and with the Continental Army, the equilibrium of balance and counterbalance was struck in poised readiness, position, and the emotions of rising patriotism commanding continental bodies and attempted American military positioning set against a counter force. A newly rehearsed performed masculinity and set of technologies and eventually imagined new technique of the Americans (such as the hit-and-run of guerilla warfare) confronted the longer practiced masculine habitus and performance of the very well-armed British within earshot on Staten Island across the river from the mainland.

General Washington wanted disciplined male bodies in his army, following orders and the officers at their head with himself responsible, in the end, for all actions in war. The army was tightening its leadership structure and chain of command and would become a regular fighting force. Freemasonry in large numbers in Washington's assembling officers corps would help provide habit correction and discipline assisted by its own rituals and symbols providing an identity of resistance and legitimacy particularly against the mythopoeic mystery and aura of the King.[168] Washington used the ritual of the freemasons for those who wanted to be freemasons in his officer's corps, consciously knowing that men would gather and bond. Washington was a savvy and pragmatic hand who understood the politics and culture of human habit and habit correction and acted accordingly to great effect.

Position at its most basic, as noted by Nathan Crick, is a "spacing as

167 "Infantry Orders: George Washington to Continental Army, July 9, 1776," *The Writings of George Washington*, ed. John Fitzpatrick (Washington, D. C.: Government Printing Office, 1932), 244-245.

168 Robert T. Kertzer, *Ritual, Politics and Power* (New Haven: Yale University Press, 1989), 161-162.

viewed from the perspective of an agent."[169] Position can be as simple as two strollers on the wood planks of a colonial Philadelphia sidewalk, jostling for position beneath an overhang to avoid a cloudburst and downpour of rain. Beyond the example of the Philadelphia strollers, the assuming of a position refers to the complexity of stances taken in a place as in the military performance of the Declaration. There was work underway, including forging habits and practical instruments for civilian control of the military in the problematic of full-scale war. The President of the Congress had dispatched the rider to begin to shape, lead, and form the army. The force of external discipline of Congress implemented in new configurations of action and objects and the alignment of the body produced new habits, conduct, and position. A position taken has an immediate qualitative value and a stance is taken to endure or even expand. The pragmatic use of freemasonry as cultural performance was powerful and effective in various ways.

There was a controlled rage in an assembling army and fighting units, making possible an instrumental aesthetics of military power, manly performance. The hot ritual performance of the Declaration made possible the more abstract, yet passionate, discourse and national territorial space laid down afterwards not only for military formation, but also in the habit correction and imagination that produced the experimental Articles of Confederation then the United States Constitution with a Bill of Rights. The Constitution to come would memorialize democratic action, with exceptions such as the exclusion of slaves from meaningful investiture. Heart and head were embodied in new habits and in assuming meaningful, value-laden positions in the symbolic and real distance and negotiated interests in the moments between the Declaration and Constitution including its Bill of Rights. And in the overlap there was a budding economy.

Even as the Continental Congress moved south along the King's Road toward Philadelphia in 1776, they were developing growing concern about possible renegade military and excessively violent actions, uncontrolled and thus an-aesthetic rage, by independent militias, or alternatively desertions, or lack of sustained fighting ability among the different militia over time if full war were to eventuate. That experience led to the 2nd Amendment in the Bill of Rights concerned with a "well-regulated militia" in

---

169 Nathan Crick (personal communication, August 5, 2010).

bearing arms. It had become a cornerstone of Washington's military strategy, ultimately to be borne out on the battlefield that local militias would turn out to fight well if there was a disciplined Continental Army around to look the British in the face in a masculine stance, in martial performance and strong position, figuratively and literally.[170] Washington also greatly valued the need for disciplined habit among the officer corps with their elite status emphasized. He considered this among the necessary predispositions of habit in the successful prosecution of war. He understood how to use freemasonry in the officer corps in this regard with all due respect yet practical, animated and inspired.

For example, if necessary, friendly and capable militia could move swiftly from the rougher terrain of the piedmont areas of Pennsylvania located to the northwest of King's Highway, or from Jersey lands, and help block major British movements through the main New York-Philadelphia corridor, with a requisite amount of confidence.[171] This was a dramatic rehearsal of possibilities (the imagination of martial actions and things not present) by Washington in the event he, and his advising officers, chose to fight along the major transportation corridor in New Jersey with his regular army.[172]

Another illustration of the actions of an officer in the Continental Army holding things together in ritual performance, using the disciplined habits of the male body, technology, and right spacing (through the deepest exigencies of war) was the Prussian soldier, and freemason, Baron Von Steuben. Steuben understood that the means (the habits of the individual soldier) were integral to the aesthetic-moral, pragmatic and intelligent ends, namely the army. At Valley Forge, he assumed control of the military training and disciplined performance of the soldier and thus the army. Old habits were broken and new ones developed. He recorded his procedures and innovations in writing and this became the *Regulations for the Order and Discipline of the Troops of the United States.*[173]

---

170 Mark Kwasny, *Washington's Partisan War, 1775-1783* (Kent: Kent State University Press, 1998), 214.

171 R. W. Hunter and J. C. G. Burrow, "The History and Archaeology of the Revolutionary War," *New Jersey in the American Revolution,* ed. Barbara J. Minick (New Brunswick: Rutgers University Press, 1983), 168.

172 Howard H. Peckham, *The Toll of Independence: Engagements and Battle Casualties of the American Revolution* (Chicago: University of Chicago Press, 1974), 168. New Jersey was the crossroads of the Revolution with 238 battles fought in New Jersey, more than any other state in the confederation.

173 United States, and Baron Friedrich Wilhelm Ludolf Gerhard Augustin von Steuben,

His training, beginning at Valley Forge, was decisive in subsequent Continental Army victories. Steuben formed a model drill company of 100 men. Their disciplined male performance captured the morale and fighting imagination of the standing army and watching militias. Congress, on March, 29, 1779, approved the printed drill manual. With the major printing of the text after the war in 1794 by the freemason and patriot printer-publisher Thomas, the book became the center of military training for the young nation's army for decades into the 19th century. Ritual performance and the transmission of a variety of print vehicles were mutually interdependent in early America.[174]

Over 40% of the generals commissioned by the Continental Congress in war were, or would become, freemasons; a stunning number, far above civil occupations. The military officers who were freemasons, perhaps beginning with the actions of a few ancient masons, or working with a Scottish patent, in war, as well as the prestige of the freemason Washington initiated in the 1750s, was antecedent to rising numbers of freemasons in civil populations. A very few inspired the rising numbers that were to come within the army and coming civilian population. In some measure, it was because of the felt, honorable ideal and defining of manhood in the revolutionary generation among masons and majority of non-masons.

G. DUNLAP'S REPORTING ON THE MARTIAL DRAMATURGY AND FREEMASONRY OF GENERAL GEORGE WASHINGTON

Dunlap printed, among so much else, a strategically chosen oration with masonic content in 1779 for publishing and circulation. The publication was put out in the blaze of war. It etched a sermon preached by William Smith at a public gathering of the Free and Accepted Masons of the State of Pennsylvania.[175] A large masonic celebration was staged on St. John's Day, December 28, as part of the proceedings of the Annual Communi-

---

Regulations for the Order and Discipline of the Troops of the United States (Boston: T. and J. Fleet, 1782).

174 Baron Von Steuben, *Revolutionary War Drill Manual* (Boston: Isaiah Thomas, 1794).

175 William Smith, *A Sermon Preached in Christ-Church, Philadelphia, [for the benefit of the poor] by Appointment of and before the General Communication of Free and Accepted Masons of the State of Pennsylvania, on Monday December 28, 1778, Celebrated Agreeable to Their Constitution, as the Anniversary of St. John the Evangelist,* ed. William Smith (Philadelphia: John Dunlap, 1779).

cation of the Grand Lodge of Pennsylvania ("Annual Communication" is a term regularly used in freemasonry by Grand Lodges since the 18th century, and perhaps by lodges in some form before). The term communication in the period of the rise of grand lodges beginning in London means a larger community assembled through a network and gathered for administration and ritualized solidarity. The communications involved masons in a gathering and drawn from a variety of geographic scales. In America, this came to mean ultimately the legally circumscribed state, for example Pennsylvania, but there were different geographic boundaries, or lack of boundaries, and different practices in the early republic that brought masons together in an Annual Communication. Pennsylvania, more than others, reached outside its boundaries in establishing lodges. St. John's Day was normally held on December 27, near the Solstice, but this year it being Sunday the masons postponed their meeting so as not to interfere with the religious ceremonies.

For the freemasons, the Annual Communication overlay a ritual form established in anthropological time in the natural cycle of the year on or near the winter solstice with another day of celebration during the summer solstice. These days were dedicated to the Saints John from the New Testament (John the Evangelist, and John the Baptist), similar to the dedications on these same days in medieval operative masonry in France to Janus the double-headed god. The fraternity often drew upon traditions carried by the Church of Rome, and others derived from or in protest to the church, as well sources lost, and widely scattered geographically, in ancient history.

Announcements of the celebrations for the regular Annual Communication were made in Dunlap's *Pennsylvania Packet* newspaper, inviting all masons under the jurisdiction of the Grand Lodge of Pennsylvania to participate with the oration delivered on St. John's day subsequently printed as a pamphlet and circulated. The ancient solstices following the annual cycle of the year, an instantiation of the dramatic play of light and dark in human embodied and emplaced experience, were replaced and performed to the honor of the two holy Saints John recorded. The St. John's event was successful, with nearly 300 masons in attendance including General Washington himself, having just arrived in Philadelphia a few days earlier.

Of interest, it was the first public masonic function in which Washington was involved of which there is record although he had been a mason for decades.[176] The likely powerful equestrian positioning and heightening of the man atop his steed, and right posturing in the assembling crowd of civilians as he led processions of freemasons, for example, into church, would be indicative of Washington's keen sense of public persona, habituated body, cultural performance, and timing evident throughout his life.

Washington was concerned with constituting and constituted habit in pursuit of the good life for himself, a meaningful and purposive life. He apparently trained himself in the development of good habits using a printed manual, in some considerable part, as his guide.[177] In this, he was exactly like Franklin. The art of incremental change in habits was the central part of his conceptualization and praxis of personal growth. He was neither a full-blown political philosopher, nor scientist, rhetorician, nor man of letters, but he was learned in body, performance, and performativity in action space—habit and habit correction—in political, socio-cultural, and military space. He did have remarkable political instincts that guided his habit correction. This was part of his genius as it was for Franklin. His art of virtue and display, anchored in the stability of the pre-reflective intentions of habit, impulse, habit correction, then imagination of possibilities—his moral imagination—took him to the pinnacle of leadership and to his standing as a global figure. His practice was remarkably akin to that of Franklin as pointed out in Chapter 3. [178] There have been efforts in contemporary neuroscience to map the coordinates of habit in the brain and its systems.[179]

---

176 Wayne Huss, *The Master Builders*, 41.

177 George Washington, *Washington's Rules of Civility and Decent Behavior in Company and Conversation*, ed. J. M. Toner (Washington, D.C.: W. H. Morrison, 1888).

178 Dewey was concerned with habit and habit correction in a meaningful, effective or good life. Both Franklin and Washington held similar views about the potency of habit, habit correction and potential pragmatic and artful action in civil or military spheres.

179 Charles Duhigg, *The Power of Habit: Why We Do Things in Life and Business* (New York: Random House: 2012), 13. Some recent neuroscience has advanced the idea that habit is situated in an oval of cells in the basal ganglia a very primitive and early part of the brain close to where the brain touches the spinal cord. This area of the brain is transactional not covered here) with other topologies of the brain, sensoriotor activity and the environment.

Before the outbreak of war, the fraternity of the freemasons was apolitical. As opening shots were fired, the Grand Lodge in Pennsylvania, typical across the colonies, issued no statements and adhered to no public position on the dispute. Members came to their own conclusions. This occurred despite the fact that American freemasonic bodies (lodges and grand lodges) were organizations, which owed allegiance to a supervisory body in England. That having been said, several subordinate lodges and individual members within the precincts of the Grand Lodge of Pennsylvania, and in Massachusetts, were not so cautious in their words or actions with some lodges showing a preponderance of support for the patriot cause but still some for the loyalist position.

Wayne Huss states:

> Many Masons played active roles in the armed forces of the United States. Lodge Nos. 2, 3, and 4 (all Philadelphia), No. 5 (New Castle County, Delaware), No. 8 (Chester County) and No. 18 (Kent County, Delaware) together provided a total of over two hundred fifty Continental Army officers. The most striking example of patriotism came from Lodge No. 3 whose membership roll contained the name of eighty-five of these individuals. [180]

The Grand Lodge of Pennsylvania and those lodges in Delaware and in other provinces initially under the jurisdiction of the Grand Lodge of Pennsylvania with its shift to ancient freemasonry likely show numbers of military men who were masons beyond the typical case across the colonies, but likely also with a larger number of military men who were freemasons occurring in Massachusetts as in Philadelphia. This was a real possibility in Massachusetts, in part because of the presence of the "ancients" in that state descended from St. Andrew's lodge of which Warren, Revere, and Hancock were early members.[181] Military lodges did appear in other places and it remains to be discerned the extent to which they were ancient. The current research tends to the conclusion that there was a strong ancient influence in the military lodges.

---

180 Huss, 41.

181 Warren had lodge brothers such as Revere, but also likely other civil and military networks who worked close to Warren in matters of military action and the flow of military intelligence and special operations at their American inception.

In effect, Dunlap, and others, participated in backstage and front stage performance, which Dunlap did on other occasions, including the later laying of the cornerstone ceremonies for the federal district at Jones Point after the war in Washington City. As discussed in Chapter 6, he reported in his newspaper the laying of the cornerstone ceremonies for Jones Point, the President's House, being the White House, and the cornerstone ceremonies at the United States Capitol building despite various difficulties including, at one point, the breakout of disease in Philadelphia.[182] Each cornerstone ceremony, as shall be seen, was an important touch-point in the developing dramaturgy of republican performance in circumscribing federal territory, following on the Declaration and Constitution.

Concerning the Philadelphia performance with General Washington, a vital likely key actor at center stage, Huss states:

> A grand procession assembled at the College and Academy of Philadelphia on the west side of Fourth Street below Arch and then proceeded to Christ Church. The religious services were conducted by two of the city's most prominent clergymen, the Rev. Dr. William White, later the first bishop of Pennsylvania, who gave the prayer, and the Rev. William Smith, now an "Ancient" Mason, who delivered the sermon, dedicated to General Washington. Smith's sermon had no single theme, but covered a wide area of concern to Masons, Christians and patriots alike. Smith extolled such Masonic virtues as wisdom, strength and beauty, temperance and charity; he re-emphasized traditional Christian beliefs; and he hailed the fledgling United States in its quest for liberty.[183]

At the end of the sermon following an elaborate program of instrumental and choral music, a collection was taken for relief of the poor totaling £400, a major sum for the period. With church bells ringing, and masonic and patriotic tunes played by a military band, the masons retired from

---

182 The cornerstone ceremony for Jones Point was reported in John Dunlap's *American Daily Advertiser*, April 28, 1791. The ceremonies for the cornerstone at the President's House were reported in the *American Daily Advertiser* October 21, 1792. There was a similar report on the cornerstone ceremonies covering the event in the United States Capitol in the *American Daily Advertiser*, September 17, 1793.

183 Huss, 41.

Christ Church to their respective meeting places, for example, alehouses transformed into lodges for the occasion, for festive dining. This major masonic dramaturgy "increased the prestige of the fraternity, associated it with the name of Washington and the cause of the United States. They helped enhance mason's reputation for support of charitable endeavors."[184] Outside of the sphere of freemasonry, and within the orb of freemasonry, Dunlap's newspapers transmitted information valuable in war and in peace. His use of the printed word involved both transmission and drama of the ritual function. Communication was only possible out of the stability of his habits. His political, socio-cultural and military strategies, tactics and ideas in worlds of print were situated in communicative action near and far from Philadelphia and in places in the overlap between near and far.

H. SUMMARY AND CONCLUSIONS

In this chapter, I have examined the ritual and transmission functions of communication in describing three different productions by Dunlap. The examples were (a) the oration as a print vehicle using the specific instance of recounting the patriot's death of Warren at Bunker Hill, (b) the transmission and ritual performance of the 1776 Declaration of Independence in the formation of multiple publics (mounting to a singular, momentary public interest) and union of states, and (c) Dunlap's reporting on the dramaturgy of General Washington in his first known public appearance as a freemason.

Washington's disciplined life-long practice of shaping new habits was a critical means of personal advancement towards the ends (the consummations and fulfillment) of military, civil groups and political life. A martial habitus among the freemasons who became officers (and a near equal number of non-masons who became officers) was developed that complemented a civic habitus and helped lead to civil control of the military. The same focus on habit and improvement of the aesthetic-moral-intellectual quality of life in performativity and habit correction was used by Franklin for building personal and commercial success in the civil sphere.

The chapter revisited the tensions in Philadelphia between ancient and modern freemasons and the growing prominence of the ancients in the

---

184 Loc. cit.

public imagination by word of mouth as American patriots but through no small measure the printed text and media strategy advanced by a small number of ancients who were also patriot printer-journalists and freemasons. The text magnified their power and helped considerably in establishing an early admiration of freemasonry in a budding nation. At the same time, the text was imagined critical in building a virtuous and informed citizenry. An informed citizenry was imagined as a practical necessity in raising up the young republic just as the occupations of printer and journalist became important even in the approach, prosecution, and consummations of war. War requires accurate information as well as the rhetorical flourishes of patriotic performance.

CHAPTER 5

THE EARLY AMERICAN EXPERIENCE OF
THE EMBODIED SELF AND OTHERS

T he subaltern, or diversity of counter publics, in America aspired for inclusion in growing civil society and the public sphere. In their desire and contested attempts at public formation, there were common psychological denominators among the disempowered groups, for example, among women and African Americans. The shared denominators in building their own civic associations as in freemasonry were (a) the meaningfulness and prizing of learning, (b) community with responsibility to past, present, and future generations, (c) ritual place, (d) faith-based values, and (e) the aspirations of upward social mobility. First Nations held a similar profile, while holding a strong allegiance to the well-being of the tribe overall and to its hierarchy and honor and freedom in self-sacrifice. Communication involves the bio-semiotics of embodied transactions such as language, cultural artifacts, and tools like the printing press or weapons and signs of war, for example the tomahawk, war paint or the peace pipe among First Nations, or additional cultural signs and artifacts such as the wampum belt.

A. PRINCE HALL IN FREEMASONRY AND THE
EARLY AFRICAN AMERICAN PUBLIC SPHERE

African-American freemasonry began in Boston largely through the initial efforts of Prince Hall (1738-1807), a manumitted slave who became the first initiated African American in American masonry, for which we have certainty in the historical record. Beginning with Prince Hall and fellow Bostonians, African-American freemasons became an important part of the cultural life of African American cultural life and leadership in America continuing until the civil rights movement of the late 1960s. There were great similarities but profound contextual differences between African-American freemasonry and its white American counterpart.

Because of the deep linkages between African-American faith traditions and cultural life, for example, the African Methodist Episcopal denomination (AME) founded in Philadelphia in 1816 with shared leadership and membership in freemasonry, there was a more religious and Christian expression in the African-American fraternity. The African-American freemasons, as well the strong majority of the wider African-American community, relied heavily on their faith derived from multiple oral/aural traditional sources and habits, involving face-to-face local community. This was a considerable source of sustenance in the face of violence, displacement, and the demeaning of their humanity. There was a socio-cultural coding of the pure and impure, of exclusion cast against the African-American community and others, such as First Nations. A deeply felt moral-aesthetics, embodied and faith-based action and intellectual position of resistance and autonomy gave a unique quality to the ritual and intellectual life of African-American freemasons.

Significantly, a common denominator between freemasons in the African-American community and those in white Euro-American civil society was the valorization of learning and its public display as a way to personal, civic, and economic progress in America.[185] In early African-American freemasonry, the inherent place of learning in the fraternity of freemasonry as an ideal may have had a more consistent expression amid a comparative paucity of institutions for self-betterment than in mainstream white American civil society and grand lodge freemasonry. The African-American population involved in freemasonry was much smaller than its white counterpart.

In Prince Hall's generation, and in the following one, newly freed African Americans often migrated to urban centers along the Atlantic seaboard like Boston and Philadelphia, and some were to become leaders in freemasonry, the church, and African-American civil society. Some leaders rose out of the slavery present in urban environments by buying their own freedom or escaping. Following in the footsteps of Prince Hall, leaders and freemasons in Philadelphia, such as James Forten, emphasized that education was the primary tool of emancipation and equality. There needed to be a "diffusion of knowledge among the African race by unfettering their thoughts and giving full scope to the energy of their minds."[186]

The emphasis by African-American freemasons on education and learning and virtue, as a core practice in the post-revolutionary period (a civic

---

185 Gary Nash, *Forging Freedom: The Formation of Philadelphia's Black Community, 1720-1840* (Cambridge: Harvard University Press, 1988), 4-7, 218, 279.

186 Julie Wynch, *The Making and Meaning of James Forten's Letters from a Man of Color* (Oxford: Oxford University Press, 2003), 156.

and learning habitus) is telling evidence of an essential aspect of freemasonry and the origins of modern wider civil society in this period and place. The lodge was a cultural expression, ritualizing, and institutionalizing of the desire for learning and self-betterment. The lodge democracy and seemingly contradictory lodge hierarchy were a weaving of integral sign systems that additionally displayed the urgency of felt qualitative place, inhabited place that could anchor action and thought.

According to the Harvard educated polymath, minister, orator, and freemason William Bentley from Salem, Prince Hall was the "leading African of Boston."[187] Hall was manumitted in 1770. In March 1775, six months prior to the battle of Lexington and Concord, he and 14 additional free African-American men were initiated into the degrees of symbolic freemasonry by members of Irish Military Lodge # 441, Irish Constitution, attached to the 38th Regiment of Foot, British Army, garrisoned at Castle Williams, now Fort Independence, Boston Harbor.[188] The British were occupying Boston at this time; all the while, Prince Hall ran a catering and leather tanning business at the Sign of the Golden Fleece on Walter Street. Hall, over the course of his life, was deeply committed to his church, the establishment of schooling for blacks, and charity in the wider community.

He was dedicated to the cause of education for African-American children. He organized the first school for African- American children in 1797, which became Boston's first public school for African American community. He also led the fight for adult literacy among African Americans, before the topic was considered seriously by anyone in Boston. Hall's passion in the totality of his life indicates the sympathetic relationship between masonic ritual performance of ethics, and spirituality, but also the ritual performance of schooling in the lodge, and schoolhouse, for the individual and group in an uncertain but promising world. "As a process ritualization helps 'create' the world for the social actor." .... "Rit-

---

187 Steven Bullock, *Revolutionary Brotherhood: Freemasonry and the Transformation of the American Social Order, 1730-1840* (Chapel Hill: University of North Carolina Press, 1998), 154.

188 Hall had been earlier promised a masonic charter by Joseph Warren but plans fell to the wayside after the death of Warren at Bunker Hill. Had Warren lived it might have influenced American freemasonry in a number of ways including a profound impact on racial relations.

ual—enacted meaning—must be seen in the very construction of reality and not simply as reflecting it." [189]

Hall matured to become the principal architect and founding father of African-American freemasonry close to the Quaker Meeting House on Quaker Lane in the usually rambunctious North End. The nearby anti-slavery Quaker environment, the local places of the Quaker community, provided some respite from the savagery of the wider racism following the stultifying effects and crimes against humanity. An environment of nurturing and safety made possible a public formation in a difficult scene. Other African Americans joined him in helping constitute the first generation of leadership of freemasons comporting themselves in the wider community. In Philadelphia, this included Absalom Jones, Richard Allen, and James Forten. All of these African-American freemasons have been referred to as among the "founding fathers" of the African-American community. [190]

A helpful work in the study of African American freemasonry in this period is Michael Gomez's *Exchanging Our Country Marks: The Transformation of African Identities in the Colonial and Antebellum South*. [191] Gomez's work concerns the transition from ethnic African identities to a racial African-American subjectivity; however, not as a withering away of African roots, but rather as the constituting and creative re-making and productive actions of hybrid identities. As a changing subjectivity transformed by contrary forces from within and without, the slave community and freed slaves were contingent in advancing to new positions. Prince Hall freemasonry was an aesthetic-moral action, and intellectual position, situated and embodied in a complex, usually hostile, sometimes nurturing, and often chaotic or violent, wider environment. The indeterminate environment produced profound ruptures in familial, individual, and community development.

Brooks states:

---

189 Peter McClaren, *Schooling as Ritual Performance: Toward a Political Economy of Educational Symbols and Gestures* (Oxford: Rowman and Littlefield Publishers, 1993), xiii.

190 David Gray, *Inside Prince Hall* (Lancaster, Anchor Communications, 2003), 97.

191 Michael Gomez, *Exchanging our Country Marks: The Transformation of African Identities in the Colonial and Antebellum South* (Chapel Hill: University of North Carolina Press, 1998).

> [Gomez's work] ... demonstrates that African Americans
> did exercise creative, politicized, and principled agency
> in the development of new identities, new cultures, and
> new discourses. This principle is critical to the study of
> early African-American literature, which yields up its se-
> crets only to faithful, suspicious, and vigilantly inductive
> readers.[192]

Recovering the historical and moral geography of African-American freemasonry is difficult because of the forces of imperialism, slavery, and racism. Each influenced the representational quality and quantity of the surviving history. As outlined by Brooks, contributing factors to the historical erasure have been "the differential documentation of African American in all spheres, unequal access to political representation, 'official' compilations of historical materials, and the assumption of history as a sequential narrative of progress rather than as a series of confrontations and cataclysms; the denial of agency to insurgents; and the failure to account for signification as a site of historical contention and negotiation."[193]

The surviving texts and literature of 18th century Prince Hall freemasonry, as illuminated by Brooks, offers fresh insights into previously written histories as well as erasures of African-American experience in the revolutionary era. Brooks notes that close attention to Prince Hall immediately challenges the enduring assumption "that black political discourse first emerged in the shadows of nineteenth-century black abolitionism."[194] In proof of this latter point, scholars have regularly cited two texts published in 1829 as the first print instances of Ethiopianist or Black Nationalist discourse in America. These were Robert Alexander Young's *Ethiopian Manifesto* and David Walker's fiery *Appeal to the Colored Citizens of the World*.[195] This has been considered as given in the literature.

---

192 Joanna Brooks. *American Lazarus: Religion and the Rise of African-American and Native American Literatures* (Oxford: Oxford University Press, 2003), 117.

193 Ibid., 118.

194 Loc. cit.

195 Robert A. Young, *The Ethiopian Manifesto: Issued in Defence of the Black Man's Rights in the Scale of Universal Freedom* (New York: privately published, 1829); David Walker, *Walker's Appeal, in Four Articles; Together with a Preamble, to the Coloured Citizens of the World, but in Particular, and Very Expressly, to Those of the United States of America,*

Three decades before this, Brooks points out that orations (including their outsourced printing and circulation) by the African American and freemasons, Hall and the Reverend John Marrant, documented a vibrant presence of Ethiopian and African ideas of culture, place, and place-making among African-American freemasons and likely others with whom they interacted[196]. The African-American lodge, self-termed African Lodge was initially working under the transmission of masons in a military lodge working from an Irish constitution. The "ancient-influenced" Irish Military lodges were likely among the most egalitarian of freemasons, which was a part of their appeal to printers, merchants, or tradesmen in the American colonies.[197] It can be added that ancient freemasonry in America likely had a stronger sense of religion than the more secular moderns they replaced.

Brooks states, "(the Irish Military lodges) ... extension of fraternity to black men invites speculation about revolutionary-era alliances between colonial subaltern groups and army soldiers who were Irish. As African-American freemasonry grew beyond its chartering, or founding, moments, the African lodge established its own version of the narrative of Masonic anciency."[198] Amid difficulties, the black freemasons in 1787 subsequently petitioned and received a charter from the "modern" Grand Lodge of England, the first "Grand Lodge," thenceforth to meet as African Lodge No. 459, a matter of great pride in African Lodge and its subsequent lineage. This was a powerful statement of legitimacy and strength of character in the post war period by the African-American freemasons, occurring at the same time Ancient freemasonry was on the rise.

Importantly, in the late 17th and 18th centuries, freemasons took on the lore and emotional appeal of "anciency" as understood by Brooks to suit their own ethnic, religious, philosophical, and political views.

> .... [A]archaeologist William Stukeley celebrated the cabalistic kernels of Freemasonry; moreover, they claimed the Druids were but displaced Semitic peoples—a lost tribe

---

Written in Boston, State of Massachusetts, September 28, 1829 (David Walker, 1830).

196 Brooks, *American Lazarus*, 118-119.

197 An important illustration is the Irish-American freemason and printer-journalist John Dunlap discussed throughout Chapter 4.

198 Brooks, *American Lazarus*, 126.

of Israel, who carried Abrahamic religion and Masonic tradition to Northern Europe. Irish freethinker John
Toland (1670-1722) rejected this Judeao-Christian or-
thodoxy and instead asserted the Celtic pagan origins
of Freemasonry. [He] proposed a Druidical Masonic
rite and located parallels to Druidism in Egyptian an-
tiquities and Pythagorean mysteries. For Toland and his
fellow republicans, these Freemasonic-Celtic research-
ers served distinctly political purposes: they discovered
in indigenous paganism a "natural" religious antidote
to the kingdom-making regimes of the Anglican and
Catholic churches, and they identified Freemasonry as
a prime venue for the development of an antimonarchi-
cal morality.[199]

The emotionally powerful, mythopoeic, or sacred and imaginative claims
of "anciency" in human experience were used to confront the exclusion-
ary practices within English freemasonry. In the 1720s, and later, work-
ing-class Irish freemasons living in London were largely banned from entry to the more aristocratic lodges in the metropolis. The Irish in London
would claim to be the true practitioners of the craft of ancient freemasonry, and therefore not subject to modern English regulations. *Ahiman
Rezon,* published and distributed widely in Britain and its colonies, fur-
nished upstart and often Irish or Scottish lineage even perhaps military
French lodges with something of a freemasonic means for self-legitimi-
zation through print. From 1751 to 1771, there were at least 140 ancient
lodges established.

The ancients were particularly resolved to charter military lodges and emphasized the granting of printed charters, or letters to operate individual
lodges to such an extent that it likely influenced the administrative practices of the moderns. The printed charters or other letters of authorization helped speed the growth of numbers which projected authority as
they were carried in saddlebags across space around the world. As has
been noted, ritual did not travel well without the tools and techniques of
transmission in the 18th century.

Freemasons in the Pennsylvania Grand Lodge, heavily influenced by ancient freemasonry since the War of Independence, repeated the story of a

---

199 Ibid., 124.

fabulous legendary document of freemasonry from the 15th century at-
tributed to King Henry the VI. The document was purportedly discussed
in a letter by Locke later, published in 1753 in the *Gentleman's Magazine*
in London.[200] Later research has deemed the letter reputed to be by Locke
a forgery. Nevertheless, the putative correspondence helps show how the
quasi-sacred aura of anciency was fashioned to conform to emerging "political sensibilities, national allegiances, and cultural identities." It also
shows the esteem in which a large number of freemasons viewed Locke.

> The document connects philosophers Pythagoras and
> Locke as well as the nations of Egypt, Greece, France,
> and England; of mystery and philosophy; mathematics
> and politics; ancient and modern. As reprinted by the
> Pennsylvania Grand Lodge, it conferred on American
> freemasons a privileged access to all of these.[201]

As was the custom each year on the festival of St. John the Baptist, June
24, drawing on the ancient cyclical festivals of the summer and winter solstice, freemasons celebrated in their normal fashion with parades, private
and public ritual performance, orations, and feasting.[202] In 1789 Prince
Hall chose this day for a public performance of African Lodge-style freemasonry in Boston. It was carefully choreographed dramaturgy.

Prior to the festivities, Hall initiated Marrant into African Lodge and
asked him to be lodge chaplain. Marrant was a remarkably capable and
well-known minister, orator, and Black Atlantic celebrity. Marrant and
Hall together combined their respective masonic and ministerial rhetorical skills—a rhetoric of becoming—to express a shared vision "of a powerful, trans-historical black community."[203] Hall engaged leaders of the

---

200 *The Gentleman's Magazine* was founded in London, England, by Edward Cave in January 1731. It contained a wide range of material of interest—in the overlap between the
near and far—intended for a learning public. It fed human interest. Cave developed
an extensive distribution system for *The Gentleman's Magazine* considerably as smart
business. It was read and discussed across the entire Anglophone world. The false letter by Locke is reprinted in *The Gentleman's Magazine, and Historical Chronicle*, 23
(1753).

201 Brooks, *American Lazarus*, 125.

202 This was discussed earlier in Chapter 4 in describing the Annual Communication of
the Grand Lodge of Pennsylvania. St. John the Evangelist was the sign of the winter
solstice and St. John the Baptist for the summer solstice

203 Ibid., 127.

African American and white communities in Boston to attend the public performance that he planned with his fellow lodge brothers.

The performers would need their audience and vice versa, and each required *objects d'art*—the working of works of art—and signs. The African-American freemasons engaged the prominent white freemasons to publish and distribute a commemorative edition of Marrant's sermon. Here is an important moment in the dramaturgical origins and spaces of the African-American public sphere, nevertheless set on an organic trajectory as something distinct from the white public sphere—the formation of multiple publics. The title and frontispiece of the edition emphasized Hall's involvement in the production.

It was entitled:

> "A Sermon Preached on the 24th Day of June 1789, Being the Festival of St. John the Baptist, at the request of the Right Worshipful Master Prince Hall and the Rest of the Brethren of the African Lodge of the Honorable Society of Free and Accepted Masons in Boston by the Reverend Brother Marrant, Chaplain." [204]

The sermon addressed itself to the difficulties of the formation of communal bonds. Marrant prioritized the shared consciousness of community. The oration and ceremony, a combinatory instrumental aesthetic-moral performance, were at the same time an intellectual critique of the status quo. It was a rhetoric of becoming in a problematic situation—a matter of inquiry (felt intelligence) and artful communication. The embodied aesthetic-moral performance and intellectual work captured the listener, and reader, first through the invocation of Anciency. This opened sacred, felt bonds of community (and the eternal return of mythos in human experience), then shifted thought and analysis to the realities of the present racist situation. The degeneracy belonged not to Creation, but to the fall, and those who lived above it could inherit not only ancient wisdom but also their original paradisiacal state. Marrant gave the ancient location (the qualitative place) of Paradise as the principal part of African Ethiopia.

To specify "African Ethiopia" is to anticipate and prevent

---

204 For full text, Joanna Brooks, and John Saillant, eds., *'Face Zion Forward': First Writers of the Black Atlantic, 1785-1798* (Boston: Northeastern University Press, 2002), 77-92.

the dissociation of North African biblical sites—like Ethiopia and Egypt—from the whole of the continent. This pan-Africanist gesture allowed Marrant to situate the African-Americans and African Lodge of Freemasons as the rightful heirs of Paradise and the chosen people of God.[205]

Marrant speaks in his sermon of gestures and signals mentioned in the Bible, of Benhadad and Ahab, leaders of warring Syrians and Israelites. In the story, somatic gestures or corporeal signs are mentioned, whereby the giver of the sign was moving toward rescue and freedom from captivity. Marrant affirmed in his sermon that these were ancient masons communicating with each other.[206] It was a practice of the embodied and ritualized transmission of information and identity going back to pre-literate societies; in this case, pointing back to guild masonry, and well before biblical times.

The practice of secret hand signs and gestures goes back outside of freemasonry; for example, it was present in the guilds and in all-male Roman Mithraism, and far more broadly in anthropological time and space.[207] It opens the question once again of the pluralist and imagined roots of freemasonry (a frequent Jesuit and Catholic critique of freemasonry is its syncretism). The Catholic Church asks where freemasonry leads and what are its pretended origins.

Marrant's hermeneutic recounting of the actions described in the surviving texts of the Bible concerning signs and gestures portends something else. On February 27, 1788, Hall and 22 lodge members petitioned the Massachusetts legislature on behalf of three free blacks kidnapped from Boston and taken to the West Indies for sale. The three African American were lured on board a ship with the promise of work, and then seized. Such incidents were common occurrences. On the day the petition was filed, the Massachusetts legislature passed "An Act to prevent the Slave-Trade, and for granting Relief to the Families of such unhappy persons as may be kidnapped or decoyed away from the Commonwealth."[208]

---

205 Brooks, *American Lazarus*, 129.

206 Ibid., 132.

207 The origin of the modern handshake, an index and proprioceptive action, is perhaps with the ancient Brotherhood of warriors, the Mithraic cult in the Roman Army.

208 Ibid., 132.

Joanna Brooks mentions a letter that recounts the action story of the eventual return and regained freedom of the three.[209] The letter written by Jeremy Belknap, on April 18, 1788, details the negotiated liberation. One of the three-kidnap victims was:

> ... a Freemason. The merchant to whom they were offered was of this fraternity. They soon became acquainted. The Negro told his story. They were carried before the Governor, with the shipmaster and the supercargo.[210]

Brooks comments:

> The key to the captives' release was their ability to engage the attention of their would-be traders and "tell their story." [It was a dramatic rehearsal indeed of possibilities.] The kidnapped black Freemason probably used special Masonic distress signals to engage the attention of his captor. Perhaps fraternal duty obliged the slave merchant, also a Freemason, to respond to the gestures of the captive, or perhaps his initial inquiry was motivated only by curiosity. Nonetheless, the "signs and tokens" of Freemasonry were powerful enough to open a discursive space which, after significant political persuasion, became an escape route. Signs and tokens demonstrated both the global character of Masonic fellowship and its anciency as well. In these gestures the ritual core of Masonic affiliation perpetuated itself through time and space.[211]

"Signs and tokens" mentioned in this quotation were (and remain) manual, lingual, and somatic gestures, acts of communication that demonstrate one's affiliation and rank within freemasonry. Only those individuals who could perform these gestures in the correct manner would be admitted into a regular lodge meeting. It was also the case that signs and tokens permitted freemasons who were traveling abroad to reliably identify each other or, in other cases, to oblige fraternal bystanders to deliver aid.

---

209 Loc. cit.

210 Loc. cit.; Harry Davis, "Documents Relating to Negro Masonry in America," *Journal of Negro History* 21/4 (1936): 430.

211 Brooks, 132.

Freemasons, years before this story, already viewed Solomon's Temple as the pinnacle of achievement in geometric proportion and symbolism, and as creating an aesthetic-moral sense of an ideal structure as a metaphor of wisdom. Freemasons thought to pattern their own lodges after its design, thinking that it held an ancient lost but also universal wisdom. As indicated earlier, Isaac Newton (not a freemason), and his friend the antiquarian, freemason, member of the Royal Society, William Stukeley, were among those who believed this about Solomon's Temple. Marrant, as his sermon proceeds, uses the occasion to describe the men of different nations and colors that worked together on the Temple, bound to each other in fraternal accord, love, and friendship. Even the completion of the edifice of the Temple of King Solomon and the geographic dispersion of the workers across the entire globe (a march of the ages across space and territory) did not diminish their loyalty to one another, and that meant relations between African American and white freemasons in America. Marrant asserted that those who refuse their brothers violate the fundamental principles of the order. "The Freemasons of history stands with the African Lodge," Marrant firmly claimed. He also stated, "The prejudicial views of their contemporaries are an unstudied, unnatural and temporary aberration."[212]

African-American freemasonry was a significant discursive resource, a hybrid oral and written tradition, both in its private ritualistic action and performance in the wider black community. Different but transactional and complementary logics of communication occurred in the delivering of sermons and conducting funerals at first in Boston, Philadelphia, Portland, Rhode Island, and ultimately in the (public) laying of cornerstones in some African communities. There was a geographically visible (not yet mapped) movement across American landscapes in laying cornerstones for African-American churches in segregated parts of rural and urban communities, in both the geographically expanding north and south.

In their public sermons and orations, and within the dramaturgical spaces of lodges they chartered, Hall and Marrant:

> ... institutionalized a crucial lexicon of gestures, keywords, phrases, and concepts, a lexicon revised and reinvigorated with each succeeding generation. They fash-

---

212 Loc. cit.

ioned from mystical, and Masonic texts an *unnatural* history, a counter narrative to eighteenth-century empiricisms and "natural histories" that classified Africa as a cipher, perpetually primitive and unintelligible. They redrew a veil of blackness around themselves and counted all who stood within it as participants in the unfolding of a mystery, a common consciousness and a culture.[213]

In this environment, freemasons and other secret societies that were already inclined to altruism and civic-mindedness moved to shape public perceptions as a way to boost their work as learned societies and as clubs of conviviality and innocence against suspicions of heresy or sedition. The black freemasons in Boston knew that their every move as a group and as individuals was under scrutiny by blacks and whites as they appeared on the public stage as freemasons.

What was freemasonry? What did it mean? What were the values visible and felt in the performance? These were among the questions on people's minds in both African-American and white communities. Public orations or ritual processions by African-American freemasons had to be distinguished in their presentation, with integral sign systems, and eloquent in their performance. There was a felt need to portray the proud reception of ancient tradition (including from biblical and African sources), while the moral imagination of African American culture was firmly situated in the present difficult situation with eyes to the future. At the same time there was an endless effort outside of slavery to demean the African persona as something beneath the fineness, development and style of white gentlemen and gentlewoman.[214]

Hall and Marrant worked in present terms to develop an admixture of counter- or non-Enlightenment sources, a history and narrative that re-established African-American subjectivity within a metaphorical and real place of self-development in Boston, namely African Lodge. This ritual construction within the revolutionary North End of Boston was transmitted orally and via print to others who became freemasons, such as Allen and Jones in Philadelphia. African-American freemasons carried the dou-

---

213 Brooks, *American Lazarus*, 150.

214 Winthrop D. Jordan, *White Over Black: American Attitudes Toward the Negro, 1550-1812* (Chapel Hill: University of North Carolina Press, 1968), 130.

ble weight that in the moral imagination of the white American public, being black, and being a freemason, might be interpreted as combining to mean rebellion and uprising among slaves and freed blacks.

African Lodge created a correlated subjectivity/place that rejected, yet engaged, America's putatively democratic public sphere. Kevin Hetherington, drawing on the terminology of Michel Foucault, calls this accounting of the potentiality of the masonic lodge (for example, by African American s) a "heterotopia" and moral ordering.

> In seeking a response to fears of social chaos and the opportunities of civil society men chose to come together in lodges to which they gave symbolic and moral significance. In joining together they formed a fraternity that through its emotive content helped to create a new type of individual identity, embedded in the idea of a strong and trustworthy social context. The alternative ordering established by freemasonry was to be found in the idea of the lodge and its associations with fraternity and moral order on the one hand and with the issue of individual freedom on the other. The space of the lodges was significant within this process .... It was a space that had significant symbolic properties, which had to be learned by members of the order once they had been initiated through the various grades. The architectural features and symbols of the lodge expressed in its layout and its architecture provided freemasons with a semiotic basis for their moral education.[215]

By the close of the first third of the 19th century, a distinct African-American public sphere using an African-American press (including newspapers) began ever so slightly to shape itself. However, even before this development, the African Lodge and the private and public performances of its members established places of gathering and resistance. Some orations were printed as small pamphlets and could be read privately, neworked or performed in public. The rhetoric and pedagogy of African Lodge can be summarized in referencing three orations that are published in full in *Face*

---

215 Kevin Heatherington, *The Badlands of Modernity: Heterotopia and Social Ordering* (London: Routledge, 1997), 97-98.

Zion forward in discussing the first writers of the Black Atlantic. These were a sermon by Marrant and two charges by Hall.[216]

The triad of orations, as such, makes three interrelated points on context and substance. First, the orations represent how the worlds of print reinforced performance and how cultural performance reinforced print. Second, the orations emphasize the notion of freemasonry as an institution of learning by Americans in the 18th century. Freemasonry was methodically engaged by African Americans as an exceptional opportunity to participate in learning, social aesthetics, moral solidarity, and social advancement at a time and place when there were almost no institutions of education and association for African Americans. Third, the orations show forth the trope and metaphor of building as something perhaps organic in the integral moral-aesthetics and sensorimotor experience of learning.

Exactly to the point, Brooks and Saillant state:

> These three speeches were designed to provide lodge members a systematic education, using the architectural tropes of Freemasonry, a "foundation" laid by Marrant and two "pillars" of "superstructure" erected by Hall— for advancement within Freemasonry. These were published by special arrangement so that lodge members not in attendance at the ceremonial feast days in Boston, including members in Philadelphia and Providence, Rhode Island, would have access to these valuable lessons.[217] [transmission, JS]

She goes on to say:

> The modernity characteristic of the Black Atlantic appears in all three speeches, which criticize the slave trade, slaver, and racism and posit a counter cultural legacy for

---

216 These orations/and subsequent printed texts were: John Marrant, *A sermon preached on the 24th of June 1789, being the festival of St. John the Baptist, at the request of the Right Worshipful the Grand Master Prince Hall, and the rest of the brethren of African Lodge of the Honorable Society of Free and Accepted Masons in Boston* (Boston, 1789); Prince Hall, *A charge delivered to the African Lodge on the 25th of June* (Boston, 1792); Hall, *A Charge Delivered to the African Lodge, June 24, 1797, at Menotomy.* (Cambridge, 1797); See also Brook and Saillant, *'Face Zion Forward'*, 77-92, 178-190, 191-198.

217 Brooks & Saillant, 29.

American blacks as heirs of Africa. Both Marrant and Hall encouraged African Lodge members to know themselves as black people.

Adapting the Masonic lore celebrating the builders of Ancient Egypt, they taught that Africa—not Europe—had been since the world's beginnings the center of human advancement. Marrant pointed out that the Bible and Biblical commentators located the Garden of Eden, or "Paradise," as bordering on Egypt, which is the principal part of African Ethiopia ... by implication Africa—not Europe—was a land chosen by God as the scene of Biblical history. The slave trade as well as anti-Black racism was, then, an assault against a holy land and holy people.[218] [Notice the ubiquitous emphasis on geographic not simply metaphorical place, among a displaced people, JS]

Marrant and Hall go on to talk about how blacks deserved the freedom to love and that freemasonry provided a universal opportunity for equality, matters of the heart, community, and fraternity. Ancient masons had enjoyed free communication with each other over the entire terrestrial globe. Everywhere masons could identify themselves in what can be termed as bio performance semiotics. Dewey stated, *"Signs and symbols, language, are the means of communication by which a fraternally shared experience is sustained and nourished."* [219] Optimally, the community can fashion a home and place to live—the formation of a public community—while giving communication vitality and depth in face-to-face communication as well movement across space in transmission. Human interest potentially integrates all forms of communication in a situation, or holistic experience including within the overlapping spaces of ritual and transmission of home and movement.

Marrant reminded his reader and audience that African American had fought in the War of Independence, remained loyal through Shay's Rebellion (with Prince Hall pledging his allegiance to fellow freemason Washington). However, he also reminded his audience of the ongoing

---

218 Ibid., 29-30.

219 Dewey, *Public and Its Problems*, 218.

revolution in St. Domingue (now Haiti) and the possibility that blacks could rise up to be free through force, if their rights were not forthcoming. Here, he affirms a key principle and aesthetic-moral imagination implicit in the Declaration of Independence. "If America was to be their physical home, then they could create spaces such as the African Lodge and the black church."[220] The individual and group aligned themselves organically with the aspirations and power of the declaring of the Declaration as a cultural sign and aesthetic field in motion. This use of the Declaration, consciously and unconsciously, occurred repeatedly in the full course and contingencies of subsequent American history among the subaltern—or counter-publics—down to the present day in a far greater number of times than perhaps imagined.

B. THE EXPERIENCE OF FIRST NATIONS IN THE OHIO

Sandra Gustafson argues in the early American crucible of cultures that orations and speeches were situated in the borderlands and places between Europeans, Native Americans, and African Americans. The orations and speeches were complex projections of power, image, and authenticity.[221] Gustafson explores the deliberations and performance semiotics among a range of North American sub-populations—including First Nations—how orators employed the shifting symbolism of speech, text, body, and environment to imbue their voices with power and to act. The spoken word could reinforce or strongly challenge text-based claims of authority, and it often did in a diverse set of embodied problematic situations—what Nathan Crick calls rhetorical situations.[222]

Joy Porter in her *Native American Freemasonry: Associationalism and Performance in America* examines the significant role of freemasonry in the history of First Nations since the colonial era.[223] She shows, among much else, correspondences between the traditions of freemasonry and

---

220 Brooks & Saillant, 31.

221 Sandra Gustafson, *Imagining Deliberative Democracy in the Early-American Republic* (Chicago: University of Chicago Press, 2011); Gustafson, *Eloquence is Power: Oratory and Performance in Early America* (Chapel Hill: University of North Carolina Press, 2011).

222 Nathan Crick, *Democracy and Rhetoric: John Dewey on the Arts of Becoming* (Columbia: University of South Carolina Press, 2010), 41-43.

223 Joy Porter, *Native American Freemasonry: Associationalism and Performance in America* (Lincoln: University of Nebraska Press, 2011).

First Nation ritual traditions concerning the spoken word and geographic place and space. The similarities may be partial explanation for the reason that freemasonry was taken up by so many First Nation men over time.

Regarding place and space Porter states:

> Much has been written about the reverences for certain numbers and directions within a number of Native American heritages and traditions, about how Indian community life, and with it Indian identity are intimately linked to and derive directly from space and place. The two are not directly comparable, but it is worth noting that Freemasonry also places great general and ritual significance on numbers, direction, and orientation and on places and spatial configuration. Place might not be "alive" in the same sense as in a number of Native traditions, but sacred power is located spatially for Masons, as opposed primarily temporally, as it is in key European and American traditions.[224]

From Porter's interesting geographic standpoint, many European and American cultural traditions give less attention to place and spatial transactions.

In the 18th and early 19th century, Thayendanegea (1742-1807) served as Principal Chief of the Six Nations, a Christian missionary of the Anglican Church, a British military officer during the American War of Independence, and an enthusiastic freemason (initiated by British military and civil forces in freemasonry) passing on the ritual heritage to his son. He was born near what is now Akron, Ohio and given the Mohawk name of Thayendanegea, although the traditional homelands of his tribe were in "the longhouse" of the Iroquois confederacy that moved nearly the length of what is now New York. Thayendanegea has been translated to mean, "He sets or places together two bets."

It was by the depth of tribal tradition that he inherited the status of Mohawk Chief from his father. He was also a student of Latin and Greek under the tutelage of the future founding head of Dartmouth, Eleazar Wheelock, and he helped translate Mark's Gospel into Mohawk. The Reverend

---

224 Ibid., 141.

Eleazar Wheelock, a Congregational minister from Connecticut, founded Dartmouth College in 1769. In an earlier time, he had established Moor's Charity School in Lebanon, Connecticut, which had a special focus on the education of Native Americans (First Nations). In seeking to expand his school into a college, Wheelock relocated his educational enterprise to Hanover, in the Royal Province of New Hampshire. Samson Occom, a Mohegan Indian and one of Wheelock's first students, was instrumental in raising substantial funds for the College, while touring and lecturing on the Christian gospel in England. Wheelock's sons became a prominent freemason.

Thayendanegea, or Chief Joseph Brant, valued each of his identities. Jessica Harland-Jacobs mentioned his regard for the fraternity and goes on to say "Freemasonry, in the eighteenth as well as the nineteenth century, could ... work to the advantage of British colonial governors in their search for collaborators." [225] In this period, freemasonry could include not only prominent indigenous collaborators around the globe, such as Chief Brant, but also freed African American slaves such as Prince Hall. Harland-Jacobs made the general point that freemasonry always was a tension of inclusion and exclusion. This is the same binary coding (deep habits) referenced earlier in this chapter in discussing narrative solidarities with aspirations and simultaneous tensions of public formation of a demos. Freemasonry was an instrument of empire in British hands but, in the process of inviting indigenous peoples into freemasonry many indigenous men around the world (and after a period some women), took up the practice of freemasonry in an emancipating sense.

In 1792 and 1793, important negotiations between the new United States and Native- American populations were underway in the rich hunting ground and agricultural lands between the Ohio River and Lake Michigan. Diplomatic journeys and negotiations were proceeding apace among the First Nations in communication with each other over considerable distances (an ancient forest diplomacy with its own forms of ritual and transmission, home and movement), and these largely concerned discussions with the United Sachems, the leaders of the United States. The dated experiences are chosen here as temporal counterparts to Washington, the freemasons, and company, laying the cornerstone for the Capitol

225 Jessica Harland-Jacobs, *Builders of Empire: Freemasons and British Imperialism, 1717-1927* (Chapel Hill: University of North Carolina Press, 2007), 80.

building in 1793, which is addressed in the next chapter, and Clinton, giving his oration at Holland Lodge in 1793 in New York on what he deemed the mutual ramifications of ritual performance and print culture in the birthing of a republic and an informed and egalitarian citizenry.

Clinton, for his part, was extremely well versed as a student of First Nation populations, and language, and knowledgeable and respectful of the Iroquois in New York. He was aware of the suffering as well as the aspirations and civilization heights of the confederation of the Iroquois nations. Clinton was not alone as a freemason or non-mason in this regard. On the other hand, freemasons as the wider population could be much more than devious as regarded First Nations, as shall be seen.

The evolving situation is simplified but accurately portrayed using the biographies of two Native American men working in the embodied oratory and habits/ritual performativity and transmission of ancient forest diplomacy, while recording their experiences in writing. Oratory and speech are juxtaposed in their lives with, and abutting, texts in deepening worlds of print. They were well aware of the printed text as a communication medium variously used. In other words, in this period they embodied the unity of what can be termed primary and secondary experience in their lives, or ritual and transmission functions of communication.[226] For the First Nations studies in this section, qualitative thought about place and community and the text, were mutually interdependent. There is a deep contrast between the written text in its feel and use compared to the depth and place making of the spoken word and focused power of ritual life of First Nations in aural/oral cultures. To arrive at this point, I first highlight prominent First Nation leaders who were on the cusp of the oral/aural traditions and the worlds of print.

First, there was Hendrick Aupaumut and his *Narrative of an Embassy to the Western Indians* (1792) and, second, Chief Joseph Brant's *Journal of the Proceedings at the General Council Held at the Foot of the Rapids of the Miamis* (1793), "These stand as the most comprehensive indigenous ac-

---

226 Dewey the American philosopher and pedagogue used the terms primary and secondary experience to lay down in scholarly studies what James Carey after reading Dewey, called "ritual" and "transmission." The latter has become a common binary term since then in communication studies. The same binary is termed "home" and "movement" by David Hansen, mentioned earlier. Human interest is situated in the overlap between "home" and "movement" or local place and more distant space in ritual and transmission embodied semiotics of communication.

counts in print of the Councils that took place in the Ohio Valley in 1792 and 1793 and they provide important counter-narratives to colonial versions of events that often misrepresent First Nations-US relations." [227]

In the promise and ambiguity of 1792, the First Nations from across the Ohio region gathered in a Great Council of Nations. Taking up a wampum belt in a powerful dramaturgical moment, Aupaumut (the representative of the new union) began his words to the assembled great council of sachems saying "we the sachems of the United States will now in one voice speak to you—we speak from our hearts—where there is a burden of sorrow" ... over the wars. The federal union of America, united as the fifteen sachems showed their putative sincerity to the First Nations "by sending their message of peace through Aupaumut ... who we trust will faithfully [deliver] to you ... the [good] dispositions of the United States."[228]

Aupaumut's larger strategic view was to use an orator's role to help fashion a (felt qualitative) place, a home, and many homes, localities, for people of the First Nations within the territories of the much younger American nation. In the cultures of First Nations, oratory was cast in embodied ritual and ceremonial form deeply felt. Aupaumut's view was that a strong native speaker could communicate in networks and across borders between First Nations and the new American nation just as his forefathers had done among the tribes in renowned forest diplomacy. His was the habituated tradition, and instrumental aesthetics of eloquence, the ethics of the spoken word, and biopsychic social skill. For Aupaumut, there was an intense struggle of agency as subject with an eye to the past, present, and future generations as shall be seen, and always an eye to the geographic environment at different scales. The living word and ritual artifact abutted the more abstract instrument of the text in the projection of power and the transmission of information.

Aupaumut was succeeding in his use of traditional ritual methods and powerful oratory across tribal cultures when things suddenly turned for the worse. Just after Aupaumut had presented the assembled sachems a wampum belt with 15 rows and 15 square marks in the middle expressing

---

227 Brooks, "Two Paths to Peace: Competing Visions of Native Space in the Old Northwest," in *The Boundaries Between Us; Natives and Newcomers Along the Frontiers of the Old Northwest Territory, 1750-1850*, ed. Daniel P. Barr (Kent: Kent State University Press, 2006) 100.

228 Gustafson, *Imagining Deliberative Democracy*, 262.

the 15 states of the new union of the United States, and after he completed his first round of spoken vital words, a representative arrived from Brant, the Mohawk sachem.

Initially, Aupaumut's sincere performance was received as "pure good Message" and the "life of all our Nations," however, Aupaumut's words were suddenly called into question by Brant's views, relayed through the memory and oratorical skill of a new messenger, Brant's own son, Ahyouwaighs (later to become a freemason). The orator arrived in the ritually constructed place to perform before the assembly. The camp clearing was situated with care and attention in along the impressive landscapes of the Ohio River.

Aupaumut stated:

> My friends I now tell you do not believe the message the Muheconneew brought to you; neither believe what he says, if you do you will be greatly deceived. I have myself seen Washington and seen his heart and bowels; and he declared that he claims from the mouth of the Miamie [This is a tributary feed into the Ohio in current southwest Ohio, JS] to the head of it—thence to the land of the Wabash River, and down the same to the mouth of it [The Wabash flows into the Ohio at the line marking the Illinois and Indiana boundaries JS]; and that he did take up dust and did declare that he would not restore so much dust to the Indians, but he is willing to have piece with the Indians. [229]

Matters then went back and forth, a deliberative and rhetorical scene, with the assembled sachems growing more cautious. The great Council of Nations disbanded in ritualistic form after close discussion and reflection in the great camp. The negotiations were planned to resume in the next year of 1793, the cycle of a season. The great forest diplomacy followed the cycles of the sun in day and year, and the movements of the moon and stars. There was inquiry using both natural signs in the land and sky and sober thought in integral experience and discourse.

Aupaumut returned to the assembled Council of Western Nations in 1793 as ambassador from the United States. Within the unfolding of the

---

229 Loc. cit.; 262.

dramaturgy of 1793, Aupaumut's rhetorical plans had turned to the 1789 United States Constitution. He was well aware of the manipulation toward First Nations that the white man had affected many times before through the traditions of weapons and text. He spoke eloquently of the United 15 Sachems and of his belief in the sincerity of the new government's words and commitment to the welfare "and learning" (Aupaumut's words) of all nations.

He informed the western Nations that since the United Sachems had achieved their liberty, the Americans now were beginning with new things. They have new laws of their own and by these laws, the tribes cannot be deceived as usual. "The United Sachems will not speak wrong." "Whatever they promise to Indians they will perform."[230] The word was a moral and powerful act. The Indians could have their ancient liberty upon the land said Aupaumut and the United States their newly discovered liberty. Each of the First Nations respected what they conceptualized as the ancient freedom of their ancestors, as well as the assembly of the great Councils of their nations. In the end, the emerging American nation-state would keep no promise given to the First Nations, and there would be great violence in manifold ways. The story of Aupaumut shows performativity and citationality of speech, text, ritual, and performance is limited within material and cultural constraints (or across cultures); yet, struggle is morally necessary in human experience and to be desired.

Returning to the work of the scholar Porter, she states:

> Another Masonic-Indian correspondence [as with place and space discussed above]... is the veneration both sets of cultures share for language. Masons call the rituals of identification and initiation the "Mason Word," connecting their activity to the almost magical qualities ascribed to God's word in John's gospel and in the Apocrypha, the Wisdom of Solomon. Similarly in many Indian traditions language has transformative spiritual power, as do symbol and thought itself.[231]

Aupaumut and Thayendanegea ended their days respectively in Wisconsin and Canada as they, their families, and communities, were relentlessly

---

230 Ibid., 261.
231 Porter, 141.

pushed westward. They were, however, in correspondence with each other using the term brother in their communicative exchange and knowing that each had meant well in their respective striving. Aupaumut and Thayendanegea believed they had done the best they could in struggle. Thayendanegea's son moved to Canada after the defeat of the British armies and became the master of a masonic lodge in British territory.

C. WOMEN IN AMERICAN CIVIL SOCIETY AT THE FOUNDING

Hannah Mather Cocker was born in Boston in 1752, lived there throughout her life, and died nearby in 1829. Her grandfather was the Puritan Minister Cotton Matter of New England and wider fame. She was home educated in literature, history, and languages, which was very rare in her time. Cotton Mather, who believed in the education of women, not only men, taught his daughters and the tradition was passed through the family. The disciplined and transmitted habits of education in her young years were rich in budding values and action. Hannah reached young adulthood in the American War of Independence. She was a proto-feminist, patriot, educator, and mother of 10 children, and a founding mother of American civil society.[232] (Note: the words feminism and feminist did not develop until the end of the 19th century, when the terms first appeared in France. Mather was also the founding master of St. Anne's lodge of freemasons in Boston, Massachusetts.)

Crocker's literary career began after the death of her husband in 1797. The husband was a Colonel in the Continental Army and a member of the Society of Cincinnati. However, prior to her literary efforts, perhaps during or even before the Revolution, while still in her 20s, Crocker founded a private society devoted to female education in Boston. This was St. Anne's lodge. With considerable courage, she modeled the lodge, a bluestocking society, in ways not yet well understood and with some of its most significant history perhaps lost forever. All-male masonic lodges in Boston and America, while espousing egalitarian ideals, deemed it entirely appropriate to exclude women from their solidarity. Crocker, however, was likely working with the assistance of a few, if not more than a few, American masons.[233]

---

232 Cokie Roberts, *Founding Mothers: The Women Who Raised Our Nation* (New York: William Morrow, 2004).

233 Crocker, Porset, Révauger, and Slifko, *The Masonic World of Enlightenment: Europe-*

St. Anne's lodge may have been suppressed before too many years by all male lodges of freemasonry, or ceased for other reasons, but not before she had gained the considerable respect of at least some prominent leaders in freemasonry and accomplished something of worth in pedagogy. When the first poem by Hannah Crocker appeared in a local newspaper, it was accompanied by a letter of support from a prominent freemason and doctor in the Boston community. Her contact with prominent figures in freemasonry was far more extensive.

One illustration came to a head in 1775, on the eve of war. In 1775, with the British occupying Boston and developing a war footing with the Americans, at the young age of 23, Crocker smuggled secret dispatches hidden in her bosom (either in an established or ad hoc intelligence network) beneath her shirt and garments out of Boston and through the British defensive perimeter of the British occupation of Boston. The dispatches she carried were headed for Warren. Warren was of singular importance in the Anglo-American fighting before the occupation or siege. The day after Crocker made it through the lines to Warren; he was killed at Bunker's Hill. She comments in her *Reminiscences* that Warren "her affectionate friend" told her she would see him the following day "as he promised he would bring her parent to see her in that morn." She worked throughout the day of Warren's death and in days afterward with the dead and wounded.

She maintained connections with proto-feminists in England and perhaps France. This is another possible source for her likely initiation into freemasonry. There may have been freemasons in the networks she had across the Atlantic. The precise source of the rituals she and her lodge used in their masonic work and the support she received at local scales has not been determined. Did they originate in lodges or individuals in France, England, or perhaps more likely in Massachusetts in some admixture or awareness of France or England?

Crocker had designed St. Anne's lodge, an all-women lodge, as a literary society in which women could read serious works of literature, philosophy, antiquarianism, "comparative religion" (before there was a discipline of comparative religion), the new science, and languages. Studies were convened in the solidarity and place of ritual performance, because as she

---

American and Colonies, A Prosopographic Dictionary, 3 vols. (Paris: Champion, 2013), 1: 908-916.

said "the aspiring female mind could no longer bear a cramp to genius."[234] She advocated in her *Letters on Freemasonry* that the establishment of female literary societies was necessary because they had the potential to "promote Science and Literature to enlarge the mind." Her use of the rhetorical device of the literary society may have been a way to deflect from the fact, and ill will of likely many male masons, that she had established a lodge of freemasonry.

Her lodge points to a fundamental understanding of freemasonry in this period, as has been seen in taking up the topic of African Lodge No. 1. Freemasonry (as an ideal type in early America) was imagined as an institution of ancient and modern learning, as well as solidarity, and a place of virtue, caring, and charity. It worked in a tension strung between processes of inclusion and exclusion no less home and movement. This was before the larger rise of 19th century institutions of education in America, and expanded development of vehicles of education for women. Crocker acknowledged in her *Letters on Freemasonry*, in all events, "that it will be thought by many, a bold attempt for a female to even dare enter on the subject at all."[235] Dorothy Ann Lipson, commenting on Crocker's *Letters on Freemasonry*, states women "seem to have reacted negatively to Masonry within the limits posed by [their domestic] roles. Mrs. Hannah Crocker's pamphlet on Masonry in 1815 suggests the complexity of women's responses."[236]

Common denominators existed between Crocker's freemasonry, African-American freemasonry in Boston in this period, and the aspirations of individuals among the First Nations, such as Aupaumut. There existed an attraction and prizing of self-improvement, and learning, a strong sense of received tradition, an instinct toward social ordering in the present and raising up of the next generation.

In both St. Ann's lodge and in lodges of African American freemasons, there were emphases on education as the means to emancipation, self-invention, and upward social mobility. This could be termed an instrumental aesthetics of indefinite perfectibility or progress from one consum-

234 Hannah M. Crocker, *A Series of Letters on Freemasonry* (Boston: Eliot, 1815), 8.

235 Ibid., 9-10.

236 Dorothy A. Lipson, *Freemasonry in Federalist Connecticut* (Princeton: Princeton University Press, 1977), 197.

mation to the next (involving interrelated processes of communication, learning and association). It is no coincidence that Prince Hall in Africa lodge launched the first public school for black children in Boston and the first school for adult literacy. There was a strong focus on the value of benevolent associations in a republic in pursuit of secular, educational, and spiritual goals. Freemasonry at its enlightenment core, like wider civil society in an ideal typical sense, concerned new forms of sociability, care, and learning.[237] There was also the presence of a non-dogmatic spirituality or what could be termed a civil religion in another inflection.

Common among St. Ann's lodge, African American freemasonry, and mainstream symbolic lodge freemasonry in post-revolutionary America, were the very strong appeals to the mythopoeic or sacred wonder of "Anciency," that which is imagined as distant in times long ago and places far away. Crocker put Anciency to use in her rhetorical defense of the real rights of women. In ancient Egypt, she believed she had discerned a greater equality between the sexes. In a true practice of Christianity, there could be a renewed experience of the position of women in relationship with man as existed before.

Crocker had a deep and abiding faith in Christianity and its capacity to strengthen the possibility of women's emancipation. After the fall in the Garden of Eden, men and women were on unequal terms and man repressed women. With the advent of Christ, however, and his mother Mary, once again man and woman were on an equal basis. Nevertheless, given man's repressive attitude toward women, which made educational opportunities profoundly unequal, women were in a difficult situation. The situation could be corrected through educational excellence and equal opportunity, all the while accounting for biological differences in the sexes. Her deeply held Christian faith was complementary to her rhetorical and written defense of the universal rights of women and their important place in society. Significantly, Crocker was a mother of 10 and she would have had ideas about these experiences.

A central emphasis in Crocker's rhetorical subtleties and written appeals concerning freemasonry was that education and benevolent associations, public formations, were of critical importance in a republican society.

---

237 These aspects of human experience were termed by male Anglo-American freemasons in their own idiom as the trinity of brotherly love, relief, and truth.

This articulation was made decades in advance of that by Tocqueville on the significance of civic associations and local community in the American democratic experience and formation and health of the state. At the same time, Crocker became an ardent federalist and saw great value in the effort toward building a union of states. The union was a monumental opportunity for an open and egalitarian society, which valued women such as Washington's wife and Franklin's childhood teacher, a woman. Crocker was arguing that society and education in the republic primarily set the bounds within which women's capacities were developed and practiced, which had occurred in all "postlapsarian" cultures (after the Garden of Eden). Crocker argued in her *Observations* that education and learning in the republic heralded the possibility of emancipation. In one sense, hers was a sophisticated search of the freemason for the "lost word" an original spoken language, felt intelligence, and means of inquiry, communication, and possibilities for association.

Crocker became, in adaptive response to the growing gendering constraints of the post-war period and place in which she lived, a skilled, subtle embodied rhetorician, and as a writer, an advocate of women's rights, duties, and education. There was a cultural backlash after the war against all things perceived radical across the United States. America, curiously, was at its most cosmopolitan in the war. Mather's stance was a practical encounter with the problems and possibilities in which she was situated in cultural and material landscapes. It was an imaginative response, cognitive mapping, democratic place making, and social aesthetics.[238]

Between 1800 and 1820, Mather evolved into the leading American political theorist on the standing of women in society and in debates regarding the rights and duties of women.[239] Her interests were not just with political theory as human rights, if this is narrowed to a specific list as in the American Bill of Rights, but also with the responsibilities of being human in difficult even tortured situations. At the American founding, she held a productive creative tension in her political studies and social aesthetics, a unified aesthetic-moral and intellectual position, of what today are presumably "thought opposing" liberal and communitarian views in political theory. She held no binary, set in an ivory tower, on this matter of political

238 Jacob Kosnoski, *John Dewey and the Habits of Ethical Life: The Aesthetics of Political Organizing in a Liquid World* (Lanham: Lexington Books, 2010).

239 Botting and Houser, 265.

understanding, but regarded the individual and group as complementary in a living regional Boston and outlying cities, state, and nation.

D. SUMMARY AND CONCLUSIONS

In this chapter I have focused on democratic conflict, efforts at solidarity and public formation by the subaltern, or what can be termed the formation of counter publics in the masonic association or lodges of African Americans, women and the Ohio camp of First Nations. The chapter touched on the romantic narrative of progress in early American expansion, the ideal of learning and valuing of equal access to education, and First Nation love of the inherited lands given to their care.

The freemason's belief in the need to recover ancient lost wisdom was for the First Nations a belief in an ancient freedom and way of life. The mythos of lost wisdom, of an earlier imagined sacred experience of ancestors cut across race, ethnicity, class, and gender. There was a social aesthetics of action and struggle in thoroughly unjust situations, an awareness of the power of words and text in shaping the present, and at the same time a valuing of traditions and an imagination of future possibilities.

Beneath the narrative of progress in the opening of American civil society, there was a deep structure and coding of self and other, inclusion and exclusion, sacred and profane, pure and impure. The binary of sacred and profane in human experience is an indicator of the presence of the eternal return of mythos in the human imagination. This is the magic of mythos as fact not fiction. Freemasonry embodies the tension of the mythos of Anciency and the logos of heart and head.

Speech and text could combine in action. Alternatively, speech could be a complex projection of power, challenging text-based claims of authority as worked in the oratory and ancient forest diplomacy of First Nations against the printed word of the white man. The American crucible of cultures in this time and place of contact and conflict involved multiple traditions of sacred, diplomatic, and political speech. The living word and community in "place" was supplemented in locale and across networks of space via the text which became increasingly English based.

CHAPTER 6

THE LAYING OF THE CORNERSTONE CEREMONIES AT THE AMERICAN FOUNDING

The cornerstone ceremonies in Washington DC demonstrate how freemasonry was used as a means of organizing civic, family, and political life *before* the rise of political parties in early America through the fraternity's inherent display of ritual, symbol and technique. The cornerstone ceremonies have been stable as an aesthetic form in masonic tradition in America since the 1790s. An initial cornerstone ceremony at Jones Point, land jutting into the Potomac, was the ritualized point of origin for the federal district. The federal district commenced as a series of abstract mathematical surveys (and related ritual ceremonies), the thrust of which was mandated in the printed Constitution culminating in the form of a ten-square mile survey of intended federal space, planned to become the District of Columbia. Subsequent related cornerstone ceremonies and surveying occurred at the President's House and later, the United States Capitol. There were other ceremonies not covered in this chapter. The cornerstones were chiseled and performed out of the artisan's habits and inherited customs that helped create the new landscape of the emerging republic. Each ceremony was reported on by John Dunlap in his Philadelphia paper with strategic intent in advancing freemasonry and nation-building now in peacetime after the war.

A. THE PUBLIC CEREMONIES OF "LAYING OF THE CORNERSTONE" IN AMERICA WAS A CULTURAL INHERITANCE, AN ACTION SPACE IN THE PRESENT, AND FORWARD LEANING

We help the poor in time of need,
The naked clothe, the hungry feed,
'Tis our foundation stone;
We build upon the noblest plan;
For friendship rivets man to man,
And makes us all as one.

—William Preston, "Song One," *Illustrations of Masonry*, 1775

Surviving accounts of the cornerstone ceremony from Scotland and England, indicated a lack of firmly set form of the rituals for most of the 18th century. The little evidence surviving from 18th century Scotland and England include three common elements, namely, the striking of the cornerstone stone with a punctuated number of times, hierarchy, and the presence of a male figure to lead the ritual performance. It appears the standard was three knocks. Number in this felt instance invokes mythos.

Pythagoras and Euclid offered a mathematics moving beyond the subjective representative capacity of mythos and language alone to mathematical science. Pythagoras is of great moment in masonic lore and considered a freemason in 18th century documents and earlier surviving masonic so called Gothic constitutions. In addition, Euclid is honored as a founding freemason. These valuations of Pythagoras and Euclid as ancient honored lineal ancestors in freemasonry, taking their rise in medieval operative freemasonry, are fictions. However, they are telling in their own way of the psychological and mythopoeic constitution and of integral qualitative thought and abstract geometry evident in lodge space and the dramaturgy of freemasonry, for example, in cornerstone ceremonies.

By the 1772 publication of William Preston's *Illustrations of Masonry*, there was an official version of the cornerstone ritual performance taking shape and it was situated in no small part in the abstract mathematical surveying of urban planners in places like Edinburgh. The text helped maintain a continuity of aesthetic form (an aesthetic field) through the artist, art object, and the changing performers of the art object and different audiences over time.[240] Preston's work was compiled in part from research on England and Scotland and in letters across diverse geographies. A quarter century later, in 1797, in Albany, New York, Thomas Smith Webb produced *The Freemasons Monitor*, a founding landmark in American freemasonry, openly stating his debt to Preston.[241]

---

240 Arnold Berleant saw art as transactional process, which he called an "aesthetic field" which changes through time and space. The processes of the aesthetic field involves the transactions of (i) the original artist, (ii) the art object, (iii) new performers of the art object [new symphonies playing Beethoven, or working masons laying the cornerstone] and (iv) constantly new active audiences. What can be called Berleant's "process aesthetics" was referenced in Chapter 2. Berleant was articulating and building on Dewey's process or transactional aesthetics.

241 Thomas S. Webb, *The Freemasons Monitor, or, Illustrations of Masonry* (New York: Southwick and Crocker, 1802).

Brent Morris wrote:

> It is instructive to compare the cornerstone ceremonies
> of Preston in 1772 with those of Webb in 1797. Both are
> quite simple, though evolved beyond [earlier 18th centu-
> ry descriptions]. Parallel versions of Preston and Webb
> from the 1775 edition of Preston and the 1816 edition
> of Webb ... [show] that Preston limits attendance to the
> Grand Lodge [the English hierarchy of modern freema-
> sons] while Webb welcomes members of private Lodges.
> Webb's ritual shows the introduction of corn, wine and
> oil, the tests of trueness of the stone, and now the almost
> universal approbation from the Grand Master that the
> stone is "well formed, true, and trusty."[242]

Both Preston and Webb describe a voluntary collection for the workers.
Such generosity may be based, states Morris, on the description in Ezra
3:7 of the preparations for the second temple in Jerusalem:

> So they gave money to the masons and the carpenters,
> and food, and drink, and oil the Sidonians and the Tyrians
> to bring cedars from Lebanon to the sea, to Joppa, accord-
> ing to the grant that they had from Cyrus King of Persia.[243]

Ritual is often drawn from common experiences such as eating, birth,
death, harvesting, hunting, and in the current case, in the act and metaphor of building through the pounding, carving and chipping of stone.
The aesthetic form of the cornerstone ceremonies changed through time
in the modern Euro-American experience, yet some of the elements have
held stable. These include: a narrative akin to baptism or birth in place
making, the use of number, male performance, the display of wealth,
power, and rank, and an active audience.

B. Creation of the Federal District

The reflective "cooler" spaces of the geometric survey of Washington City
and the District of Columbia took their point of origin in felt, qualitative

---

242 Brent Morris, *Cornerstone of Freedom: A Masonic Tradition* (Washington, D.C.: The
Supreme Council, 1993), 138, 142.

243 Ezra 3:7, King James Bible, quoted op. cit.

mythopoeic time and space, with the "hot "affective ritual performances of the working of the cornerstone and cornerstone ceremonies. The initial foundational ritual performance of the American nation-state occurred first at Jones Point. The ceremony etched an embedded/emplaced sign on the landscape, a geo-semiotic, that anchored the city's square, diamond, or rhombus outline, as seen in Figure 7. The north-south axis of Washington very clearly cuts through the northern and southern angles of the rhombus rising out of Jones Point. At the same time, geometric, socio-cultural and celestial survey pinpointed the most opportune cultural and material spot for launching public ritual performance.

Early American founders studying ancient periods and places drew upon diverse traditions, moral-aesthetics of ritual and practices from Roman, Greek, and sometimes Egyptian culture. In this case, the north-south axis intersects a perpendicular east-west axis and echoes, intentionally or unintentionally, ancient Roman urban planning. These lines of intersection precipitate four imagined cardinal directions of space. This was a repetition with a difference reflecting the ritualistic and geometrized origins of a Roman city. Washington City, in no small part, was planned as "Rome reborn" on western shores.[244]

Masonic ritual, communicative action and symbolism valorize spatial referents. In the ritual performances of the freemasons, and their relevant texts, a language is developed in transaction with underlying spatial referents of the body in an environment, for example, the cardinal directions in the horizontal, an orientation of up and down, and an emphasis on the East as the place of the rising sun.

The felt, integral quality of masonic ritual performance and integral sign systems situated the federal space at the metaphorical heart of the new republican nation-state, a step up in geographic scale from the city-state of Athens. The federal space demonstrated an expanded moral imagination in which the modern demos could function beyond place and the smaller geographic scale of the ancient demos. The ritual founding of the national-space in the cornerstone ceremonies, in addition, was part of the larger ritual healing needed by the union after the war.

---

244 Eran Shelav, *Rome Reborn on Western Shores: Historical Imagination and the Creation of the American Republic* (Charlottesville: University of Virginia Press, 2009).

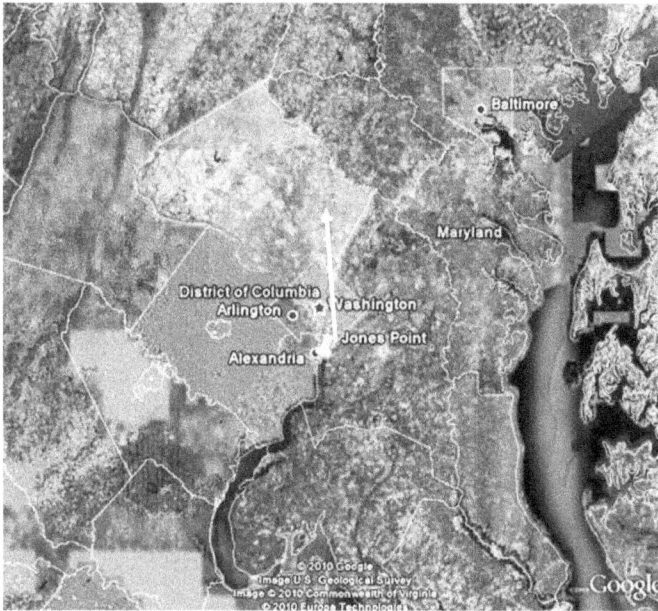

Figure 7. Jones Point at the southernmost point of the Federal District diamond. Jones Point is highlighted with a yellow pushpin. An axis (white arrow) runs through the southern tip of the diamond and the northern point in a perfect north/south alignment. Satellite photo, with borders, taken from Google Earth Pro (Access Date March 20, 2010).

Sir William Brewster's writing on the history of freemasonry in Scotland, published by the Secretary of the Scottish Grand Lodge, Alexander Lawrie, in 1804, gives descriptions of processions held by Scottish masons in the 18th century for the laying of foundation stones.[245] "The chief ceremonial expression of the urban development of Edinburgh from the 1760's was the large scale Masonic processions connected with the building and opening of such major new works as the Royal Exchange, various new bridges, new university buildings, and the National Monument on Carlton Hill."[246]

---

245 This book is ascribed to David Brewster, who wrote it at the request of Alexander Lawrie, who is often erroneously considered the author. Lawrie was the printer and publisher. See Brewster, *The History of Freemasonry: Drawn from Authentic Sources of Information with an Account of the Grand Lodge of Scotland* (Edinburgh: Alexander Lawrie and Company, 1804).

246 Prescott, 2.

An earlier masonic procession was the dedication at St. Martin-in-the Fields of a stone at St. Martin-in-the-Fields in 1722. Yet another early formal masonic ceremony was the laying of the foundation stone of the New Royal Infirmary of Edinburgh by the Earl of Cromarty, Grand Master of the Scottish Masons on August 2, 1738. David Brewster wrote a description of this last event 66 years later in 1804.

> When the company came to the ground, the Grand Master, and his Freemasons surrounded the plan of the foundation hand-in-hand [the performance was locative or place making] and the Grand Master-Mason, along with the press (representatives) of the Managers of the Royal Infirmary, having come to the east corner of the foundation where the stone was to be laid, place the same in its bed; and after the Right Honorable the Lord Provost had laid a medal under it each their turns strikes three strokes upon the stone with an iron mallet. Which was succeeded by three clarions of the trumpet, three huzzas, and three claps of the hands.[247]

The ceremony was known in America, perhaps through oral transmission of sojourning and migrating masons from England, Scotland, and Ireland as well as through print, such as with parts of the ceremony coming to America by way of Preston's *Book of Illustrations*. In 1797, Thomas Smith Webb published his landmark book *Freemason's Monitor or Illustrations of Masonry in America*. Webb relied heavily on Preston's 1772 *Book of Illustrations* for his thoughts on the cornerstone ceremony, as he also drew on *Jachin and Boaz* (both discussed in Chapter 2) from England concerning ritual matters in lodge. Ritual did not travel well in the 18th century without print.

The federal district was fashioned from gifts of land presented by Maryland and Virginia. The masons were given a leading part in the cultural, semiotic, and material making of the American capital. It was stipulated, after due deliberation, in Article 1, Section 8 of the printed *Constitution* that "Congress shall have power ... over such District, not exceeding ten miles square, as may, by cession of particular States, and the acceptance of the Congress become the seat of the government of the United States

---

247 David Flather, "The Foundation Stone," *Ars Quatour Coronoatum* 48, (1939): 222.

...." Then, in 1790, Congress designated Philadelphia as the temporary location of the capital and specified its permanent location to be located on the Potomac River, at a location to be selected by the President. President Washington, himself a surveyor, appointed three commissioners permitted by Congress to survey what he perceived as the wondrous Potomac, connecting the great inland with the sea. The surveyed land was to become the District of Columbia, the federal district.

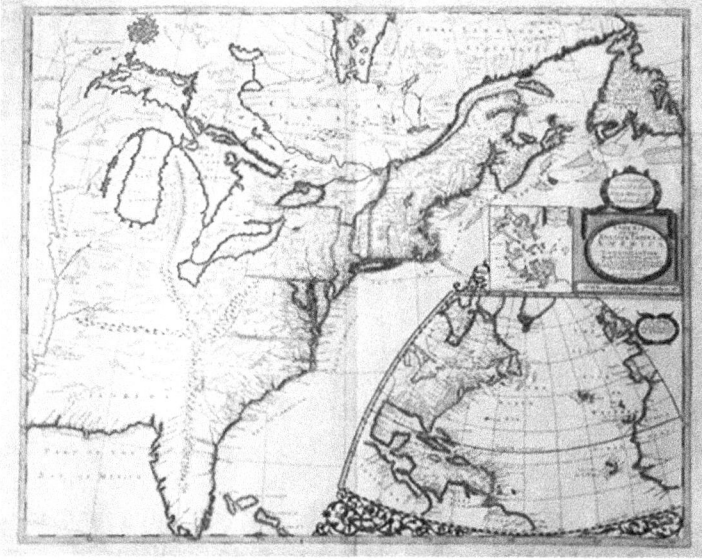

Figure 8. John Senex, *A New Map of the English Empire in America,* colored engraving, London: D. Brown, 1721 (Courtesy of the New York Public Library Digital Collections).

The movement of people into the continental interior was constant in the Euro-American imagination where rivers served as routes for these migrations. This theme is the basis of the strong magnification and framed centrality of the Potomac River in the map by Senex (Figure 8).[248] Washington embodied this geographic imagination and praxis throughout his life, beginning as a young British military officer and gatherer of intelligence and likely studying maps by Senex among others. Once inland to Pennsyl-

248 The central role of Senex in laying the foundations for the period of modern Grand Lodges as a civil society (not in this case as a mapping of Empire) was discussed in Chapter 1 in reviewing his role in printing and publishing the 1723 *Book of the Constitutions of the Free-Masons.*

Figure 9. Andrew Ellicot, "The Territory of Columbia," 1793, engraving. Jones Point is a small spit of land at the very bottom of the rhombus barely visible butting into the waters of the Potomac River from the left side. Above it and to the left is the compass rose pointing to the North and cardinal directions. This was Washington at its masculine birth. (Library of Congress image in the public domain).

vania, he would sometimes use pathways skirting the Monongahela River, or move on the Monongahela, flowing toward the great Ohio River.

Senex was busy drafting this map precisely in the same period as the forming of the Grand Lodge of London, between its first communication in 1717 and the printing and public presentation of its *Book of Constitutions* in 1723. In an ideal sense there is overlap yet difference between the state, civil society and the economy since the 17th and 18th centuries. As discussed in Chapter 2, Senex was of considerable importance in the founding of modern speculative freemasonry, although he may have left the fraternity by the end of his life, a telling action given the vitality and intelligence he poured into the fraternity at its founding moment.

The first task in establishing the mandated federal district was to locate the geographic position where a founding ceremony would be ritually enacted (similar to ancient Rome but different in ceremony) and from which the isomorphic lines of geometric survey were to radiate. The story published with dateline in Philadelphia by Dunlap in his *The American Daily Advertiser* on April 21, 1792 is informative. The reporting recounts Rev. James Muir's proclamation in the cornerstone ceremony of a new nation in an ethos and rhetoric of becoming anchored in mythopoeic space and Anciency. The exact ceremony does not survive. We know it, in part, from the newspaper reporting of Dunlap, the freemason and printer-journalist of the Declaration writing from Philadelphia and the central figure of examination in Chapter 4.

The story published by Dunlap on April 21, 1792 recounts Rev. James Muir's proclamation in the cornerstone ceremony of a new nation in an ethos and rhetoric of becoming anchored in mythopoeic space and agency. The exact ceremony does not survive but Dunlap's reporting is invaluable.

In Dunlap's *Advertiser*, repeating the oration, it was reported that:

> Of America it may be said, as it was of Judea of old, that it is a good land, and large, a land of brooks of waters, of fountains and depths that spring out of valleys and hills—a land of wheat and barley, and vines, and fig-trees, and pomegranates; a land of oil olive and honey, a land wherein we eat bread without scarceness, and have lack of nothing; a land whose stones are iron, and out of whose hills though mayest dig brass; a land which the Lord thy God careth for, the eyes of the Lord thy God are always upon it, from the beginning of the year even unto the end of the year!—May Americans be grateful and virtuous, and they shall secure the indulgence of Providence! ... May this Stone ... long commemorate the goodness of God in those uncommon events, which have given America a name amongst the nations—Under this Stone may jealousy and selfishness be forever buried! From this Stone may a superstructure arise, whose glory, whose magnificence, show stability, unequaled hitherto, shall astonish the world and invite even the savage of the wilderness to take shelter under its roof.[249]

---

249 Brent Morris, *Cornerstones of Freedom: A Masonic Tradition* (Washington, D.C.: The Supreme Council, Southern Jurisdiction, 1993), 28, 33.

The inclusion of the American First Nations is in contrast to the displacement of First Nations examined in Chapter 5.

Figure 10. Ellicot and Bannekar with Washington surveying the Federal District. Painting by Peter Waddell with permission of the Grand Lodge of the District of Columbia of Free and Accepted Masons.

African-American slaves, or freed slaves, were an important part of the overworked labor force used to build the nation's capital city. A freed slave, Bannekar, was involved seminally in the surveying of the District of Columbia. Bannekaer, the surveyor is depicted in the painting by Peter Wadell (Figure 10). The painting shows an integration of the ritual construction of place and more abstract transmission logics of communication for example in the tools for surveying. A brazier warms the scene and place of face-to-face communication in the tent. The canvas tent—a tent lodge, in one sense—is filled with instruments of surveying, symbols, the warming brazier, and the play of light affirming quietly the simultaneous ritual and transmission or embodied and emplaced semiotics of communication.

In freemasonry, symbols and artifacts (for example, the terrestrial and celestial globes seen in the "tent lodge") were imported from the Enlightenment, Renaissance, and the earlier Classical period of the Mediterranean.[250] The globes made their way into the lodges of freemasonry at some unknown point in the 18th century quite possibly through the direct

250 Denis Cosgrove, *Apollo's Eye: A Cartographic Genealogy of the Earth in the Western Imagination* (Baltimore: The Johns Hopkins University Press, 2003).

influence of the work of Senex, who was a world-renowned globe- and map-maker. The unity and semiotic transactions of the globes as an aesthetic form anchor the project of freemasonry in celestial and terrestrial worlds, but these were and are conceptualized differently in diverse periods and places, including in ancient and modern science, mathematics, surveying, and philosophy.

A prominent symbol in freemasonry is the checkered floor of opposites—the dark and light squares that mark the contingency and ambiguity of action in the world no less a sense of the sacred and profane, and the known and unknown. This pattern is termed the mosaic pavement. Early texts in masonry that mention the floor related to Moses were incorrect, as the pavement does not have Hebraic origins. Daniel Beresniak, the French scholar of freemasonry, pointed out:

> [The mosaic pavement] first appeared in the first century
> B.C. in Rome. At that time, the term was used for mosa-
> ics decorating natural or artificial caves, and fountains.
> Dedicated to the Muses, the nine goddesses of the arts,
> such places of rest and relaxation were called *musaea*. The
> decorations found here were known as *museum opus*, ab-
> breviated to *mussinum*. This is the origin of the word.[251]

The mosaic pavement in the tent is part of the stylization of a *musaea*, a place of rest, originally a natural cave. The floor existed in each masonic lodge from the 18th century forward. It signifies opposites of existence and the endless dynamic play and utter mystery of imaginative inquiry and journey—a pilgrimage into the unfathomable, a contemplative crisis, and spatial patterning, attaching itself to the linked metaphors of light, building, and journey. The symbols of freemasonry are polyvalent. The art object of the geographic survey was transactional with the artisan-surveyor's environment and wide audience outside the tent-lodge. The internal-volume and exterior express an integral moving whole of parts, including the forming habits and imagination of nation-building and soon wealth-production. The lozenges show precariousness, the often unconscious sense of the "sacred" play of light and darkness in contingent human experience.

---

251 Daniel Beresniak, *Symbols of Freemasonry* (New York: Saint Martin's Press, 1997), 52.

C. SIGNIFICANCE OF FREEMASONS IN BUILDING
THE PRESIDENT'S HOUSE

At President Washington's suggestion, the Irish-born architect and opera-tive stonemason James Hoban (1762-1831), a freemason of the Scottish constitution, travelled to the federal capital from South Carolina to submit a plan for the presidential palace. The "palace" or President's House, later to become the White House, proposed by Hoban was a refined Georgian mansion, in the Palladian style, which was very popular in London and English landscapes as reference in Chapter 2. Some Palladian elements appeared in Ireland, including the Irish Parliament House, likely impact-ing Hoban's architectural sensibilities. On October 13, 1792, Dunlap in Philadelphia reported the cornerstone was laid in masonic fashion.[252] It was very dissimilar from the grand palace proposed by Pierre L'Enfant who was the original grand planner of the city. There was aesthetic-moral logic scaling back from the vision of an American Versailles held by the freemason L'Enfant.[253]

The President's House was a latter day expression of the plain Palladian style of architecture and in distinct contrast to the grandeur of the Cap-itol building. More elegant Classical elements were added to the White House in later periods by the often acknowledged "father of American en-gineering and American architecture" the freemason Benjamin Latrobe. He was an important influence on the first generation of builders working on the American Capitol after Hoban, in what he considered not Palladi-anism but a more eloquent classical style.

The stone mason's lodge depicted in Figure 11 was Maryland Lodge #15, which became Federal Lodge #1. Waddell, the painter, as earlier hinted, is well known for his images of geographic place in history using lighting, drapery, objects, people, and other effects. Here, he captures something of the history of place making, the builder's art of an operative lodge of freemasons, and the rhythmic cycles (day and night) of temporal flow. His work animates an iconic sense, the icon as a sign of the felt, qualita-tive immediacy and pervasive whole of place. People have a first raw, im-mediate sense of a place before they come to "know it." Waddell depicts

252 John Dunlap, *The American Daily Advertiser* (October 13, 1792, Philadelphia).

253 It appears L' Enfant was initiated as an entered apprentice in the important Holland Lodge in New York, but did not proceed to the next degrees of the symbolic lodge.

the men and women who designed, and sometimes built and inhabited, homes and the wider built environment.

Figure 11. Peter Waddell, *A Meeting at the End of the Day,* Artist:. *"The first Stone of the President's House was laid on the 13th Day of October, 1792, and the 17th Year of Independence of the United States of America."* *The Charleston City Gazette,* November 15, 1792. Permission granted by the Grand Lodge of Freemasons of the District of Columbia.[254]

Aspects of the painting by Waddell depict the ritual and transmission functions of communication. The builder's plans for the day on the table symbolized by the scroll (the tracing board used for designing in ancient operative freemasonry) are presumably an accurate, repeatable mirroring of the landscape and built environment. It is an exacting measure-intensive twining between representation and fact. An example is the exactness required in the building of a flying buttress in a medieval cathedral, or laying the foundation of the President's House.

At the same time, the ritual view of communication—potentially constituting something never seen before—is depicted in the interior of the working lodge, the tracing board roughly symbolized by the scroll and table, and a glimpse of the environment and shifting light of the sun on the outside. The tracing board captures a point of view offered in com-

---

254 As pointed out earlier in displacing the King new rituals, monuments and symbols of self-identity were necessary and this was easily provided by freemasonry, including the masculinity of its ritual and symbolic secrecy depicted in the painting by Waddell. The Declaration of Independence was the vital turning point in the radical break with the king by America civil society as a whole in 1776. The building of the President's House is another important moment in the death of a Kingly view and Royal House.

munication studies drawing on John Dewey's inquiry into the embodied ritual and transmission functions of communication. Carey stipulated our models of communication, like all models, have a dual aspect—an 'of' aspect and a 'for' aspect. In one mode of communication models [the tracing board] tell us what the process is; in their second mode they produce the behavior they have described.[255]

The ritual view of communication constitutes what it finds in (inquiry) imaginative intelligence, deliberation and artful communication. Transmission mirrors cultural and material landscapes in place and across networks. The imagination in Wadell's painting is the seeming tension between inner and outer vision,, inside and outside the framing of the window, one instance of absence and presence, and the endless seeking of a new equilibrium in ongoing processes of human embodied, temporalized and emplaced experience in a medium. Yet, to re-emphasize, imagination is situated or disciplined within rule-making with the abstract "model" of the tracing board.

D. THE UNITED STATES CAPITOL CORNERSTONE CEREMONIES IN 1793

The gendered performance of the cornerstone of the Capitol was enacted on Wednesday, September 18, 1793 as reported by the seemingly ubiquitous Dunlap in Philadelphia and by the local Washington paper.[256] (See Appendix B.) The day's events, the temporal flow and rhythm, began when the real yet semi-mythical hero Washington moved from his estate on to the banks of the Potomac River to meet the lodge assembled on the water's edge, perhaps with masons and non-masons on both sides of the river. The river-crossing was the first consummation and trans-liminal moment in the day leading to the next consummation, in a developing, emotionally charged procession moving toward the rise that, with time, became known as Capitol Hill.

---

255 James Cary, *Communications as Culture: Essays on Media and Society* (London: Routledge, 1988).

256 Dunlap, John. *The American Daily Advertiser* (September 10, 1792, Philadelphia). Dunlap's report was dated September 10, and he referred to ongoing plans in preparation for the Capitol. In the same article he states that the sale of lots of real-estate will take place. Appendix B is a complete account of the actual ceremony as reported in the *Columbian Mirror & Alexandria Gazette*, George Town, September 25, 1793, concerning the ritual ceremony on Sept. 21.

Lodge No. 15, which was at the center of much of the activity on that day, had been chartered to work as a lodge only six days earlier, with the founding master of the lodge of freemasons none other than Hoban, the Irish operative stone mason, freemason, and architect of the President's House. Washington, while officially on the rolls of Alexandria, was on this day heading up Lodge No. 15, a symbolic act pointing toward the presumed coming importance when it was to become Federal Lodge No. 1. The freemasons were not the only civic association attempting to work equally at local levels and national scale. The strongest desire for a national Grand Lodge of Freemasonry seems to have been from the military lodges and their remnants after the War of Independence. Theda Skocpol has pointed to the growth in scale and importance of these national civic associations contra Alexis de Tocqueville's emphasis on the local New England village as the source of American democratic civil society.[257]

It is important to note that in the movement into war, during the war and in the immediate years after, there was no such thing as a political party. In this environment, as demonstrated in this chapter the civil association of the masonic lodge and freemasonry acted to organize the situation at hand in ways akin to a "political party." The Kings ritual had been displaced and a substitute was needed and this was provided by freemasonry to some not insignificant degree. In the ritual performance founding of the District of Columbia freemasonry as a civic association and overlapping or additional civic associations were the equivalent organizing solidarity of a political party. There were ongoing transitions in American politics, civic and governmental organizing up ahead including the opening of an ultimately expanding voting franchise.

A published news account from the local *Gazette* newspaper began by stating the great success and attendance of the event of the laying of the cornerstone of the Capitol was no doubt a result of an advertisement that had been placed in more than one local newspaper. It was a well-done attempt at a media event, building constructively on the media mistakes made in the Jones point ceremony. It was thought by some, such as Dunlap in Philadelphia, that Jones Point did not receive sufficient press attention due to a lack of strategy and follow-through. A mural in the halls of Congress recounting the laying of the cornerstone ceremonies of the Capitol is depicted in Figure 12.

257 Theda Skocpol, *Social Revolutions in the Modern World* (Cambridge: Cambridge University Press, 1994), 33.

Figure 12. A gendered interpretation of the laying of the cornerstone at the Capitol by President Washington Freemasons and company in regalia in 1793. Allyn Cox's mural on the vaulted hallway ceiling of the House wing of the U.S. Capitol, 1953. (Permission from Architect of the Capitol)

One way to analyze the cornerstone ceremonies is to focus on the temporal stages of the ritual performance and build from these essential elements of rituals emplacement and embodiment in a medium. Len Travers articulates these levels in his *In the Greatest Solemn Dignity: The Capitol Ceremony in the Early Republic.*[258] Travers, for his part, has divided the ritual working at Capitol Hill on September 18, 1793 into four distinct temporal phases to which I add a sense of place making. The temporal phases are:

(i)   The establishment of ceremonial, mythopoeic time, place and style;

(ii) The procession from the staging area at President's square to Capitol Hill;

---

258 Len Travers, "'In the Greatest Solemn Dignity': The Capitol Ceremony in the Early Republic," in *A Republic for the Ages: The United States Capitol and the Political Culture of the Early Republic,* ed. Donald Kennon (Charlottesville and London: The United States Capitol Historical Society, 1999), 155-176.

(iii) The consecration ceremony of the day, a baptism of the cornerstone and nation; and

(iv) The ending communal feast, festival.

For Travers, the first temporal phase of the ritual performances began that sunny day in September 1793, as President Washington's group came into sight of the assembling crowds and then abruptly when an artillery unit at the south bank of the Potomac opened fire and made solemn the very sense of the place. The fire of cannon in sequence (and as mythopoeic number) in an instant commanded all who were within earshot that the suspension of ordinary time, and space, had commenced. Repeated cannon fire throughout the day helped sustain the magic spell between habit and dramatic performance.

Having made the journey over the Potomac, a band, gleefully playing music, was added as artful accompaniment to the procession. The assembly moved toward the staging area prepared for the event at the Presidents House. That waiting area included a makeshift masonic lodge of some sort at what became known as the White House. At the President's house, there was a pause and dramatic imagining of things to come, but also the rehearsal of how the group would proceed to the ground and rise of the future Capitol. The group again began to move after the planned pause, reconnoiter, and dramatic rehearsal of possibilities.

The second phase of the day's performance was now beginning, according to Travers. This started at high noon, the symbolic time when freemasons work in modern speculative, philosophic lodges. In that measure-intensive moment based in nature, there began another advance of the procession.[259] The dignitaries, groups, and masons approached the hill and the forward position of the civic authorities had the effect of "making way"—clearing—the public streets.[260] The individual and group remade the pub-

---

259 Procession is the mounting of a qualitative and proprioceptive performance, the habit, and habit correction innate in walking each step. Processions are sometimes anchored in the perceived larger sacred cycles of the year or upon special observances, ruptures, and reorientation such as a burial. Processions can also mark secular festivals.

260 The masons, and others assembled, knew something of ceremonial tradition. In earlier days in Europe, tradesmen's guilds often celebrated including parading on their patron saint's day, just as the American masons had proceeded in colonial times on their two St.'s John days mentioned roughly at the summer and winter ceremonies of solstice.

lic space in the ritual performance in the simple act of walking and the integral communicative sign vehicles, habits, and instrumental aesthetics of procession. The elites were reestablishing and signaling to others their position in society as holders of the authority of public office.

In the cornerstone ceremonies under discussion, classes and stations were moving in segregated form, but as a unity with "all" classes ostensibly having their own dignified place, except for the ethnic, gendered, and racial subaltern who were likely watching from the side in a segregated place. The display was of order, orientation, and authority, yet a sense of the liminal was in the air. In this evolving situation, the white male was permitted to rise and was nurtured by his fraternity of civic priests. Freemasonry, in part, was a support network for men. Women were made invisible especially after the war.

The actions and booming sounds of the artillerymen as they shifted their vantage point lent martial power, visual gravitas, and support for the mayor, local, state, and federal offices present and the assembled publics.

As described by Travers:

> The Freemasons marched as a discrete unit in the procession. In their fine clothes, white gloves, and ceremonial aprons, they commanded the most attention. Sword bearers at their front and rear separated them from non-members in the procession—symbolic of the majesty of the virtues they guarded, as well as the exclusiveness of their fraternity. Between the sword bearers, the brotherhood marched in distinct subdivisions. Degreed Masons came first with deacons, stewards, and treasurers of the order separating the different degrees. The marching band came next, isolating officers and degreed men from the rank-and-file membership of Lodge No. 22, who were disposed in their own order. Bearers of the sacramental objects—the corn, wine and oil [to be deposited on the cornerstone, JS]—came next, and last in line walked Washington flanked by two grand masters of the [masonic, JS] order.[261]

---

261 Travers, 169.

Approaching the stately hill, the procession opened outward at the spoken command of the director of ceremonies, with participants then moving to the left and right by two steps. The players halted and turned toward each other. The procession turned into itself as it moved forward, like a coat sleeve being turned inside out. The rear sword bearer walked ahead through the newly shaping passageway of people and public, followed by the President and his entourage. The freemasons were now in front, with the newest apprentice perhaps to the fore for all to see.

At the Capitol laying of the cornerstone ceremonies the young men at the front, the newest apprentices, and fellows of the craft, along with master masons, were being raised up in prominence in public and masonic eyes. There was a polar tension of the symbolic young and old and a powerful transmission to the young. The new babe was nurtured and, in return, there was an expectation of acquired skillful service to the group. The stonecutters and mechanics were behind the elegantly bedecked front group of newly initiated philosophical or speculative freemasons, and the local mayor and officials now took up the rear. A reversal of position had taken place within the guiding light and stability of a tight hierarchy and social ordering, anchored by the body-mind and perceived aesthetic moral virtue, profound gravitas, and performance of Washington, the commander-in-chief, the republican Cicero reincarnate. There was a disciplined masculinity of the army behind him, the animated crowds at hand, and the physical performativity and bio-performance-semiotics of a new republic before him.

Travers sees this shift in place as the beginning of another, a third, phase of the ritual working of that day. "When the ritual space changed, so did the rules of preeminence and the roles of everyone in the procession."[262] Up until this moment, the local representatives of the people, such as the mayor, had been in pride of place. Now, the freemasons—with their student apprentices, fellows of the craft, and master masons, assumed what seemingly no one denied was their rightful place of honor—the honor of marching out front. The reputation of the freemasons in the republic had been sparked at first by printed reports and oral communication around the rebelling colonies, as depicted in Chapter 4 with the discussion of Dunlap in Philadelphia and newspaper reports and word of mouth in Bos-

---

262 Ibid., 171.

ton on the actions of increasing numbers of ancient freemasons. The masculine performance of the freemasons, and their fraternal lodges, on many an occasion took hold in the social imaginary for decades until the Morgan affair, briefly discussed in Chapter 1. After the Morgan incident there would be a strong revival of freemasonry across the nation moving into what has been termed the golden age of fraternalism after the Civil War.

The third phase of the ritual performance commenced as each assumed their place around the large quasi-sacred corner stone and stood for a period in silence. It was another pregnant pause in the rhythm. The baptism was underway. The stone was held by ropes under a tripod, and lowered and set in Masonic ritualistic form. The cannon sounded. The cornerstone was positioned at the right angles and corner of a load bearing east to west foundational wall and one running north and south. There was the obligatory numbered tapping on the stone. The abstractions of language, speech and number were integral to the performance. There was a sanctifying and performative utterance that the stone had been well formed, trusted and true. Corn, wine, and oil were poured. A plate was attached beneath, on top, or to the side of the stone, and the deed was done. It was a very public moment in the ritual founding of the nation-state. There followed remarks of those officiating at the site, including a strong statement wishing the new city commercial success in the laying out of plots of land. There was ideally the mutual interdependence of the state, the economy and civil society in modernity.

A fourth and final phase of the ceremony followed the birthing. Ritual often moves to festivity. People turn to refreshment and celebration after creative or physical tension. In this case, communal dining on oxen and drink reinforced the identity no less the unity and diversity of groups and the close ties between the individual and group. It was a festival astride a ritual and a sealing instrumental aesthetic consummation, building on earlier consummations in the procession, and then offering a release of the tensions. The work had been well done and now it was time for exaltation and the sharing of food and drink. The simple act of communal feasting with its ritual origins lost in the night of time rooted the magic and habits of family, community, stability, and renewal in time.

One way that the channeled energies of habit and custom are visible in the vaulted painting of the cornerstone ceremony in Figure 12 at the Capitol is through the gendered performance and habits of the women smiling and in an elevated yet sequestered public space on the platform above Washington. The smile is a developed habit, and conduct, that in the specific and general case can often act to show women as non-threatening to manly performance in masculine public space, here constituted by the masons and company.

Women are seemingly elevated in the new republican social contract with their special place in nurturing the young generation to come. There is a child visible behind the women in the painted vault, pointing to the importance of the woman in the home. The sequestering shows women put in a smaller space and an elevated manageable place in public space in a situation dominated by the men. Agency as subject is possible. The women can raise their hands and weight from the bannister to stand up and step into the coerced action and creativity of activity underway. The child behind the women can gain learning ability to walk firmly, stand, gesture, and speak in doing and undergoing, supported by the mother and inheritance of the enveloping culture or family support.

The two women are likely attended to at some point, situated in a new place, perhaps catering to the men, or providing decorations after the serious work of the day, in this case in the festival that follows the cornerstone ceremonies. The scene at the cornerstone is reminiscent of what Carol Pateman has called the sexual contract in contemporary society.[263] Pateman challenges the interpretation of an idea deeply embodied in Anglo-American political philosophy: the intellectual view that women are set on an equal footing in the rights and freedoms obtained in the modern republic. The modern republic gives emphasis to the abstractions of political philosophy following on the theory of the social contract, and other theories, from Locke, Hobbes, Rousseau, and others. The intellectual traditions maintain an invisible legacy, however, of gendered coercion, the deeply habituated body in an environment, and subsequent conduct, a sexual contract. Freemasonry in the early republic was representative of gendered civil society at its origins in the new union.

In the ritual of the laying of the cornerstone ceremonies by Washington in the federal district it can be seen how freemasonry was an extremely important instrument and expression of human bonding in civil society as well in the formation of the United State of America with its growing

---

263 Carol Pateman, *The Sexual Contract* (Cambridge: Polity, 1988).

economy. The associative power of freemasonry, however, after the presidency of Washington and the prominence of freemasonry in the 1790s and opening decades of the 19th century would be replaced by the formation of political parties as an organizing mechanism. Nevertheless, white male lodge democracy would endure and grow in numbers in local place and reach through ritual bonds of solidarity across great distances of the American continent. At the same time there grew a social imaginary of the public, a people, and the demos. Despite the cohesive aspects of its ritual communication and networks of print, cosmopolitan freemasonry could not endure with such singular importance and formative power as a civil society, both in the international republic of letters and in the growing power and dynamics of the formation of territory—the new union of states—and growing economy.[264] In addition, the Morgan affair had wreaked havoc. Cosmopolitan freemasonry as an educational and learning enterprise in the international republic of letters began to wane.

E. The Quality of the Transactional Self, Embodied Place and Light

The participants in the cornerstone ceremonies had a symbolic language oriented in the qualitative whole of a place, in temporal flow, in a surveyed space, and in a medium. That medium included the presence of the sun and its warmth after sunrise in the easterly sky. The enduring but shifting aesthetic form of the cornerstone ceremonies was situated in the natural cycles of the sun for both the work of the day and the cycle of seasons. With the sun rising in the east, and moving along its east-west path, it etched the earthly course of one load-bearing wall that would support the cornerstone. The other load-bearing wall ran at a right angle to the first moving precisely north and south, etching the human sensibility of the four cardinal directions—a geo-semiotics—and echoing the annual cyclic movement of the sun and its phenomenological movement north and south, east and west, in time-space. Ernst Cassirer, with an eye on the philosophical anthropology of experience said:

> [The] grandiose and self-contained intuition of the spatial-physical world and cosmos ... is [a] late manifesta-

264 John L. Brooke, *Columbia Rising: Civil Life on the Upper Hudson from the Revolution to the Age of Jackson*, Omohundro Institute of Early American History and Culture (Chapel Hill: University of North Carolina Press, 2013).

tion [with] astrology being a later manifestation. Even
the mythical worldview starts from the most restricted
sphere of sensuous-spatial existence, which is extended
only very gradually .... [as] we have seen [in language]
... the terms of spatial orientation, the words for "before,
and "behind" "above" and "below are usually taken from
man's intuition of his own body ... myth starts from a
spatial-physical *correspondence* [emphasis in the orig-
inal] between the world and man and from this correspondence infers a unity of origin [of man and world, JS]
.... By virtue of this peculiar principle mythical thinking
seems to negate and suspend spatial distance. The distant
merges with what is close at hand, since the one in some
way copies the other.[265]

Cassirer argued that both language and science remove man from the immediacy of lived experience and introduces a mediating symbolic sphere
between man and reality. The American pragmatist Dewey offered the
same argument. In this similarity they were both drawing on and working
to re-shape the *Bildung* tradition fit for their time. As much as this process
of abstraction from the organic world is a necessary condition for scientific discovery, freedom making, and progress, as well as the basis for all
linguistic communication, it inevitably leads to reduced vividness of life.
It is artful experience and wholeness of bio-performance-semiotics, the
live creature in an environment—including the cultural lifestyles, habits,
learning habits and moral imagination of the individual and group in the
civil sphere in deliberative democracy—that restores the richness of life
against linguistic and scientific impoverishment and closed habits. In the
polyvalent interpretation of symbols, Cassirer is from one perspective
describing the masonic "word which has been lost" but now found in embodied inquiry and artful, valuing and meaningful communication.

F. SUMMARY AND CONCLUSIONS

After the American War of Independence, American civil society
emerged. The earlier concourse of ritual performance, habit, social drama, and self-presentation of the King and his public realm had been displaced in the redress of war. There was a profound crisis generated by the

265 Cassirer, *The Philosophy of Symbolic Forms,* 2:90-91.

inevitable schisms and sacrifices of war and a small part of the later rituals of healing were the cornerstone ceremonies in the building of Washington DC. The three cornerstone ceremonies examined in the chapter were rituals of separation and birth, but also of healing after the violence of the War of Independence. The ceremonies actively symbolized and enacted a new local and growing national community.

CHAPTER 7

CONCLUSIONS

In the previous pages I have outlined the role freemasonry played the significant cultural and material transformation that occurred in the transition from oral/aural cultures to an increasingly literate and (ideally) informed citizenry commencing in the period immediately before the American Revolution. This transition occurred via growing literacy and increasingly diverse vehicles of print such as pamphlets, ancient and modern books, circulated weekly edition newspapers, broadsides, declarations or civic constitutions (such as for a philosophical society) at home in the ritual life of local community and in the communication across networks of civic associations and communities. Freemasons helped valorize the moral imagination of an informed citizenry in no small measure through the value they, along with other Americans, placed on worlds of print as vital for the functioning and promise of the early American republic in a difficult but promising postwar environment.

This collective imagination emerged in part through the civic habitus and the valuing of knowledge cultivated in the practice of the freemason's inherited ritual and symbolic work in lodge, knowledge of the geographically expansive American republic, as well as the praxis and potential of the emerging professional occupation of printer and printer-journalist. Leading freemasons such as Clinton championed the cause of an informed citizenry in the new republic in engaging problematic or promising situations in commerce, actionable governance, and experimentation in education from primary school to the support of universities. These were inheritances from the War of Independence and the deliberations of civil society in a social and physical world turned upside down yet full of promise. Clinton was representative of this emerging collective vision in articulating the expansive republic in projects like the Erie Canal. Freemasonry and wider civil society were situated in the *overlap between the near and far* in networks of print and place in 1a potentially continental geography. Freemasonry provides a focused area of study of emerging moral imagination of the new republic.

Unlike in England where there had been an acceptance of social hierarchies, there arose in the new republic a willingness to criticize the existing state of affairs. Brown states that there was a growing view in the new union that an informed citizenry ought to be more comprehensive and inclusive and involve more than liberally educated gentlemen alone. Equally, as critical inquiry was necessary in the search for religious and scientific truth, a politically informed citizenry was vital for evaluating public policy and thus for the well-being of the state and the liberty of its people. Ideas arose as well that unfair actions by the Crown, for example the profound list of grievances outlined in the Declaration of Independence (see Appendix A), demanded immediate discussion and transformation. By the third quarter of the 18th century, the view which valued a politically informed citizenry over a realm populated by subjects indoctrinated in the channeled habits of religious, monarchical and political conformity had become part of the American discourse.

In America a budding narrative of progress (indefinite perfectibility to use Tocqueville's term) underwent a dramatization and reality check just prior to the crisis of the American War of Independence. The notion of an informed citizenry had been advocated rarely, or ethereally, in the mid-18th century and earlier in England and later in the colonies. Brown points out that between 1763 and 1775, the idea *[moral imagination]* of an informed citizenry was activated in the colonies and would expand in the early 19th century. The initial catalyst was a series of parliamentary acts and administrative policies the British initiated in their efforts to reform (for them} the benign imperial system. Unanticipated negative consequences by the good King's action in commerce and taxation as well as punitive actions as matters of legal and socio-cultural practices instituted to discipline his subjects became a point of focus and resistance.

The British actions which effected overseas trade, imported and exported consumer goods, western lands, and newspapers, and all legal transactions, aroused repeated protests from the elite political and economic classes in the colonies. Planters and merchants were joined by almost everyone with a college degree or aspiration to the gentry's class as well as master tradesmen like shipbuilders, carpenters, wheelwrights, printers, printer-journalists, and workers in iron. When these self-styled gentlemen sought to mobilize opposition to the British measures via legislative resolutions, public meetings, newspapers, and pamphlets, they discovered the importance of the idea of an informed citizenry and the value of print communication as an effective tool of communication between and among groups and community. The profound transition from oral/aural habits to the aesthetic-moral habitus and deliberation made possible in worlds of print and the civil sphere at different geographic scales was influenced by the valorization of ancient and modern learning in the symbolism, traditions, and rituals of the lodges of freemasonry. There was a keen and deliberate awareness of the theoretical and practical impact of emerging print culture in the Constitution and federal postal acts as legislation in the new union of states, in public discourse and in freemasonry.

Early American freemasonry presents a rich and focused opportunity for sustained empirical and theoretical studies of the origins and development of modern civil society (especially in moments before the rise of political parties), the moral imagination of an informed citizenry and democratic praxis in deliberative democracy. Democracy emerges in the early republic as more than voting. At its core democracy as stated by Dewey in Chapter 1 is *"primarily a mode of associated living and conjoint communicative experience."* Women, First Nations (Native Americans) and African Americans often fought boldly as a counter public for democratic position and solid communication in the republic long before they could vote, while some well-established men like the leading freemason Clinton imagined and fought for an informed citizenry built through universal education, experiments in pedagogy, and opportunities for life-long learning. At the same time, ideas of an informed citizenry concerned varying opinions about the relative merit, and value of, ancient and modern learning, for example, the contest of Greek and Roman classics, Christian and Renaissance ideals, and modern Newtonian experimentation and science.

I have used the model of ritual and transmission semiotics drawn from the discipline of communication studies, and the focus on freemasonry, to illuminate the past historical geography of American worlds of print and the demos, but these open a door to an extended discussion of apposite human association, moral imagination and communicative experience in deliberative democracy. Ritual communication involves levels of trust in embodied face-to-face communication, the emotional and imaginative searching and construction of values and meaning, and embodied moral-aesthetics in local-place and landscape. Transmission concerns processes of "representation" and abstract movements of information, goods and people across space and networks of place, and "representation" in situ. In actuality, these embodied functions, logics or semiotics of communication are combinatorial and contributory to the struggle for the good life, a practical, effective, expressive life in a difficult world. Different forms or types of communicative action are mutually interdependent—holistic—in the fusion of laughing, sighing, crying, plotting, lifting and learning experience in an environment. Learning and the arc of meaning, purpose and values in artful-aesthetic living all thrive in the give and take and natural social curiosity of the individual and group in an environment.

The ostensible secrecy of freemasonry as a civic association remains a contradiction, yet the American Constitution was drafted in secrecy. Out of responsible discretion there can be a greater capacity for republican service, liberal self-reflection and healthy identification of sorts. Alternatively a stifling and potentially violent suffocation can take place in closely held community. A stupidly superstitious secrecy led to the Morgan affair, in the kidnapping of an American citizen by fellow citizens hoping to maintain the "secrecy" of the actual often valued practice of widely circulating printed rituals. Alternatively, the private or secret practice of ritual of early freemasonry was intended and did develop an aesthetic-moral civic habitus of republican virtue and valorization of self-development in the private and public world.

In this work I barely scratch the surface of the moral-aesthetic-intellectual action and material artifact of thousands of pamphlets, declarations, constitutions, books, newspapers, broadsides and other vehicles of print (and writing) that need to be folded together in situating freemasonry and early American print culture in comparative and global studies of print culture in the 18th and 19th century. Three world class bibliographies that show the scale of the work ahead in the American case alone are Kent Logan Walgen's *Freemasonry, Anti-Masonry and Illuminism in the United States: 1734-1850; American Masonic Periodicals 1811- 2001,* by Larissa Watkins; and Watkins, *International Masonic Periodicals 1738-2005.*

By the time of the death of Hezekiah Niles and his first national American newspaper, worlds of print were experiencing blistering expansion with the advent of new technologies like the steam powered press, rotating plates of type, steam boats on the Ohio, and expanding roads and railroads. A core system of cities and networks of print took shape with a density of printing establishments and endless transactional play, in the end, unequalled anywhere on the globe. The moral imagination of an informed citizenry, a dramatic rehearsal of possibilities and process aesthetics, experimentation, and egalitarian possibilities in education, were the potential life blood in the heart of deliberative democracy and the extensive republic.

THE AMERICAN DECLARATION OF INDEPENDENCE

Adopted by Congress on July 4, 1776

The Unanimous Declaration
of the Thirteen United States of America

When, in the course of human events, it becomes necessary for one people to dissolve the political bands which have connected them with another, and to assume among the powers of the earth, the separate and equal station to which the laws of nature and of nature's God entitle them, a decent respect to the opinions of mankind requires that they should declare the causes which impel them to the separation.

We hold these truths to be self-evident, that all men are created equal, that they are endowed by their Creator with certain unalienable rights, that among these are life, liberty and the pursuit of happiness. That to secure these rights, governments are instituted among men, deriving their just powers from the consent of the governed. That whenever any form of government becomes destructive to these ends, it is the right of the people to alter or to abolish it, and to institute new government, laying its foundation on such principles and organizing its powers in such form, as to them shall seem most likely to effect their safety and happiness. Prudence, indeed, will dictate that governments long established should not be changed for light and transient causes; and accordingly all experience hath shown that mankind are more disposed to suffer, while evils are sufferable, than to right themselves by abolishing the forms to which they are accustomed. But when a long train of abuses and usurpations, pursuing invariably the same object evinces a design to reduce them under absolute despotism, it is their right, it is their duty, to throw off such government, and to provide new guards for their future security. --Such has been the patient sufferance of these colonies; and such is now the necessity which constrains them to alter their former systems of government. The history of the present King of Great Britain is a history of repeated injuries and usurpations, all having in direct object the establishment of an absolute tyranny over these states. To prove this, let facts be submitted to a candid world.

He has refused his assent to laws, the most wholesome and necessary for the public good.

He has forbidden his governors to pass laws of immediate and pressing importance, unless suspended in their operation till his assent should be obtained; and when so suspended, he has utterly neglected to attend to them.

He has refused to pass other laws for the accommodation of large districts of people, unless those people would relinquish the right of representation in the legislature, a right inestimable to them and formidable to tyrants only.

He has called together legislative bodies at places unusual, uncomfortable, and distant from the depository of their public records, for the sole purpose of fatiguing them into compliance with his measures.

He has dissolved representative houses repeatedly, for opposing with manly firmness his invasions on the rights of the people.

He has refused for a long time, after such dissolutions, to cause others to be elected; whereby the legislative powers, incapable of annihilation, have returned to the people at large for their exercise; the state remaining in the meantime exposed to all the dangers of invasion from without, and convulsions within.

He has endeavored to prevent the population of these states; for that purpose obstructing the laws for naturalization of foreigners; refusing to pass others to encourage their migration hither, and raising the conditions of new appropriations of lands.

He has obstructed the administration of justice, by refusing his assent to laws for establishing judiciary powers.

He has made judges dependent on his will alone, for the tenure of their offices, and the amount and payment of their salaries.

He has erected a multitude of new offices, and sent hither swarms of officers to harass our people, and eat out their substance.

He has kept among us, in times of peace, standing armies without the consent of our legislature.

He has affected to render the military independent of and superior to civil power.

He has combined with others to subject us to a jurisdiction foreign to our constitution, and unacknowledged by our laws; giving his assent to their acts of pretended legislation:

For quartering large bodies of armed troops among us:

For protecting them, by mock trial, from punishment for any murders which they should commit on the inhabitants of these states:

For cutting off our trade with all parts of the world:

For imposing taxes on us without our consent:

For depriving us in many cases, of the benefits of trial by jury:

For transporting us beyond seas to be tried for pretended offenses:

For abolishing the free system of English laws in a neighboring province, establishing therein an arbitrary government, and enlarging its boundaries so as to render it at once an example and fit instrument for introducing the same absolute rule in these colonies:

For taking away our charters, abolishing our most valuable laws, and altering fundamentally the forms of our governments:

For suspending our own legislatures, and declaring themselves invested with power to legislate for us in all cases whatsoever.

He has abdicated government here, by declaring us out of his protection and waging war against us.

He has plundered our seas, ravaged our coasts, burned our towns, and destroyed the lives of our people.

He is at this time transporting large armies of foreign mercenaries to complete the works of death, desolation and tyranny, already begun with circumstances of cruelty and perfidy scarcely paralleled in the most barbarous ages, and totally unworthy the head of a civilized nation.

He has constrained our fellow citizens taken captive on the high seas to bear arms against their country, to become the executioners of their friends and brethren, or to fall themselves by their hands.

He has excited domestic insurrections amongst us, and has endeavored to bring on the inhabitants of our frontiers, the merciless Indian savages, whose known rule of warfare, is undistinguished destruction of all ages, sexes and conditions.

In every stage of these oppressions we have petitioned for redress in the most humble terms: our repeated petitions have been answered only by repeated injury. A prince, whose character is thus marked by every act which may define a tyrant, is unfit to be the ruler of a free people.

Nor have we been wanting in attention to our British brethren. We have warned them from time to time of attempts by their legislature to extend an unwarrantable jurisdiction over us. We have reminded them of the circumstances of our emigration and settlement here. We have appealed to their native justice and magnanimity, and we have conjured them by the ties of our common kindred to disavow these usurpations, which, would inevitably interrupt our connections and correspondence. They too have been deaf to the voice of justice and of consanguinity. We must, therefore, acquiesce in the necessity, which denounces our separation, and hold them, as we hold the rest of mankind, enemies in war, in peace friends.

We, therefore, the representatives of the United States of America, in General Congress, assembled, appealing to the Supreme Judge of the world for the rectitude of our intentions, do, in the name, and by the authority of the good people of these colonies, solemnly publish and declare, that these united colonies are, and of right ought to be free and independent states; that they are absolved from all allegiance to the British Crown, and that all political connection between them and the state of Great Britain, is and ought to be totally dissolved; and that as free and independent states, they have full power to levy war, conclude peace, contract alliances, establish commerce, and to do all other acts and things which independent states may of right do. And for the support of this declaration, with a firm reliance on the protection of Divine Providence, we mutually pledge to each other our lives, our fortunes and our sacred honor.

New Hampshire: Josiah Bartlett, William Whipple, Matthew Thornton

Massachusetts: John Hancock, Samuel Adams, John Adams, Robert Treat Paine, Elbridge Gerry

Rhode Island: Stephen Hopkins, William Ellery

Connecticut: Roger Sherman, Samuel Huntington, William Williams, Oliver Wolcott

New York: William Floyd, Philip Livingston, Francis Lewis, Lewis Morris

New Jersey: Richard Stockton, John Witherspoon, Francis Hopkinson, John Hart, Abraham Clark

Pennsylvania: Robert Morris, Benjamin Rush, Benjamin Franklin, John Morton, George Clymer, James Smith, George Taylor, James Wilson, George Ross

Delaware: Caesar Rodney, George Read, Thomas McKean

Maryland: Samuel Chase, William Paca, Thomas Stone, Charles Carroll of Carrollton

Virginia: George Wythe, Richard Henry Lee, Thomas Jefferson, Benjamin Harrison, Thomas Nelson, Jr., Francis Lightfoot Lee, Carter Braxton

North Carolina: William Hooper, Joseph Hewes, John Penn

South Carolina: Edward Rutledge, Thomas Heyward, Jr., Thomas Lynch, Jr., Arthur Middleton

Georgia: Button Gwinnett, Lyman Hall, George Walton

Source: The Pennsylvania Packet, July 8, 1776

From *The Columbian Mirror* *& Alexandria Gazette*

September 25, 1793

George Town, Sept. 21.

On Wednesday last one of the grandest MASONIC Processions took place, which perhaps ever was exhibited on the like important occasion: It was in all probability much facilitated by an advertisement which appeared many days before in several news-papers of this state.

About 10 o'clock, Lodge, No. 9, were visited by that Congregation, so graceful to the Craft, Lodge, No. 22, of Virginia, with all their Officers and Regalia, and directly afterwards appeared on the southern banks of the Grand River Potomack: one of the finest companies of Volunteer Artillery that has been lately seen, parading to receive the President of the United States, who shortly came in sight with his suite -- to whom the Artillery paid their military honors, and his Excellency and suite crossed the Potomack, and was received in Maryland, by the Officers and Brethren of No. 22, Virginia and No. 9, Maryland whom the President headed, and preceded by a bank of music; the rear brought up by the Alexandria Volunteer Artillery; with grand solemnity of march, proceeded to the President's square in the City of Washington: where they were met and saluted, by No. 15, of the City of Washington, in all their elegant regalia, headed by Brother Joseph Clark, Rt. W.G.M. --- P.T. and conducted to a large Lodge, prepared for the purpose of their reception. After a short space of time, by the vigilance of Brother C. Worthy Stephenson, Grand Marshall, P.T. the Brotherhood and other Bodies were disposed in a second order of procession, which took place amid a brilliant crowd of spectators of both sexes, according to the following arrangement.

Viz. --- The Surveying department of the City of Washington.

Mayor and Corporation of George Town.

Virginia Artillery.

Commissioners of the City of Washington, and their attendants.

Stone Cutters,   Mechanics,

Two Sword Bearers.

Masons of the 1st. Degree.

Bibles &c. on the Grand Cushions.

Deacons with Staffs of Office.

Masons of the 2d degree.

Stewards with wands.

Masons of the 3d degree.

Wardens with truncheons

Secretaries with tools of office.

Past Master with their Regalia.

Treasurers with their Jewels.

Band of music.

Lodge No. 22, of Virginia, disposed in their own order.

Corn, Wine, and Oil

Grand Master P.T. George Washington , W.M. No. 22, Virginia,

Grand Sword Bearer.

The procession marched two a-breast, in the greatest solemn dignity, with music playing, drums beating, colors flying, and spectators rejoicing; from the President's Square to the Capitol, in the City of Washington; where the Grand Marshall called a halt, and directed each file in the procession, to incline two steps, one to the right, and one to the left, and face each other, which formed a hollow oblong square; through which the Grand Sword Bearer led the van; followed by the Grand Master P.T. on the left --- the President of the United States in the Centre [heading up at this point lodge No. 9], and the Worshipful Master of Number 22, Virginia, on the right --- all the other orders, that composed the procession advanced, in the reverse of their order of march from the President's Square, to the south-east corner of the Capitol; and the Artillery filed off to a defined ground to display their maneuvers and discharge their cannon: The President of the United States, the Grand Master, P.T. and the Worshipful M. of No. 22, taking their stand to the East of a huge stone; and all the Craft, forming a circle westward, stood a short time in silent awful order;

The Artillery discharged a Volley.

The Grand Marshall delivered the Commissioners, a large Silver Plate with an Inscription thereon which the commissioners ordered to be read, and was as follows:

This South East corner Stone, of the Capitol of the United States of America in the City of Washington, was laid on the 18th day of September 1793, in the thirteenth year of American Independence, in the first year of the second term of the Presidency of George Washington, whose virtues in the civil administration of his country have been as conspicuous and beneficial, as his Military valor and prudence have been useful in establishing her liberties, and in the year of Masonry 5793, by the Grand Lodge of Maryland, several Lodges under its jurisdiction, and Lodge No. 22, from Alexandria, Virginia.

[signed] Thomas Johnson, David Steuart and Daniel Carroll, Commissioners, Joseph Clark, R.W.G.M. [Right Worshipful Grand Master] pro tem, James Hoban and Stephen Hallate, Architects. Collin Williamson, Master Mason.

The Artillery discharged a volley.

The Plate was then delivered to the President, who, attended by the Grand Master pro tem., and three Most worshipful Masters, descended to the carazion trench and deposited the plate, and laid it on the corner-stone of the Capitol of the United States of America, on which were deposited corn, wine, and oil, when the whole congregation joined in reverential prayer, which was succeeded by Masonic chanting honors, and a volley from the Artillery.

The President of the United States, and his attendant brethren, ascended from the carazion to the East of the corner-stone, and there the Grand Master pro tem, elevated on a triple rostrum, delivered an oration fitting the occasion, which was received with brotherly love and commendation. At intervals during the delivery of the oration the Artillery discharged several volleys. The ceremony ended in prayer, Masonic chanting honors, and a 15-volley from the Artillery.

The whole company retired to an extensive booth, where an ox of five hundred pounds weight was barbecued, of which the company generally partook with every abundance of other recreation. The festival concluded with fifteen successive volleys from the Artillery, whose military discipline and maneuvers merit every commendation. Before dark the whole company departed with joyful hopes of the production of their labor.

BIBLIOGRAPHY

Primary Sources

Addison, Joseph, and Sir Richard Steele. *The Spectator*. 12th ed. London: J. and R. Tonson, 1726.

———. *The Spectator*. Collected ed. London, 1788.

American Daily Advertiser (Philadelphia, PA)

Anderson, James. *The Constitutions of the Free–Masons*. London: John Senex and John Hooke, 1723.

Anderson, James A.M., Benjamin Franklin, and Royster, Paul (editor & depositor). *The Constitutions of the Free-Masons (1734)*. Faculty Publications, UNL Libraries. Paper 25. http://digitalcommons.unl.edu/libraryscience/25

Anonymous. [lead article across the upperfold.] *Columbian Mirror & Alexandria Gazette*. George Town, September 25, 1793.

Anonymous, or, A Gentleman Belonging To The Jerusalem Lodge. *Jachin and Boaz; Or an Authentic Key to the Door of Free-Masonry*. Pamphlet. London: W. Nicol, 1762.

Anonymous. *The Sentiments of an American Woman*, Philadelphia: A broadside printed by John Dunlap, 1780.

Aupaumut Hendrick. *A Narrative of an Embassy to the Western Indians, from the Original Manuscript of Hendrick Aupaumut, with Prefatory Remarks by Dr. B. H. Coates*. Philadelphia: Memoirs of the Historical Society of Pennsylvania, 1827.

Bernard, David. *Light on Masonry: A Collection of All the Most Important Documents on the Subject of Speculative Free Masonry: Embracing the Reports of the Western Committees in Relation to the Abduction of William Morgan, with All the Degrees of the Order Conferred in a Master's Lodge, as Written by Captain William Morgan*. Utica: William Williams, 1829.

Brant, Joseph. *Journal of the Proceedings at the General Council Held at the Foot of the Rapids of the Miamis, in W.L. Stone, Life of Joseph Brant Thayendanegea Including the Indian Wars of the American Revolution*. 2 vols. Reprint 1793. New York: Alexander V. Blake, 1838.

Brewster, David, Sir. *The History of Freemasonry: Drawn from Authentic Sources of Information with an Account of the Grand Lodge of Scotland.* Edinburgh: A. Lawrie, 1804.

The William Bentley Papers, 1700-1820. Mss. 259. Tisch Library, Tufts University, Medford, MA.

Carr, Harry. *Three Distinct Knocks and Jachin and Boaz.* Reprint 1760, 1762. Bloomington: Masonic Book Club, 1981.

Clinton, DeWitt. *An Address delivered before Holland Lodge, December 24, 1793.* New York: Childs and Swaine, 1794.

Columbian Mirror & Alexandria Gazette (Alexandria, VA)

Crocker, Hannah Mather. *A Series of Letters on Freemasonry.* Boston: Eliot, 1815.

Delegates of the Constitutional Convention. *United States Constitution.* Reprint 1787. National Center for Constitutional Studies, 2005.

Dermot, Laurence. *Ahiman Rezon: or, A help to a brother; shewing the excellency of secrecy, and the first cause, or motive, of the institution of free-masonry, &c. Followed by a choice selection of songs.* London, 1756.

De Tocqueville, Alexis. *Democracy in America.* Trans. Harvey C. Mansfield. Ed. Delba Winthrop. Reprint 1835. Chicago: University of Chicago Press, 2011.

Dunlap. John. *An Oration, Delivered at King's Chapel in Boston, April 8, 1776, on the Re-Internment of the Remains of the Late Most Worshipful Grand-Master Warren, Esquire, President of the Late Congress of this Colony, and Major-General of the Massachusetts Forces; Who Was Slain in the Battle of Bunker's Hill, June 17, 1775.* Philadelphia: *The American Daily Advertiser,* April 21, 1791; Philadelphia: *The American Daily Advertiser,* Oct. 13, 1792; Philadelphia: *The American Daily Advertiser,* September, 10, 1793, Philadelphia: *Claypoole's American Daily Advertiser.* September 21, 1796.

Franklin, Benjamin. *Autobiography.* Reprint 1791. New York: Dover Publications, 1996.

The Gentleman's Magazine, and Historical Chronicle, London, 1753.

Grand Lodge of Freemasons in New York. *The Constitutions of the Ancient and Honorable Fraternity of Free and Accepted Masons in the State of New-York.* New York: Shepherd Kollock, corner of Wall and Water Streets, 1805.

Hall, Prince. *A Charge Delivered to the African Lodge on the 25th of June.* Boston, 1792.

———. *A Charge Delivered to the African Lodge, June 24, 1797, at Menotomy.* Cambridge, 1797.

Halliwell, James Orchard. "A Poem on the Constitutions of Masonry" (unpublished translation of *The Regius Poem* or, *The Halliwell Manuscript,* c. 1390, from the original manuscript in the King's Library of the British Museum, London, 1840), http://www.pagrandlodge.org/district37/D37_Pdfs/TheRegiusPoem.PDF

Hutchinson, William. *Spirit of Masonry in Moral and Elucidatory Lectures by WM of the Barnardcastle Lodge of Concord.* Boston: J. Wilkie and W. Goldsmith, 1775.

Jefferson, Thomas. *The Papers of Thomas Jefferson.* 42 vols. Ed. Julian P. Boyd et al. Princeton: Princeton University Press, 1950-2015.

Marrant, John. *A sermon preached on the 24th of June 1789, being the festival of St. John the Baptist, at the request of the Right Worshipful the Grand Master Prince Hall, and the rest of the brethren of African Lodge of the Honorable Society of Free and Accepted Masons in Boston.* Boston, 1789.

Morton, Perez. *An Oration, Delivered at King's Chapel in Boston, April 8, 1776, on the Re-Internment of the Remains of the Late Most Worshipful Grand-Master Warren, Esquire, President of the Late Congress of this Colony, and Major-General of the Massachusetts Forces; Who Was Slain in the Battle of Bunker's Hill, June 1775.* Philadelphia: John Dunlap, 1776.

M-O-V-N. *Three Distinct Knocks* (London: H. Serjeant without Temple Bar, 1756)

Paine, Thomas. *The American Crisis,* Reprint 1776. Boston: Nathaniel Coverly, 1803.

Preston, William. *Illustrations of masonry: By William Preston, Past Master of the Lodge of Antiquity Acting by Immemorial Constitution.* London: G. and T. Wilkie, 1792.

Perrault, Charles. *Parallèle des anciens et des modernes en ce qui regarde les arts et les sciences: Dialogues.* Paris: Jean Baptiste Coignard, 1693.

Picart, Bernard, and Jean Frederic Bernard, *Cérémonies et coutumes réligieuses de tous les peuples du monde.* 7 vols. Second edition. Amsterdam: J. F. Bernard, 1733-1739.

Poe, Edgar Allan. "Cask of Amontillado." *Godey's Ladies Journal* 33 no. 5 (New York, 1846): 216-218.

Preston, William. *Illustrations of Masonry: By William Preston, Past Master of the Lodge of Antiquity Acting by Immemorial Constitution.* London: 1792.

Pritchard, Samuel. *Masonry Dissected.* London: J. Wilford, 1730.

Rush, Benjamin. *An Address to the Inhabitants of the British Settlements in America, upon Slave-keeping.* Philadelphia: J. Dunlap, 1773.

Smith, William. *A Sermon Preached in Christ-Church, Philadelphia, (for the benefit of the poor) by Appointment of and before the General Communication of Free and Accepted Masons of the State of Pennsylvania, on Monday December 28, 1778.* Philadelphia. John Dunlap, 1779.

Von Steuben, Baron, F. W. L. G. A., *Regulations for the Order and Discipline of the Troops of the United States: Part I.* Commonwealth of Massachusetts. Boston: T. and J. Fleet, 1782.

———. *Regulations, for the order and discipline of the troops of the United States.* Boston: Isaiah Thomas, 1794.

———. *Revolutionary war drill manual.* Boston: Isaiah Thomas, 1781.

Smith, Fairbairn J. *Michigan Masonic Tracing Board, 1764 to 1976: A Panorama of Masonic History, Sesquicentennial of the Grand Lodge of Free and Accepted Masons of Michigan, 1826-1976.* Sesquicentennial Commission.: Grand Lodge of Free and Accepted Masons of Michigan, N.d..

Smith, William. *A Sermon Preached in Christ-Church, Philadelphia, [for the benefit of the poor] by Appointment of and before the General Com-*

munication of Free and Accepted Masons of the State of Pennsylvania, on Monday December 28, 1778, Celebrated Agreeable to Their Constitution, as the Anniversary of St. John the Evangelist, ed. William Smith. Philadelphia: John Dunlap, 1779.

Steele, Richard, Sir. *The Tattler,* London, 1709.

Steele, Richard, Sir, and Joseph Addison. *The Spectator.* London, 1726.

Thomas, Isaiah. *The History of Printing in America. With a Biography of Printers, and an Account of Newspapers.* Worcester, 1810.

United States Congress, Thomas Jefferson, and the Congressional Committee. *The Declaration of Independence.* Philadelphia: John Dunlap for the United States Congress, 1776.

Walker, David. "Appeal to the coloured citizens of the world but in particular, and very expressly, to those of the United States of America." Reprint 1830. In *Walker's Appeal and Garnet's Address to the Slaves of the United States of America.* Nashville: James C. Winston, 1994.

Washington, George. *Orders to his troops on July 9, 1776, General Orders.* George Washington Papers at the Library of Congress, 1741-1799: Series 3g Varick Transcripts. Washington, D.C.: Library of Congress, Manuscript Division. http://memory.loc.gov/cgi-bin/ampage?collId =mgw3&fileName=mgw3g/ gwpage001.db&recNum=307

Washington, George, and J.M. Toner. *Washington's rules of civility and decent behavior in company and conversation. A paper found among the early writings of George Washington.* Copied from the original with literal exactness, and edited with notes. Washington, D.C.: W.H. Morrison, 1888.

Webb, Thomas Smith, and Robert Morris. *The Freemasons Monitor, or, Illustrations of Masonry.* New York: Southwick and Crocker, 1802.

Webb, Thomas Smith. *The Freemason's Monitor; or, Illustrations of Masonry.* Albany: Fry and Southwick for Spencer and Webb, 1797.

Young, Robert Alexander. "The Ethiopian manifesto: issued in defence of the black man's rights in the scale of universal freedom." In *Pamphlets of Protest: An Anthology of Early African American Protest Literature, 1790-1860.* New York: Routledge, 2000.

———— . *The Ethiopian manifesto: issued in defence of the black man's rights in the scale of universal freedom.* New York, 1829.

Secondary Sources

Ackerman, James. *Palladio.* New York London: Penguin, 1996.

Alexander Thomas M. *The Human Eros: Eco-Ontology and the Aesthetics of Existence.* New York: Fordham University Press, 2013.

Anderson, Benedict. *Imagined Communities: Reflections on the Origin and Spread of Nationalism.* London: Verso, 2006.

Anderson, Christy. *Inigo Jones and the Classical Tradition.* Cambridge: Cambridge University Press, 2010.

Appleby, Joyce. *Inheriting the Revolution: The First Generation of Americans.* Cambridge: Belknap Press, 2000.

Bailyn, Bernard, and John B. Hench, eds. *The Press and the American Revolution.* Worcester: American Antiquarian Society, 1980.

Bell, Charles Henry. *History of Exeter, New Hampshire.* Hanover: J. E. Farwell & Co. Press, 1888.

Beresniak, Daniel. *Symbols of Freemasonry.* New York: St. Martin's Press, 1997.

Berleant, Arnold. *The Aesthetic Field: A Phenomenology of Aesthetic Experience.* Christchurch: Cybereditions, 2000.

Berman, Ric. *The Foundations of Modern Freemasonry: The Grand Architects – Political Change and the Scientific Enlightenment, 1720-1740.* East Sussex: Sussex Press, 2012.

Blanchard, Rae. "Was Richard Steele a Freemason?" *PMLA* 63 no. 3 (1948): 903-917.

Botein, Stephen. "Printers and the American Revolution." *The Press and the American Revolution.* Eds. Bernard Bailyn and J. Hench. Boston: Northeastern University Press, 1981.

Botting, Eileen Hunt, and Sarah L Houser. "'Drawing the Line of Equality': Hannah Mather Crocker on Women's Rights." *American Political Science Review.* 100 no. 2 (May, 2006): 265-278.

Bradley, Patricia. *Slavery, Propaganda, and the American Revolution.* Jackson: University of Mississippi Press, 1988.

Brewer, John. *The Pleasures of the Imagination: English Culture in the Eighteenth Century.* New York: Brown Farrar Straus Giroux, 1997.

Brooke, John L., and Omohundro Institute of Early American History & Culture. *Columbia Rising: Civil Life on the Upper Hudson from the Revolution to the Age of Jackson.* Chapel Hill: University of North Carolina Press, 2013.

Brooks, Joanna. *American Lazarus: Religion and the Rise of African-American and Native-American Literatures.* Oxford: Oxford University Press, 2003.

Brooks, Joanna, and John Saillant, eds. *Face Zion Forward: First Writers of the Black Atlantic, 1785-1798.* Boston: Northeastern University Press, 2002.

Brooks, Lisa. "Two Paths to Peace: Competing Visions of Native Space in the Old Northwest." *The Boundaries Between Us: Natives and Newcomers Along the Frontiers of the Old Northwest Territory, 1750-1850.* Kent: Kent State University Press, 2006.

Brown, John Seely, and Paul Duguid. *The Social Life of Information.* Boston: Harvard Business School Press, 2000.

Brown Richard D. *Knowledge is Power: The Diffusion of Information in Early America, 1700-1865.* New York: Oxford University Press, 1989.

———. *The Strength of a People: The Idea of an Informed Citizenry in America, 1650-1870.* Chapel Hill: University of North Carolina Press, 1996.

Bullock, Steven. *The Revolutionary Brotherhood.* Chapel Hill and London: University of North Carolina Press, 1996.

Burrow, Ian C., and Richard W. Hunter. "The Historical Geography and Archaeology of the Revolutionary War." *New Jersey in the American Revolution.* Ed. Barbara J. Mitnick. New Brunswick: Rutgers University Press, 2005.

Carey, James W. *Communication as Culture: Essays on Media and Society.* London and Boston: Routledge, 2009.

Carpenter, Audrey T. *John Theophilus Desaguliers: A Natural Philosopher, Engineer, and Freemason in Newtonian England.* London and New York: Continuum, 2011.

Carpo, Mario. *Architecture in the Age of Printing: Orality, Writing, Typography, and Printed Images in the History of Architectural Theory.* Trans. Sarah Benson. Cambridge: M.I.T. Press, 2001.

Cassirer, Ernst. *The Philosophy of Symbolic Forms.* 3 vols. New Haven: Yale University Press, 1953.

Clark, Peter. *British Clubs and Societies, 1580-1800: The Origins of an Associational World.* Oxford: Oxford University Press, 2000.

Coil, Henry H. "Gothic Constitutions." *Coil's Masonic Encyclopedia.* Richmond: Macoy Publishing and Masonic Supply Company, 1995.

Cosgrove, Denis. *Apollo's Eye: A Cartographic Genealogy of the Earth in the Western Imagination.* Baltimore: The Johns Hopkins University Press, 2003.

Crick, Nathan. *Democracy and Rhetoric: John Dewey on the Arts of Becoming.* Studies in Rhetoric/Communication. Columbia: University of South Carolina Press, 2010.

Davis, Harry E. "Documents Relating to Negro Masonry in America." *The Journal of Negro History* 21 no. 4 (1936): 411-432.

Davis-Unidiano, Robert Con. "Poe and the American Affiliation with Freemasonry." *Symploke* 7 nos. 1/2 (1999): 119-138.

Dewey, John. *Democracy and Education: An Introduction to the Philosophy of Education.* New York: The Macmillan Company, 1916.

———. *The Public and Its Problems.* Athens: Ohio University Press, 1927.

———. *Art as Experience.* New York: Minton, Balch, & Company, 1934.

Dibble, Vernon. "Occupations and Ideologies." *The American Journal of Sociology* 68 no. 2 (September, 1962): 229-241.

Duhigg, Charles. *The Power of Habit: Why We Do Things in Life and Business.* New York: Random House, 2012.

Dyer, Colin. *William Preston and His Work.* London: Lewis Masonic, 1987.

Elliott, Paul, and Stephen Daniels. "The 'school of true, useful and universal science': Freemasonry, Natural Philosophy and Scientific Culture in Eighteenth-Century England." *British Journal of the History of Science* 39, no. 2 (2006): 207-229.

Fesmire, Steven. *John Dewey and Moral Imagination: Pragmatism in Ethics.* Bloomington: Indiana University Press, 2003.

——— . *Dewey.* Routledge Philosophers. London: Routledge, 2014.

Fiske, John. *Introduction to Communication Studies.* London: Methuen, 1982.

Fitzpatrick, Edward A. "The Educational Views and Influence of DeWitt Clinton." PhD diss., Teachers College, Columbia University, 1911.

Flather, David. "The Foundation Stone." *Ars Quatuor Coronatum,* 48 (1939): 221.

Fleming, Thomas. "Crossroads of the American Revolution." *New Jersey and the American Revolution.* B. J. Minick, ed. New Brunswick: Rutgers University Press, 2005.

Fliegelman, Jay. *Declaring Independence: Jefferson, Natural Language, and the Culture of Performance.* Stanford: Stanford University Press, 1993.

Frasca, Ralph. *Benjamin Franklin's Printing Network: Disseminating Virtue in Early America.* New York: Columbia: Columbia University Press, 2006.

Gilmore, William J. *Reading Becomes a Necessity of Life: Material and Cultural Life in Rural New England, 1780-1835.* Knoxville: University of Tennessee Press, 1989.

Gomez, Michael A. *Exchanging Our Country Marks: The Transformation of African Identities in the Colonial and Antebellum South.* Chapel Hill: University of North Carolina Press, 1998.

Goodman, Roy E. "Hezekiah Niles, His Weekly Register, and the Atlantic Revolutionary World." *Profiles of the Revolutionaries in Atlantic History,*

1700-1850. R. William Weisberger, Dennis P. Hupchick, and David L. Anderson, eds. New York: Columbia University Press, 2007.

Goodman, Russell B. *American Philosophy and the Romantic Tradition*. Cambridge: Cambridge University Press, 1990.

Gottdiener, Mark. *Postmodern Semiotics: Material Culture and the Forms of Postmodern Life*. Oxford: Blackwell, 1995.

Gray, David L. *Inside Prince Hall*. Virginia: Anchor Communications, 2003.

Gross, Robert and Marky Kelly, eds. *A History of the Book in America—An Extensive Republic: Print, Culture, and Society in the New Nation, 1790s-1840*. Volume Two. Chapel Hill: University of North Carolina Press, 2010.

Gustafson Sandra M. *Eloquence is Power: Oratory and Performance in Early America*. Chapel Hill and London: University of North Carolina Press, 2000.

———. *Imagining Deliberative Democracy in the Early American Republic*. Chicago: University of Chicago Press, 2011.

Habermas, Jürgen. *The Structural Transformation of the Public Sphere: An Inquiry into a Category of Bourgeois Society*. Trans. Thomas Burger. Cambridge: M.I.T. Press, 1991.

Hansen, David T. "Dewey and Cosmopolitanism." *John Dewey at 150: Reflections for a New Century*. Eds. A.G. Rudd, Jim Garrison, and Linda Stone. West Lafayette: Purdue University Press, 2009. 104-116.

Harland-Jacobs, Jessica L. *Builders of Empire: Freemasons and British Imperialism, 1717-1927*. Chapel Hill: University of North Carolina Press, 2007.

Hasselmann, Kristiane. "Performing Freemasonry: The Practical-Symbolic Constitution of a Civic Habitus in Eighteenth-Century England." *Journal for Research into Freemasonry and Fraternalism* 1 no. 2 (2010): 184-194.

Hetherington, Kevin. *The Badlands of Modernity: Heterotopia and Social Ordering*. London and New York: Routledge, 1997.

Hunter, R.W., and J. C. G. Burrow, "The History and Archaeology of the Revolutionary War," *New Jersey in the American Revolution*, ed. Barbara J. Minick (New Brunswick: Rutgers University Press, 1983). [Huss, Wayne A. *The Master Builders: A History of the Grand Lodge of Free and Accepted Masons of Pennsylvania*. 3 vols. Philadelphia: The Grand Lodge, 1986.

Huyler, Jerome. *Locke in America: The Moral Philosophy of the Founding Era*. Lawrence: University Press of Kansas, 1995.

Jackson, Alexander Cosby Fishburn. *English Masonic Exposures 1760-1769*. London: Lewis Masonic Publications, 1986.

Jacob, Margaret. *Living the Enlightenment: Freemasonry and Politics in Eighteenth-Century Europe*. Oxford: Oxford University Press, 1991.

Jensen, Merrill. *The Founding of a Nation: A History of the American Revolution, 1763-1776*. Oxford: Oxford University Press, 1968.

Jordan, Winthrop. *White over Black: American Attitudes Toward the Negro, 1550-1812*. Chapel Hill: University of North Carolina Press, 1968.

Kertzer, Robert. *Ritual, Politics, and Power*. New Haven: Yale University Press, 1989.

Kielbowicz, Richard B. "The Press, Post Office, and Flow of News in the Early Republic." *Journal of the Early Republic* 3 no. 3 (1983): 255-280.

Kosnoski, Jacob. *John Dewey and the Habits of Ethical Life: The Aesthetics of Political Organizing in a Liquid World*. Lanham: Lexington Books, 2010.

Kwasny, Mark V. *Washington's Partisan War, 1775-1783*. Kent: Kent State University Press, 1998.

Lawrence, Snezna. "Geometry of Architecture and Freemasonry in Nineteenth-Century England." PhD diss. Open University, 2002.

Levin, Joseph M. *Between the Ancients and Moderns: Baroque Culture in Restoration England*. New Haven and London: Yale University Press, 1999.

Lipson, Dorothy Ann. *Freemasonry in Federalist Connecticut*. Princeton: Princeton University Press, 1977.

Lofts, Steve G. *Ernst Cassirer: A "Repetition" of Modernity*. Albany: State University of New York Press, 2000.

London, Daniel. "Building the Great Community: John Dewey and the Public Spaces of Social Democracy." Unpublished manuscript, University of Exeter. https://www.academia.edu/934760/Building_the_Great_Community_John_Dewey_and_The_Public_Spaces_of_Social_Democracy.

Luxon, Norval Neil. *Niles' Weekly Register: News Magazine of the Nineteenth Century*. Baton Rouge: Louisiana State University Press, 1947.

Marble, Annie Russell. *From 'Prentice' to Patron: The Life Story of Isaiah Thomas*. New York and London: D. Appleton-Century Company, 1935.

McClaren, Peter. *Schooling as Ritual Performance: Toward a Political Economy of Educational Symbols and Gestures*. Oxford: Rowman and Littlefield Publishers, 1993.

Meinig, Donald W. *The Shaping of America: A Geographical Perspective on 500 Years of History*. 3 vols. New Haven: Yale University Press, 1995.

Miller, Kerby A., Arnold Schrier, Bruce D. Boling, and David N. Doyle. *Irish Immigrants in the Land of Canaan: Letters and Memoirs from Colonial and Revolutionary America, 1775-1815*. Oxford: Oxford University Press, 2003.

Morris, Brent S. *Cornerstones of Freedom: A Masonic Tradition*. Washington, D.C.: The Supreme Council the Southern Jurisdiction, 1993.

Munson, Eve Stryker, and Catherine A. Warren. *James Carey: A Critical Reader*. Minneapolis: University of Minnesota Press, 1997.

Nash, Gary B. *First City: Philadelphia and the Forging of Historical Memory*. Philadelphia: University of Pennsylvania Press, 2002.

———. *Forging Freedom: The Formation of Philadelphia's Black Community, 1720-1840*. Cambridge: Harvard University Press, 1988.

Olwig, Kenneth. *Landscape, Nature, and the Body Politic: From Britain's Renaissance to Americas New World*. Madison: University of Wisconsin Press, 2002.

Ong, Walter J. *Orality and Literacy: The Technologizing of the Word*. London and New York: Routledge, 2006.

Pateman, Carol. *The Sexual Contract*. Cambridge: Polity, 1988.

———. *The Disorder of Women: Democracy, Feminism, and Political Theory*. Stanford: Stanford University Press, 1990.

Peckham, Howard H. *The Toll of Independence: Engagements and Battle Casualties of the American Revolution*. Chicago: The University of Chicago Press, 1974.

Peirson, George Wilson. *Tocqueville in America*. Baltimore and London: The Johns Hopkins University Press, 1996.

Pérez-Gómez, Alberto. *Architecture and the Crisis of Modern Science*. Cambridge and London: Cambridge University Press, 1992.

Peter, Robert, Cécile Révauger, and Jan A. M. Snoek, eds. *British Freemasonry, 1717-1813: A Primary Source Guide*. 5 vols. London: Pickering & Chatto, 2015 (forthcoming).

Porter, Joy. *Native-American Freemasonry: Associationalism and Performance in America*. Lincoln: University of Nebraska Press, 2011.

Pred, Allan. *Urban Growth and the Circulation of Information: The United States System of Cities, 1790-1840*. Cambridge: Harvard University Press, 1973.

Prescott, Andrew. "The Productions of the English Books of Constitutions in the Eighteenth Century." Unpublished manuscript. Ronde table, Le Monde Maçonnique, University of Sorbonne, Paris, 2005,

Purdy, Daniel L. *On the Ruins of Babel: Architectural Metaphor in German Thought*. Cornell: Cornell University Press. 2011.

———. "The Building in *Bildung*: Goethe, Palladio, and the Architectural Media." *Goethe Yearbook*. 15 no.1 (2008): 57-73.

Pushee, George D. "Joseph Warren Martyr of Bunker Hill." Conference paper, C. B. Vance Council # 85, Allied Masonic Degrees, Chesapeake, Virginia, April 7, 1994.

Remer, Rosalind, *Printers and Men of Book Publishers in the New Republic*. Philadelphia: University of Pennsylvania Press, 1996.

Révauger, Cécile. "Thomas Jefferson." *Le monde maçonnique des Lumières: l'Europe, l'Amérique et de ses colonies, prosopographique Dictionnaire.* Cécile Révauger & Charles Porset, eds. Paris: Champion, 2014. 1522-1525.

Révauger, Cécile, and Charles Porset. *Le monde maçonnique des Lumières: l'Europe, l'Amérique et de ses colonies, prosopographique Dictionnaire.* 3 vols. Paris: Champion, 2014.

Roberts, Cokie. *Founding Mothers: The Women Who Raised Our Nation.* New York: William Morrow, 2004.

Rotundo, E. Anthony. *American Manhood: Transformations in Masculinity from the Revolution to the Modern Era.* New York: Basic Books, 1993.

Rudd, A. G., Jay Garrison, and Linda Stone, eds. *John Dewey at 150: Reflections for a New Century.* West Lafayette: Purdue University Press, 2009.

Ruffin, Rixey. *A Paradise of Reason: William Bentley and Enlightenment Christianity in the Early Republic.* Oxford: Oxford University Press, 2008.

Rykwert, Joseph. *The First Moderns: The Architects of the Eighteenth Century.* Cambridge: M.I.T. Press, 1980.

Sachse, Julius F., and Norris F Barratt. *Freemasonry in Pennsylvania, 1727-1907.* Vol. 1. Lancaster: New Era Printing Company, 1908.

Schlereth, Thomas J. *The Cosmopolitan Ideal in Enlightenment Thought: Its Form and Function in the Ideas of Franklin, Hume, and Voltaire, 1694-1790.* Notre-Dame: University of Notre Dame Press, 1977.

Seely, John Brown, and Paul Duguid, *The Social Life of Information.* Boston: Harvard Business School Press, 2000.

Sella, Zohar Kadmon. "The Journey of Ritual Communication." *Studies in Communication Sciences* 7 no. 1 (2007): 103-124.

Sharman, Will. "Ahiman Rezon: a Look at the Hebraic Terms and prayers used by Dermott." *Ars Quatuor Coronatorum: Transactions of Quauour Coronati Lodge* 105 no. 2076 (1993): 49-68.

Shelav, Eran. *Rome Reborn on Western Shores: Historical Imagination and the Creation of the American Republic (Jeffersonian America)*. Charlottesville: University of Virginia Press, 2009.

Sherrard, Thomas Roy. *Stalwart Builders: A History of the Grand Lodge of Masons in Massachusetts, 1733-1970*. Boston: The Masonic Education and Charity Trust of the Grand Lodge of Massachusetts, 1971.

Skocpol, Theda. *Social Revolutions in the Modern World*. Cambridge: Cambridge University Press, 1994.

Slifko, John. "Hannah Mather Crocker." *Le monde maçonnique des Lumières: l'Europe, l'Amérique et de ses colonies, prosopographique Dictionnaire*. Cécile Révauger and Charles Porset, eds. 3 Vols. Paris: Champion, 2013, Vol. 1, 908-917.

Smith, James Fairbairn, *Michigan Masonic Tracing Board, 1764 to 1976: A Panorama of Masonic History*. N.p.: Sesquicentennial of the Grand Lodge of Free and Accepted Masons of Michigan, 1976.

Stankiewicz, Steven. "Qualitative Thought, Thinking Through the Body, and Embodied Thinking: Dewey and his Successors." *The Continuing Relevance of John Dewey: Reflections on Aesthetics, Morality, Science, and Society*, Larry A. Hickman, Matthew Caleb Flamm, Krzysztof Piotr Skowro Ski, eds. Amsterdam: Rodolpi, 2011. 101-118.

Stevenson, David. *The Origins of Freemasonry: Scotland's Century 1590-1710*. Cambridge: Cambridge University Press, 1988.

————. "James Anderson" *Le monde maçonnique des Lumières: Europe-Amérique et de ses colonies, prosopographique Dictionnaire*. Cécile Révauger and Charles Porset, eds. 3 Vols. Paris: Champion, 2013. Vol. 1, 89-96.

Stewart, John Robert, Olivier Gapenne, Ezequiel A. Di Paolo, and L'Association pour la récherche cognitive (France). *Enaction: Toward a New Paradigm for Cognitive Science*. Cambridge: M.I.T. Press, 2010.

Tanselle, G. Thomas. "Statistics on American Printing, 1764-1783." *The Press and the American Revolution*. Bernard Bailyn and John B. Hench, eds. Boston: Northeastern University Press, 1981.

Thomas, Isaiah. *The History of Printing in America, with a Biography of*

Printers & an Account of Newspapers. New York: Weathervane Books, 1970.

Travers, Len. "'In the greatest solemn dignity': The Capitol Cornerstone and Ceremony in the Early Republic." *A Republic for the Ages: The United States Capitol and the Political Culture of the Early Republic.* Donald R.Kennon, ed. Charlottesville and London: University of Virginia Press, 1999. 155-176.

Walgren, Kent Logan. Steven Bullock, Preface, *Freemasonry, Anti-Masonry and Illuminism in the United States: A Bibliography, 1734-1850.* Vol. 1.Worcester: American Antiquarian Society, 2003.

Watkins, Larissa P. *American Masonic Periodicals, 1811-2001.* New Castle: Oak Knoll Press, 2003.

———— . *International Masonic Periodicals 1738-2005.* New Castle: Oak Knoll Press, 2005.

Wigglesworth, Robert J., Jr. "Competing to Popularize Newtonian Philosophy: John Theophilus Desaguliers and the Preservation of Reputation." *Isis* 94 no. 3 (2003): 434-455.

Wynch, Julie. *The Making and Meaning of James Forten's Letters from a Man of Color.* Oxford: Oxford University Press, 2003.

About the Author

John Slifko (1950-2018) was an expert in the fields of Freemasonry and Esotericism. He dedicated much of his scholarly and charitable work to studying democratic civil societies.

In 2015, John was awarded the Degree of Doctor of Philosophy in Geography from University of California, Los Angeles. He completed a joint Bachelor's degree in Urban Planning and Geography in 1987 from San Francisco State and a Master's degree in 1989 from University of California, Los Angeles in Urban Planning. John worked as a Planning Deputy for the Los Angeles City Council and as a Legislative Aide Field Representative for the United States Congress.

He was a founding member and served on the Board of Advisors at the Hannah Mather Crocker Society, Notre Dame University. He was also a Founder and co-Director of the Roosevelt Center for the Study of Civil Society and Freemasonry and Project AWE, which is dedicated to exploring connections between Western esotericism and the arts.

John was described by Zhenya Gershman, an Artist and Art Historian, as someone who "had a thirst for knowledge and a striving for improvement of life conditions for others that continues to be contagious. The concept of 'Moral Imagination' represented to John a combination of the reverie for artistic creativity with simultaneous responsibility for the world."

www.ingramcontent.com/pod-product-compliance
Lightning Source LLC
LaVergne TN
LVHW091216080426
835509LV00009B/1027